The Mystery of Redemption
and Christian Discipleship

The Didache Series

SEMESTER EDITION

The Didache

[DID-uh-kay]

The *Didache* is the first known Christian catechesis. Written in the first century, the *Didache* is the earliest known Christian writing outside of Scripture. The name of the work, "*Didache*," is indeed appropriate for such a catechesis because it comes from the Greek word for "teaching," and indicates that this writing contains the teaching of the Apostles.

The *Didache* is a catechetical summary of Christian Sacraments, practices, and morality. Though written in the first century, its teaching is timeless. The *Didache* was probably written by the disciples of the Twelve Apostles, and it presents the Apostolic Faith as taught by those closest to Jesus Christ. This series of books takes the name of this early catechesis because it shares in the Church's mission of passing on that same Faith, in its rich entirety, to new generations.

Below is an excerpt from the *Didache* in which we see a clear example of its lasting message, a message that speaks to Christians of today as much as it did to the first generations of the Church. The world is different, but the struggle for holiness is the same. In the *Didache*, we are instructed to embrace virtue, to avoid sin, and to live the Beatitudes of our Lord.

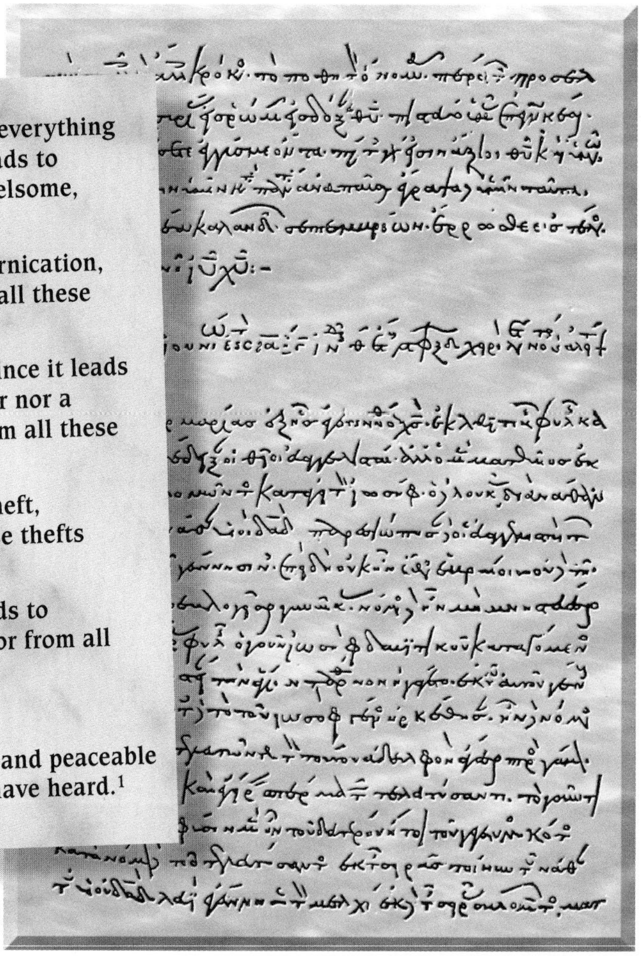

My child, flee from everything that is evil and everything that is like it. Do not be wrathful, for wrath leads to murder, nor jealous nor contentious nor quarrelsome, for from all these murder ensues.

My child, do not be lustful, for lust leads to fornication, nor a filthy-talker nor a lewd-looker, for from all these adulteries ensue.

My child, do not be an interpreter of omens, since it leads to idolatry, nor an enchanter nor an astrologer nor a magical purifier, nor wish to see them, for from all these idolatry arises.

My child, do not be a liar, for lying leads to theft, nor avaricious nor conceited, for from all these thefts are produced.

My child, do not be a complainer, since it leads to blasphemy, nor self-willed nor evil-minded, for from all these blasphemies are produced.

Be meek, for the meek will inherit the earth.

Be long-suffering and merciful and guileless and peaceable and good, and revere always the words you have heard.[1]

The *Didache* is the teaching of the Apostles and, as such, it is the teaching of the Church. Accordingly, this book series makes extensive use of the most recent comprehensive catechesis provided to us, the *Catechism of the Catholic Church*. The *Didache* series also relies heavily on Sacred Scripture, the lives of the saints, the Fathers of the Church, and the teaching of Vatican II as witnessed by the pontificates of John Paul II and Benedict XVI.

1. Swett, Ben H. "The Didache (The Teaching)." © January 30, 1998. http://bswett.com/1998-01Didache.html

The Mystery of Redemption
and Christian Discipleship

Author: Rev. Peter V. Armenio
General Editor: Rev. James Socias

MIDWEST THEOLOGICAL FORUM
Woodridge, Illinois

Published in the United States of America by

Midwest Theological Forum
1420 Davey Road
Woodridge, IL 60517

Tel: 630-739-9750
Fax: 630-739-9758
mail@mwtf.org
www.theologicalforum.org

First Edition
ISBN 978-1-936045-06-8

Acknowledgements

Excerpts from the English translation of the *Catechism of the Catholic Church* for the United States of America, copyright ©1994, United States Catholic Conference, Inc.—Libreria Editrice Vaticana. Used with permission.

Excerpts from the English translation of the *Catechism of the Catholic Church: Modifications from the Editio Typica*, copyright ©1997, United States Catholic Conference, Inc.—Libreria Editrice Vaticana. Used with permission.

Scripture quotations are adapted from the *Revised Standard Version of the Bible*, copyright ©1946, 1952, 1971, and the *New Revised Standard Version of the Bible*, copyright ©1989, by the Division of Christian Education of the National Council of the Churches of Christ in the United States of America, and are used by permission. All rights reserved.

Excerpts from the *Code of Canon Law, Latin/English Edition*, are used with permission, copyright ©1983 Canon Law Society of America, Washington, DC.

Citations of official Church documents from Neuner, Josef, SJ and Dupuis, Jacques, SJ, eds., *The Christian Faith: Doctrinal Documents of the Catholic Church*, 5th ed. (New York: Alba House, 1992). Used with permission.

Excerpts from *Vatican II: The Conciliar and Post Conciliar Documents, New Revised Edition* edited by Austin Flannery, OP, copyright ©1992, Costello Publishing Company, Inc., Northport, NY, are used with permission of the publisher, all rights reserved. No part of these excerpts may be reproduced, stored in a retrieval system, or transmitted in any form or by any means—electronic, mechanical, photocopying, recording or otherwise, without express written permission of Costello Publishing Company.

Disclaimer: The editor of this book has attempted to give proper credit to all sources used in the text and illustrations. Any miscredit or lack of credit is unintended and will be corrected in the next edition.

Library of Congress Cataloging-in-Publication Data
Armenio, Peter V.
The mystery of redemption and Christian discipleship / author, Peter V. Armenio ; general editor, James Socias.
p. cm.
Originally published: 1st ed. c2001.
Includes index.
ISBN 978-1-936045-06-8
1. Christian education – Textbooks for teenagers – Catholic. I. Socias, James. II. Title
BX930.A76 2010
234'.3 – dc22
2010018593

In accordance with c. 827, permission to publish is granted on October 30, 2009 by the Very Reverend John F. Canary, Vicar General of the Archdiocese of Chicago. Permission to publish is an official declaration of ecclesiastical authority that the material is free from doctrinal and moral error. No implication is contained therein that those who have granted it agree with the content, opinions, or statements expressed in the work; nor do they assume any legal responsibility associated with the publication.

Printed in Canada

Foreword

No one has ever wanted anything more than God wants to share the communion of Trinitarian life with us. The Father, Son and Holy Spirit—as St. Irenæus once wrote—who have no need of company gave participation in the divine life to those who need them. This is the tremendous mystery of our faith, and it is at the heart of this wonderful book by Father Peter Armenio, *The Mystery of Redemption and Christian Discipleship.*

The Catholic tradition has not hesitated to call our participation in the life of God a true friendship. From the beginning, God has desired nothing less than to share this friendship with us and to give us the participation in his divine life that makes this friendship possible. It is only through Christ that this can happen. He is the only-begotten Son of the Father and by assuming our nature he makes us the *adopted* sons and daughters of God. But it is not only our nature that needs to be transformed by Christ through grace of the Holy Spirit. Another obstacle to our participation in the divine life arose from the failure of the first human beings to embrace the invitation to divine intimacy. This refusal wounded our nature and caused a fundamental alienation between the human race and God—one which he, out of his great love for us, immediately undertook to repair through the promised Redeemer who reconciles us with the Father. As Father Armenio demonstrates with great clarity, this remarkable plan of salvation gradually unfolded through the call of Abraham and then the election of the people of Israel from whom the Savior of the world would come—the Incarnate Son, true God and true man.

Through his passion, death, and resurrection, Jesus Christ merited the salvation of all people and, through the Church he founded, he continues his saving work until he comes again. Christ instituted the Sacraments of the Church as the primary means of conveying the grace of his Redemption, and, in the Holy Mass, his redemptive sacrifice is actually made present. In the words of the *Catechism of the Catholic Church*, "Christ's death is both the *Paschal sacrifice* that accomplishes the definitive redemption of men, through 'the Lamb of God, who takes away the sin of the world,' and the *sacrifice of the New Covenant*, which restores man to communion with God by reconciling him to God through the 'blood of the covenant, which was poured out for many for the forgiveness of sins'" (§613).

I have no doubt that readers of this splendid book will be led to a deeper understanding of the Redemption that Christ has won for us, and I warmly recommend it for use by high schools, parishes, and Catholic families.

✠ **J. Augustine Di Noia, O.P.**
Vatican City

Tree of Life by Pacino.
This altarpiece, ca. 1300, illustrates a devotional text, the *Lignum Vitæ* of St. Bonaventure, in which the life and Passion of Jesus Christ is described symbolically as the flowering of the "tree of the cross."

The Mystery of Redemption

CHAPTER 1

In the Beginning

Though Adam and Eve had disobeyed God, he did not abandon them; instead, he introduced a new and marvelous plan of redemption to restore the friendship they had lost.

The Mystery of Redemption

CHAPTER 1

In the Beginning

Man was created for greatness—for God himself; he was created to be filled by God. But his heart is too small for the greatness to which it is destined. It must be stretched. "By delaying [his gift], God strengthens our desire; through desire he enlarges our soul and by expanding it he increases its capacity [for receiving him]."[1]

Ultimately we want only one thing—"the blessed life," the life which is simply life, simply "happiness." In the final analysis, there is nothing else that we ask for in prayer. Our journey has no other goal—it is about this alone.[2]

INTRODUCTION

The Scriptures had foretold this divine plan of salvation through the putting to death of "the righteous one, my Servant" as a mystery of universal redemption, that is, as the ransom that would free men from the slavery of sin.[3] (CCC 601)

In the context of theology, redemption refers to the atonement or deliverance from sins merited by the sacrifice of Jesus Christ on the Cross. The story of this redemption of the human race, which culminated on the Cross, began at the very dawn of creation.

The opening chapters of the Book of Genesis relate how man and woman were created out of God's great love and were intended to share in his intimate friendship. They alone, among all of God's visible creatures on earth, were created to know and love God so as to share in his own divine life. In the creation narrative, man and woman were made in God's image and likeness,[4] thereby enjoying an exalted dignity and a special relationship with the Creator. In fact, the creation of Adam and Eve was the pinnacle of God's visible creation. In this sense, the entire world was created to serve human people.

God entrusted his creation to the care of Adam and Eve. They lived in a paradise God had created for them, and they had dominion over all things. However, God gave one commandment to our first parents: not to eat the fruit of the Tree of the Knowledge of Good and Evil.[5]

Adam and Eve's disobedience of this one command disrupted the harmony of God's creation and inflicted sin on humanity—a sin with consequences for our first parents and their descendants. This first, or Original, Sin introduced sin, suffering, and death into the world. From that moment, every descendant of Adam and Eve—every human person—would suffer from the effects of Original Sin and would need a Redeemer to reconcile him- or herself with God. (Later, this text will present how the Blessed Virgin Mary, by the merits of Christ, was preserved from all stain of Original Sin.)

Though Adam and Eve had disobeyed God, he did not abandon them; instead, he introduced a new and marvelous plan of redemption to restore the friendship they had lost. This first chapter will examine the creation of our first parents and their Fall so as to provide a background for understanding the necessity and importance of Christ's work of redemption.

The Expulsion from Paradise (detail) by Natoire.
Every descendant of Adam and Eve—every human person—would suffer from the effects of Original Sin and would need a Redeemer to reconcile him- or herself with God.

THIS CHAPTER WILL ADDRESS SEVERAL QUESTIONS:

- What is man's original vocation?
- What does the Church mean when she says Adam and Eve were created in an original state of holiness and justice?
- What is Original Sin?
- What are the consequences of Original Sin?
- How can a person overcome the effects of Original Sin?

God Creating the Sun, the Moon and the Stars in the Firmament by Jan Brueghel II.
God is the First Cause and Creator of the universe both in its vast immensity and in its detailed components.

THE CREATION OF THE WORLD

The Book of Genesis—its name coming from the Greek for *origin*—opens with an account of the creation of the world. The first verse reads, "In the beginning God created the heavens and the earth."[6] Thus, the Sacred Author makes one thing abundantly clear: God is the First Cause and Creator of the universe both in its vast immensity and in its detailed components.

> **"In the beginning God created the heavens and the earth":[7] three things are affirmed in these first words of Scripture: the eternal God gave a beginning to all that exists outside of himself; he alone is Creator (the verb "create"—Hebrew *bara*—always has God for its subject). The totality of what exists (expressed by the formula "the heavens and the earth") depends on the One who gives it being. (CCC 290)**

The Sacred Author then describes how God created the world and everything in it. We are told, in metaphorical imagery, God created the universe in six days. The literary style employed in the creation narrative is not intended to shed light on the scientific intricacies of creation or the exact dates on which each part of the universe came into existence; rather, it teaches God created the world according to his divine plan and intention. Throughout the opening chapter of Genesis, the obvious protagonist is God, who displays his omnipotent power simply by speaking the universe into being.

One aid to understanding the creation narrative in Genesis is to note how creation is arranged in two sets of three days. According to Genesis 1: 2, "The earth was without form and void." In the first three days, God

Scenes from Genesis, Bulgarian Revival Period.
The literary style employed in the creation narrative is not intended to shed light on the scientific intricacies of creation or the exact dates on which each part of the universe came into existence.

created the forms of the world: day and night, sky and sea, land and vegetation. In the second set of three days, God created the inhabitants that would fill these forms: sun and moon, birds and fish, animals and man.

In this way, it becomes clear the universe was created for its inhabitants, the greatest of whom were Adam and Eve, who would be given dominion over all creation.

Day 1: Day and Night	RULED BY	Day 4: Sun and Moon
Day 2: Sky and Sea	RULED BY	Day 5: Birds and Fish
Day 3: Land and Vegetation	RULED BY	Day 6: Animals and Man

The creation narrative in Genesis culminates on the sixth day with the creation of Adam and Eve, thus making it clear why God created everything else. The world was created for human beings, who are the only creatures God made in his own image and likeness.

> God created everything for man,[8] but man in turn was created to serve and love God and to offer all creation back to him. (CCC 358)

God created the world to serve human beings. He intended for them and their descendants to subdue the earth and exercise dominion over all creation.

> **"Be fruitful and multiply, and fill the earth and subdue it; and have dominion over the fish of the sea and over the birds of the air and over every living thing that moves upon the earth."** (Gn 1:28)

However, this dominion over God's creation does not mean human beings are free to do whatever they desire in the world. Rather, our first parents were called to be stewards, or caretakers, of creation, "to till it and keep it,"[9] according to the will of God, the Creator.

> In God's plan man and woman have the vocation of "subduing" the earth[10] as stewards of God. This sovereignty is not to be an arbitrary and destructive domination. God calls man and woman, made in the image of the Creator "who loves everything that exists,"[11] to share in his providence toward other creatures; hence their responsibility for the world God has entrusted to them. (CCC 373)

Creation set the stage for God's relationship with his people. God created the world as a gift to our first parents and their descendants. In order for it to serve human needs, however, creation requires the intervention of human work. For this reason, Adam and Eve were called to subdue and complete what God had already created for them.

The world God made is the arena for human work and, at the same time, is a constant, visible reminder of God's infinite love for the human family. In a certain sense, we are in a partnership with God, whereby we participate in his creation. God wants man to discover the deep mysteries of the created world and the ways creation can be "subdued," or used. This is a task the human race has been accomplishing in a most astonishing way throughout history. Through human work, people give glory to God and gratefully offer his creation back to him.[12]

God the Father by Batoni.
God created the world as a gift to our first parents and their descendants.

GOOD STEWARDSHIP

Creation of the Animals by Tintoretto. "Man's dominion over inanimate and other living beings granted by the Creator is not absolute; it is limited by concern for the quality of life of his neighbor,..." (CCC 2415)

When God created our first parents, he placed them in the Garden of Eden as stewards of his creation. He invited them to cooperate with him in his creation and instructed them, "Be fruitful and multiply, and fill the earth and subdue it."[13] This phrase, "be fruitful and multiply," can be applied by extension to the goods of the earth as well. If mankind is to "fill the earth," people must make wise use of natural resources to support themselves and future generations.

> **The seventh commandment enjoins respect for the integrity of creation. Animals, like plants and inanimate beings, are by nature destined for the common good of past, present, and future humanity.[14] Use of the mineral, vegetable, and animal resources of the universe cannot be divorced from respect for moral imperatives. Man's dominion over inanimate and other living beings granted by the Creator is not absolute; it is limited by concern for the quality of life of his neighbor, including generations to come; it requires a religious respect for the integrity of creation.[15] (CCC 2415)**

"The goods of creation are destined for the whole human race."[16] In the modern era, a majority of the world's goods are consumed by a minority of the world's population. As man is called to imitate Christ, it is clear personal wealth can never be an excuse for rampant consumerism.

As stewards of creation, people must not only be *just* when dealing with each other but also avoid excessive consumption. Care must be taken to protect the "goods of creation," and every Christian has a personal obligation to use the goods of the earth as God wills, according to the promptings of the Holy Spirit.

> **An increased sense of God and increased self-awareness are fundamental to any *full development of human society*. This development multiplies material goods and puts them at the service of the person and his freedom. It reduces dire poverty and economic exploitation. It makes for growth in respect for cultural identities and openness to the transcendent.[17] (CCC 2441)**

CREATION AS THE WORK OF THE BLESSED TRINITY

In the Nicene Creed, Christians pray, "I believe in one God, the Father almighty, maker of heaven and earth." Although God the Father is generally referred to as the Creator, each Person of the Blessed Trinity acts in concert with the other divine Persons; thus, creation was an act of each Person of the Blessed Trinity: Father, Son, and Holy Spirit.

The Holy Trinity by Pereda. Creation of the world through the "Word" foreshadowed God's re-creation or redemption of the world through the "Word of God."

Each act of creation was intimately connected to the "Word of God." For example, the creation of light occurred when God said, "Let there be light."[18] Everything God created is preceded by a verbal command, including the creation of the first man and woman.

This creation of the world through the "Word" foreshadowed God's re-creation or redemption of the world through the "Word of God." This correspondence between creation and re-creation is beautifully detailed in the opening verses of St. John's Gospel.

> **In the beginning was the Word, and the Word was with God, and the Word was God. He was in the beginning with God; all things were made through him, and without him was not anything made that was made....And the Word became flesh and dwelt among us, full of grace and truth; we have beheld his glory, glory as of the only Son from the Father.** (Jn 1:1-3, 14)

The "Word of God" in the creation narrative is none other than Jesus Christ, the Son of God, the Second Person of the Blessed Trinity. Through him all things were created. He holds all things together in himself; through his redemption, all things will be made new.

The creation narrative in Genesis also mentions the "Spirit of God" moving over the waters.[19] This "Spirit of God" is likely an allusion to the Holy Spirit, the Third Person of the Blessed Trinity. The Sacred Author also mentions the "breath of life,"[20] which brought Adam into being. *Breath*, *wind*, and *spirit* are images of the Holy Spirit, and they feature prominently in the creation narrative.

> **"O Lord, my God," the Psalmist sings, "when you send forth your spirit, they are created, and you renew the face of the earth" (Ps 104:30). These words evoke the first creation, when the Spirit of God hovered over the deep (cf. Gn 1:2). And they look forward to the new creation, at Pentecost, when the Holy Spirit descended upon the Apostles and established the Church as the first fruits of a redeemed humanity (cf. Jn 20:22-23). These words summon us to ever deeper faith in God's infinite power to transform every human situation, to create life from death, and to light up even**

WHAT CATHOLICS BELIEVE ABOUT THE BIBLE

The seventy-three books of the Bible (twenty-seven in the New Testament and forty-six in the Old), often called Sacred Scripture, tells the story of how God's plan of salvation has unfolded throughout history. This is called *salvation history*. Salvation history, however, is different from other kinds of history. The Bible not only teaches the meaning of past events but also reveals how those events affect every person's life in every age.

The Bible is inspired and inerrant. It is *inspired* because God himself guided the Sacred Authors, who were enlightened by God the Holy Spirit to write what he wanted and nothing more. Thus, God the Holy Spirit is the principal author of Scripture; the human writers were the instruments through which he chose to reveal himself to his people. Scripture is *inerrant* because it does not err. God can neither deceive nor be deceived. Because the Holy Spirit is the principal author of Sacred Scripture, it is true and contains no errors.

> **"Since therefore all that the inspired authors or sacred writers affirm should be regarded as affirmed by the Holy Spirit, we must acknowledge that the books of Scripture firmly, faithfully, and without error teach that truth which God, for the sake of our salvation, wished to see confided to the Sacred Scriptures."[21] (CCC 107)**

The Bible is sacred literature. It is *sacred* because God the Holy Spirit is its author. It is *literature* because it uses literary forms and techniques—stories, poems, dialogues, figurative language, and the like—to convey its meaning. Unless how these forms and techniques function is understood, the meaning of the Sacred Authors cannot be understood.

The Bible has a purpose different than any other work of human literature. The Bible is *religious*. Though the Sacred Authors told great stories and wrote great poetry, their literary techniques were placed at the service of the religious purpose of the Bible.

The Bible is ancient literature. Even the most recent books of the New Testament were written almost 2000 years ago. The Sacred Authors did not write in the same manner as modern authors. In order to understand what they meant to say, the historical context in which they lived and an appreciation of their worldviews must be understood.

Sacred Scripture is not intended by God or by the Sacred Authors to be either a scientific treatise or a mere historical record. It is much more. The purpose of the Bible is to show the way to salvation. By presenting stories such as the creation narrative in Genesis, the Bible transmits a religious message—a message that is true, inspired, and inerrant.

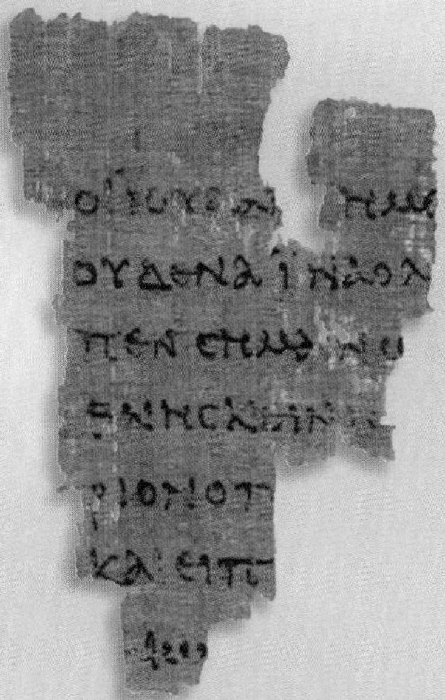

St. John's Fragment or Rylands P52 is a papyrus fragment written in Greek on both sides. Measuring only 3.5" by 2.5", it is conserved at the John Rylands Library, Manchester, UK. Rylands P52 is generally accepted as the earliest extant record of a canonical New Testament text. A scholarly range of dates is set at before AD 100 to 160. The front (recto), shown above, contains lines from Jn 18: 31-33. The back (verso) contains lines from Jn 18: 37-38.

the darkest night. And they make us think of another magnificent phrase of Saint Irenæus: "where the Church is, there is the Spirit of God; where the Spirit of God is, there is the Church and all grace."[22] (Pope Benedict XVI, Homily, St. Patrick's Cathedral, New York, April 19, 2008)

The early Christians viewed the use of plural pronouns in the creation of man as a reference to the Blessed Trinity: "Let *us* make man in *our* image."[23] Thus, in a veiled way, Genesis communicates creation is the work of all three Persons of the Blessed Trinity.[24] This implicit reference to the Blessed Trinity becomes explicit with the Revelation of Jesus Christ in the New Testament.

Though the work of creation is attributed to the Father in particular, it is equally a truth of faith that the Father, Son and Holy Spirit together are the one, indivisible principle of creation. (CCC 316)

Why did God Create the universe?

THE CREATION OF ADAM AND EVE

Nothing in creation can add to the perfection of God; he is already perfect. Nor can it add to his happiness; he is infinitely and eternally content. Creation, then, is a manifestation of God's infinite goodness and love. God wants his creatures to share in his happiness. This is especially true in the creation of Adam and Eve, the only rational beings in all of visible creation. Only they had the capacity to understand God's infinite goodness and reflect his glory.

"The world was made for the glory of God."[25] St. Bonaventure explains that God created all things "not to increase his glory, but to show it forth and to communicate it,"[26] for God has no other reason for creating than his love and goodness: "Creatures came into existence when the key of love opened his hand."[27] (CCC 293)

Man and woman are the high point of visible creation. Human beings are radically different from and far superior to all other earthly creatures. The reason for this is given in Sacred Scripture: man and woman are created in the image and likeness of God.[28]

"Let us make man in our own image, after our likeness."... So God created man in his own image, in the image of God he created him; male and female he created them. (Gn 1:26-27)

Creation of Adam by Michelangelo.
While the body of Adam was created from pre-existing material, i.e., the dust from the ground, his soul was created directly by God.

Creation of Eve, Byzantine Mosaic. While a person's biological nature comes from his or her parents, the soul is created and infused into the body directly by God at conception without mediation or human intervention.

Bearing the image and likeness of God means, first of all, each human person has a rational soul with the spiritual powers of intellect and will. Human beings, unlike animals, have a body and a rational soul.

> **In Sacred Scripture the term "soul" often refers to human *life* or the entire human *person*.[29] But "soul" also refers to the innermost aspect of man, that which is of greatest value in him,[30] that by which he is most especially in God's image: "soul" signifies the *spiritual principle* in man. (CCC 363)**

What's the effect of being Created unique?

"The LORD God formed man of dust from the ground, and breathed into his nostrils the breath of life; and man became a living being."[31] While the body of Adam was created from pre-existing material, i.e., the dust from the ground, his soul was created directly by God. The same is true for each human being. While a person's biological nature comes from his or her parents, the soul is created and infused into the body directly by God at conception without mediation or human intervention.

The human soul is the spiritual component of each human person. While intimately united to the body, enlivening it and giving it form, the soul carries out strictly spiritual operations.

Through these spiritual operations, the human person reflects the power of God and "images" the divine life in a finite way. Through the spiritual soul, human beings can form concepts, know God, make choices, and love. They also have the capacity to know themselves, possess themselves, give themselves, and enter into communion with God and other persons.[32]

His or her spiritual component enables a human person to discover the secrets of created reality through the intellect. The human mind can decipher the laws of the universe and describe them in mathematical formulas. Thus, a natural consequence of the spiritual capacity for thought and reason is the development of science. This is a great gift that can lead to a deeper understanding and appreciation of God's creation and, ultimately, God himself.

The findings of modern science attest to the power and grandeur of God. The rich complexity and finely tuned harmony of the created world reflect an infinitely intelligent and powerful Creator. The laws, design, and inner secrets of the material world are an invitation to acknowledge not only the greatness of a divine Creator but also his immeasurable love.

Why are we Created unique?

MARRIAGE IN GOD'S PLAN

God created man—male and female—in his image and likeness.

> **God blessed them, and God said to them, "Be fruitful and multiply, and fill the earth and subdue it; and have dominion over the fish of the sea and over the birds of the air and over every living thing that moves upon the earth." (Gn 1:28)**

With this command, "be fruitful and multiply," God intended much more for mankind than simply to reproduce. Instead, God created man and woman as equal and complementary persons, joining them in a loving relationship sealed by a marriage covenant. This brings to light an important fact: marriage was not invented by people or by society but was instituted by God at the moment he created man *male and female*.

In the New Testament, the Pharisees questioned Christ about why Moses allowed divorce.[33] He answered them by quoting the Book of Genesis to clarify the doctrine of marital indissolubility:

> **"Have you not read that he who made them from the beginning made them male and female, and said, 'For this reason a man shall leave his father and mother and be joined to his wife, and the two shall become one flesh'? So they are no longer two but one flesh. What therefore God has joined together, let not man put asunder." (Mt 19:4-6)**

God created marriage to be permanent, life-long, and indissoluble. Because God creates each marriage bond, no human effort can break it.

God also calls husband and wife to be *fruitful*. Marital love is meant to be life-giving: the two become one flesh, and then, if God wills, three, four, and five, etc. In this way, the husband and wife become co-creators with God. Together they bring into being a child, a new human person with an immortal soul. This new human being, then, deserves to be cared for and educated in a family environment of love and virtue. The family—husband, wife, and children—is an image of the Blessed Trinity, which is itself a community of three divine Persons.

Scenes from the Life of the Virgin: Marriage of the Virgin (detail) by Giotto.
God created man and woman as equal and complementary persons, joining them in a loving relationship sealed by a marriage covenant.

Some people, however, have mistakenly argued the field of human knowledge is restricted to that which can be deduced from empirical data, i.e., information gathered from experiments and observations of the natural world. They argue the created world can reveal nothing about God, if he exists at all. These views, however, place artificial limitations on the human mind, which was created to seek the truth.

God has endowed each human person with the capacity for metaphysical ("beyond the physical") knowledge that transcends empirical data. This ability to see more than what can be measured or observed in the created world leads the human person to sense a Creator who loves and provides for the needs of his creation.

The spiritual soul enables every person to know, love, and serve God in this life and consequently share in his friendship and love for all of eternity. Thus, the human soul is the key component that gives each individual his or her exalted dignity and reflects a spark of divine life.

THE ORIGINAL STATE OF MAN

> **Of all visible creatures only man is "able to know and love his creator."[34] He is "the only creature on earth that God has willed for its own sake,"[35] and he alone is called to share, by knowledge and love, in God's own life. It was for this end that he was created, and this is the fundamental reason for his dignity. (CCC 356)**

God created our first parents to share in his love and friendship. For this reason, he gave them preternatural virtues and his supernatural grace, endowing them with the capacity for knowledge and love that were indispensable for their participation in his divine life.

Before the Fall, Adam and Eve possessed a clear awareness of God's presence and enjoyed a profound and loving relationship with him. They were exceedingly happy in the paradise God had created for them and were destined for a blissful life in Heaven.

The Garden of Eden by Field. As outlined in the Book of Genesis, it was clearly God's intention for man and woman to find pleasure and fulfillment in every aspect of their lives.

THE CREATION OF ANGELS

> The Apostles' Creed professes that God is "Creator of heaven and earth." The Nicene Creed makes it explicit that this profession includes "all that is, seen and unseen." (CCC 325)

Sacred Scripture and Sacred Tradition clearly teach God's creation includes both the material and spiritual reality. God's spiritual creations include the human soul as well as the angels.

Angels are purely spiritual, or noncorporeal, beings. As such, they possess intelligence and will but do not have physical bodies and are, therefore, immortal.

> Angels are spiritual creatures who glorify God without ceasing and who serve his saving plans for other creatures: "The angels work together for the benefit of us all."[36] (CCC 350)

The angels exist to serve God and have, from the moment of creation, cooperated in God's plan of salvation for his people. Often they act as messengers; for example, the Archangel Gabriel announced to the Blessed Virgin Mary she had been chosen to be the Mother of the Redeemer. At other times, they assist people to follow God's will; for example, the Archangel Raphael guided Tobias in the Book of Tobit.

Christ often spoke of angels during his public ministry. Referring to little children, he said, "Their angels always behold the face of my Father who is in heaven."[37] Christ was consoled by an angel during his agony in the Garden of Gethsemane,[38] and angels announced the Resurrection to the holy women who had come to visit Christ's tomb.[39] "The Church venerates the angels who help her on her earthly pilgrimage and protect every human being."[40]

Catholic tradition maintains each person has a guardian angel who accompanies him or her at every moment and who can protect from physical and moral harm. A guardian angel can be a person's "spiritual best friend" whose greatest desire is to help him or her get to Heaven.

The Guardian Angel by Pietro.
Each human being is entrusted by God to the custody of a guardian angel from childhood to death.

PRAYER TO ONE'S GUARDIAN ANGEL

Angel of God, my guardian dear,
to whom God's love commits me here,
Ever this day (night) be at my side,
to light and guard, to rule and guide.
Amen.

The *Catechism* relates how God blessed our first parents by creating them in a "state of holiness and justice."

> **The Church, interpreting the symbolism of biblical language in an authentic way, in the light of the New Testament and Tradition, teaches that our first parents, Adam and Eve, were constituted in an original "state of holiness and justice."[41] This grace of original holiness was "to share in...divine life."[42]** (CCC 375)

This state enjoyed by Adam and Eve included a number of gifts that were lost due to Original Sin. These preternatural gifts included immunity from sickness, suffering, and death as well as freedom from disordered appetites and passions. Our first parents' natural inclinations were subject to the control of their minds and wills, and they enjoyed harmony and self-mastery inside their hearts.

As long as Adam and Eve remained close to God through fidelity to his will, they did not suffer, become sick, or die. God intended they have a joyful relationship with him, with each other, and with the rest of creation. This perfect state bestowed on our first parents is called original justice.[43]

In the state of original holiness and justice, work was not a burden but rather an easy and rewarding activity. Without toil or fatigue, Adam and Eve cultivated the earth as stewards of God's creation. As outlined in the Book of Genesis, it was clearly God's intention for man and woman to find pleasure and fulfillment in every aspect of their lives.

ORIGINAL SIN

God placed Adam and Eve in the Garden of Eden to cultivate it and watch over it. They lived in harmony with God, with each other, and with all of creation. They had dominion over all of creation, and everything they did was gratifying and fulfilling, without any trace of harm to themselves, to each other, or to creation.

God gave them complete freedom in the Garden of Eden with only one prohibition: they were forbidden to eat the fruit of the Tree of the Knowledge of Good and Evil.[44] When forbidding them from eating this fruit, God warned them disobedience would result in death.

We do not know how long Adam and Eve remained in their original state of holiness and justice before they were visited by the Devil in the form of a serpent.

The Fall of Man (detail) by Mantegna.
God gave them complete freedom in the Garden of Eden with only one prohibition: they were forbidden to eat the fruit of the tree of the knowledge of good and evil.

> **The serpent was more subtle than any other wild creature that the LORD God had made. He said to the woman, "Did God say, 'You shall not eat of any tree of the garden'?" And the woman said to the serpent, "We may eat of the fruit of the trees of the garden; but God said, 'You shall not eat of the fruit of the tree which is in the midst of the garden, neither shall you touch it, lest you die.'" But the serpent said to the woman, "You will not die. For God knows that when you eat of it your eyes will be opened, and you will be like God, knowing good and evil." So when the woman saw that the tree was good for food, and that it was a delight to the eyes, and that the tree was to be desired to make one wise, she took of its fruit and ate; and she also gave some to her husband, and he ate.** (Gn 3:1-6)

Paradise by Lucas Cranach the Elder.
The mission of Satan and his followers has always been to sabotage God's loving plan for his people.

The Hebrew word used to describe the serpent, *nahash*, is used throughout the Old Testament in reference to powerfully evil creatures. For example, Numbers 21: 6 uses the term to describe "fiery serpents" that attacked the Israelites in the desert; in Isaiah 27: 1, the term is used to depict the great mythical serpent or dragon, the Leviathan.

Thus, the serpent described in Genesis 3 is not a harmless snake; it is a deadly, lying murderer.

> **Scripture witnesses to the disastrous influence of the one Jesus calls "a murderer from the beginning," who would even try to divert Jesus from the mission received from his Father.[45] "The reason the Son of God appeared was to destroy the works of the devil."[46] In its consequences the gravest of these works was the mendacious seduction that led man to disobey God. (CCC 394)**

Sacred Scripture and Sacred Tradition reveal Satan is a fallen angel. Though he was one of God's chief angels, he rejected God's friendship and refused to abide by God's will. As an angel, Satan is pure spirit and thus superior in intellect and power to human beings. His followers, also fallen angels, are normally referred to as devils or demons.

> **Behind the disobedient choice of our first parents lurks a seductive voice, opposed to God, which makes them fall into death out of envy.[47] Scripture and the Church's Tradition see in this being a fallen angel, called "Satan" or the "devil."[48] The Church teaches that Satan was at first a good angel, made by God: "The devil and the other demons were indeed created naturally good by God, but they became evil by their own doing."[49] (CCC 391)**

The mission of Satan and his followers has always been to sabotage God's loving plan for his people. He achieves this through temptations, lies, and deceits that lead people away from God and toward destruction. For this reason, Christ called Satan a "murderer from the beginning" and the "father of lies."[50]

SATAN AND THE FALLEN ANGELS

At some point after their creation, God submitted the angels to a test. While the nature of this test is not known, some have speculated it concerned pride or envy. These ideas seem plausible since Scripture records, "The beginning of man's pride is to depart from the Lord," and, "The beginning of pride is sin."[51] The adage, "pride cometh before the fall," is, in fact, a nice summary of Scripture's treatment of this particular sin. Regarding the sin of envy, the Book of Wisdom teaches, "God created man for incorruption, and made him in the image of his own eternity, but through the devil's envy death entered the world."[52]

Whatever their particular sin, Satan and many other angels rebelled against God and were cast from Heaven. About him, the Book of Isaiah relates:

> **"How you are fallen from heaven, O Day Star, son of Dawn! How you are cut down to the ground, you who laid the nations low! You said in your heart, 'I will ascend to heaven; above the stars of God I will set my throne on high; I will sit on the mount of assembly in the far north; I will ascend above the heights of the clouds, I will make myself like the Most High.' But you are brought down to Sheol, to the depths of the Pit." (Is 14: 12-15)**

In the New Testament, Christ spoke about the Devil frequently. He called Satan the tempter, the father of lies, the enemy who sows evil, and a murderer. As in the Fall of Adam and Eve, the Devil can tempt human beings. God allows these temptations in order to test fidelity and to manifest the merits of Christ. He also gives the grace to resist these temptations. Among the divine weapons is recourse to the angels, especially guardian angels, and the saints, particularly the Blessed Virgin Mary.

St. Michael and the Devil by Raphael.
Christ called Satan the tempter, the father of lies, the enemy who sows evil, and a murderer.

PRAYER TO ST. MICHAEL THE ARCHANGEL

Saint Michael the Archangel, defend us in battle; be our defense against the wickedness and snares of the Devil. May God rebuke him, we humbly pray. And do you, O prince of the heavenly host, by the power of God thrust into Hell Satan and all the evil spirits who prowl about the world for the ruin of souls. Amen.

In the case of our first parents, Satan tempted Eve with the promise she would become like God with knowledge of good and evil. He insinuated God did not want them to become like him. Upon hearing the serpent's deceptive words, Eve chose to put her own desires before God's will and then convinced Adam to do the same.

THE NATURE OF ORIGINAL SIN

The sin that our first parents committed was the sin of *disobedience*. As St. Paul explained, "By one man's disobedience many were made sinners."[53] Adam and Eve had been destined to the beatific vision of God in Heaven. As St. Maximus observed, however, they wanted to "be like God" but "without God, ahead of God, and not according to God."[54]

In their sin, they deliberately and disobediently decided to reach for the absolute freedom and knowledge that can belong only to God. They distrusted God despite the compelling proofs of his love. The *Catechism* clearly explains the seriousness of our first parents' disobedience:

> **In that sin man *preferred* himself to God and by that very act scorned him. He chose himself over and against God, against the requirements of his creaturely status and therefore against his own good. (CCC 398)**

In order to understand the gravity of Original Sin, it is helpful to contrast the sin of our first parents with all subsequent human sins. While every sin involves a choice to disobey God, human beings have, since the Fall, been greatly influenced by a weakness of soul, a disorder of appetites and passions, and an inclination to sin called *concupiscence*. These human weaknesses, however, were not a factor in the sin of our first parents. Adam and Eve were certainly human, but, because of their original, preternatural gifts, their sin involved a deliberate choice to disobey God by distrusting him and usurping his authority.

The Creation and the Expulsion from the Paradise by Giovanni di Paolo.
In their sin, Adam and Eve deliberately and disobediently decided to reach for the absolute freedom and knowledge that can belong only to God.

THE CONSEQUENCES OF ORIGINAL SIN

The consequences of Original Sin were immediate. Adam and Eve lost their state of original holiness and justice as well as their friendship with God; they were consequently expelled from the Garden of Eden.

Their transgression also had consequences for the whole human race. As St. Paul teaches, "Sin came into the world through one man and death through sin."[55] By their offense, Adam and Eve harmed not only themselves but also all their descendants. They forfeited the state of original holiness and justice for themselves and for all their descendants—including us—and introduced suffering and death, including death of the soul (sin), to the whole human race.

The human mind and will were damaged; thus, our first parents could no longer know and love God as a close, loving friend. A chasm opened between our first parents and God that could not be bridged by human effort alone. In a certain sense, Adam and Eve had lost the means to be united with God. This rupture of their relationship with God left a wound in the human soul.

The human intellect became clouded and incapable of fully discerning God's Laws. This caused the human conscience to become lax and unreliable to judge truthfully between good and evil actions. As an intimate unity of body and spirit, the human person became inclined to immoderation and disorder to such an extent people were enslaved to bodily desires and passions. From this point on, the human person tended to focus inwardly on the self, which led to a further alienation from God.

> **"Man, enticed by the Evil One, abused his freedom at the very beginning of history."[56] He succumbed to temptation and did what was evil. He still desires the good, but his nature bears the wound of original sin. He is now inclined to evil and subject to error:**
>
> > **Man is divided in himself. As a result, the whole life of men, both individual and social, shows itself to be a struggle, and a dramatic one, between good and evil, between light and darkness.[57] (CCC 1707)**

Before the Fall, Adam and Eve lived in harmony with each other and viewed each other with innocence and purity. However, the newly acquired knowledge of evil promised by Satan caused them to experience disorder in their passions and appetites. They experienced concupiscence, or the inclination to sin, and, for the first time, they noticed their mutual nakedness. They were seduced by the lie that they had to experience evil in order to know what is evil.

The Denunciation of Adam and Eve by Watts.
A chasm opened between our first parents and God that could not be bridged by human effort alone.

The eyes of both were opened, and they knew that they were naked; and they sewed fig leaves together and made themselves aprons. And they heard the sound of the LORD God walking in the garden in the cool of the day, and the man and his wife hid themselves from the presence of the LORD God among the trees of the garden. (Gn 3: 7-8)

God's creation is inherently good, which is clearly taught in the first chapter of Genesis; following every act of creation, God beheld his creation and declared it "good." The great wonders and inherent goodness of God's creation apply especially to the human person. In fact, after having made man and woman, God declared his creation "very good."[58]

The Expulsion from the Garden of Eden (detail) by Masaccio. Adam and Eve were ashamed when they noticed their nakedness and felt the need to cover themselves.

The body is an essential component of the human person and, in and of itself, is nothing of which to be ashamed. However, once the intimate harmony between God and man—and between man and woman—had been damaged, the body became an object of lust. Adam and Eve were ashamed when they noticed their nakedness and felt the need to cover themselves. According to the *Catechism*:

The union of man and woman becomes subject to tensions, their relations henceforth marked by lust and domination.[59] (CCC 400)

Satan told our first parents they would be like God, possessing knowledge of good and evil. Adam and Eve thereafter experienced knowledge of evil; however, knowledge of evil is not an addition to true knowledge. For example, the experience of a debilitating disease is not a positive increase to knowledge. In like manner, the experience of sin causes a loss of freedom, happiness, dignity, and self-worth. Satan's lie beguiled our first parents, causing them to relinquish the wonderful gifts connected with their state of original holiness and justice and their exalted status in the eyes of God.

Though Original Sin did not destroy completely free will or the ability to know the truths of natural religion, it damaged natural human powers of body and soul and left human nature in a wounded condition.

The wounds caused by Original Sin stand in opposition to the four cardinal virtues:

- *Malice* inclines the will to sin and weakens it in the face of temptation. This is opposed to the cardinal virtue of *justice*.
- *Ignorance* impedes the ability to discern the truth. This is opposed to the cardinal virtue of *prudence*.
- *Weakness* causes a person to avoid effort or difficulties. This is opposed to the cardinal virtue of *fortitude*.
- *Concupiscence* fosters the appetite to escape the dominion of reason. This is opposed to the cardinal virtue of *temperance*.

Expulsion of Adam and Eve (detail) by Milani.
This exclusion signified the loss of sanctifying grace and of the intimate friendship they had previously enjoyed with God as well as the impossibility of entering Heaven without redemption.

GOD CONFRONTS ADAM AND EVE

After the Fall, Adam and Eve tried to hide from God. Having sought them out, God informed Eve she would suffer pain in childbearing as well as mistreatment from her husband. God had created Eve to be a companion and equal of Adam;[60] she would henceforth be under his domination.

God then addressed Adam, the father of the human race. He told Adam that the pleasures of work and his domination over creation had come to an end. From now on, Adam's work would require toil and would often end in futility ("thorns and thistles").[61] Thus, because of Original Sin:

> **Harmony with creation is broken: visible creation has become alien and hostile to man.**[62] (CCC 400)

One of the disastrous consequences for Adam and Eve, however, was the elimination of their preternatural gifts, which formed part of their original state of holiness and justice. Both body and soul suffer the consequences of Original Sin. God told our first parents, "You are dust and to dust you shall return";[63] i.e., they would suffer death of the body. Their immunity from sickness had also been lost; the body would be subject to disease and physical frailty, which would culminate in the separation of the body and soul at death.

Along with physical sickness and death, Original Sin left a permanent wound in the spiritual component of the human person. The former self-control typified by the dominion of mind and will over bodily passions was gone, never to return.[64]

The last punishment due to Original Sin was the banishment of Adam and Eve from the Garden of Eden. This exclusion signified the loss of sanctifying grace and of the intimate friendship they had previously enjoyed with God as well as the impossibility of entering Heaven without redemption. The exile of our first parents from the Garden of Eden also prefigured the agony later suffered by the New Adam, Jesus Christ, in the Garden of Gethsemane. His suffering, however, opened the gates of Paradise that had been shut.

TRANSMISSION OF ORIGINAL SIN

Cain Killing Abel (detail) by Crespi.
Adam's state of holiness and justice was meant to be transmitted to his descendants; instead, his fallen nature is transmitted.

The consequences of Original Sin afflicted not only Adam and Eve but also all of their descendants. This has been clear from the outset of human history, when Cain killed his brother Abel out of envy and hatred.

This terrible deed is tangible proof sin had entered the world. The effects of Original Sin continue to cause tragedy upon tragedy in the form of injustices, violations of human dignity, and untold destruction of human life. All of creation has in some way suffered from Original Sin.

> **After that first sin, the world is virtually inundated by sin. There is Cain's murder of his brother Abel and the universal corruption which follows in the wake of sin. (CCC 401)**

Every human person, with the exception of the Blessed Virgin Mary, has been conceived with the stain of Original Sin on his or her soul. As opposed to personal sin, which by its nature consists in a free and deliberate violation of God's Law, Original Sin is transmitted by human propagation and deprives human nature of the original holiness and justice God intended for his people.

> **Adam had received original holiness and justice not for himself alone, but for all human nature. By yielding to the tempter, Adam and Eve committed a *personal sin*, but this sin affected the *human nature* that they would then transmit *in a fallen state*.[65] It is a sin which will be transmitted by propagation to all mankind, that is, by the transmission of a human nature deprived of original holiness and justice. And that is why original sin is called "sin" only in an analogical sense: it is a sin "contracted" and not "committed"—a state and not an act. (CCC 404)**

In some sense, the whole human race was present in Adam and is, therefore, ensnared in his sin. Adam's state of holiness and justice was meant to be transmitted to his descendants; instead, his fallen nature is transmitted. Since every human person receives his or her nature ultimately from Adam, every human person shares Adam's fallen state. The *Catechism* cogently explains the universal impact of Original Sin:

> **The whole human race is in Adam "as one body of one man."[66] By this "unity of the human race" all men are implicated in Adam's sin, as all are implicated in Christ's justice. (CCC 404)**

ST. ELIZABETH ANN SETON

St. Elizabeth Ann Seton was the first native-born citizen of the United States of America to be canonized. She was born in New York City in 1774. Her family was wealthy, well respected in New York society, and strongly Episcopalian. As a young girl, St. Elizabeth was an avid reader who loved novels, but in time she developed a love for Sacred Scripture—a love that would last throughout her life.

At age 19, St. Elizabeth married William Seton, a wealthy New York businessman with whom she was deeply in love. Within a few years, they had five children. St. Elizabeth's blissful life, however, was soon to end. After a series of setbacks, William lost his business and had to file for bankruptcy. Shortly thereafter, he developed tuberculosis. The doctors advised William to go to Italy, whose climate might help cure his illness.

In Italy, St. Elizabeth was first exposed to Catholicism. She made many good, Catholic friends who helped her to understand the teachings of the Church. Two years later, she decided to be received into the Church.

Following William's death, St. Elizabeth returned to New York, where she suffered from the anti-Catholic bigotry rampant at the time. Abandoned by many of her family and friends, she struggled for several years to take care of her family. At the invitation of the president of Mount St. Mary's College and Seminary, she moved to Emittsburg, Maryland, where she established the St. Joseph's Academy and Free School for Catholic girls. This was the first free Catholic school in the United States of America.

In 1809, St. Elizabeth Ann Seton made vows of poverty, chastity, and obedience, and from that moment on, she was known as Mother Seton. With the help of two young women, Mother Seton established the Sisters of Charity of St. Joseph, the first religious community for women in the United States of America. Within a decade, the sisters had two orphanages and another school entrusted to their care. She devoted the rest of her life to the religious order, and today there are six religious communities derived from the community she established.

Throughout her life, St. Elizabeth suffered many trials and misunderstandings. She lost her mother at an early age. She lost her husband after just a few years of marriage. She struggled to raise her children. She was abandoned by many and misunderstood by others. However, she bore these crosses with grace and serenity. In fact, her contemporaries described her as always courteous and cultured, full of kindness, patience, and wit.

Throughout her life, St. Elizabeth maintained a great devotion to Sacred Scripture as well as to the Holy Eucharist and the Blessed Virgin Mary. As a woman of intense prayer, she taught those around her to maintain the constant presence of God.

> "We must pray literally without ceasing—without ceasing; in every occurrence and employment of our lives. You know I mean that prayer of the heart which is independent of place or situation, or which is, rather, a habit of lifting up the heart to God, as in a constant communication with Him."

St. Elizabeth Ann Seton died from tuberculosis in 1821. She was canonized in 1975 and is a patron of Catholic schools. Her feast day is January 4.

Illustration: *Mother Seton*, unknown artist, ca. 1804.

At the moment of conception, each new human person receives Adam's fallen nature by virtue of being his descendant. Even an infant, who cannot commit personal sins, has inherited Original Sin. As the fallen state of our first parents excluded them from the original earthly paradise, so is each of his descendants excluded from Heaven as long as Original Sin remains on the soul. This in no way detracts from God's infinite mercy; rather, it indicates the indispensability of redemption for every person. The Church teaches Original Sin affects each individual, and the whole of human history is affirmed in Sacred Scripture when Christ is said to have redeemed everyone. This is why St. Paul affirmed Christ "died for all."[67]

WOUNDED HUMAN NATURE

Pope John Paul II Baptizes an Infant in the Vatican's Sistine Chapel. The Sacrament of Baptism, which is an immediate fruit of Christ's redemption, removes the stain of Original Sin by infusing God's sanctifying grace into the soul.

The stain of Original Sin inherited from Adam and Eve has left each human person with a wounded nature. Spiritually speaking, people are born with an infection that can never heal on its own. Human nature, which is damaged but not utterly corrupted, leaves each person with a strong inclination toward all forms of selfishness.

As human history overwhelmingly attests, this sinful state leads people to violence, treachery, greed, and lust. Unless Original Sin is removed and the soul purified, there can be no hope of true happiness in this life or salvation in the life to come.

Original Sin damages the spiritual operations of the intellect and will. The mind's capacity to distinguish between good and evil is limited. Without Divine Revelation—such as the Ten Commandments and the Beatitudes—it would be very difficult to know or understand the moral law. Furthermore, without the aid of God's grace, it would be impossible to grow in holiness.

Personal experience demonstrates the impossibility of conforming one's life to the teachings of Jesus Christ without the help of God's grace. Living the Gospel message requires both a serious sacramental life and personal struggle. Each person must, for example, work hard to have kind thoughts, be gracious and pleasant to others, speak truthfully, and keep a pure heart. Perhaps in a given instance, an individual can conduct him- or herself according to objective moral standards, but to do this habitually is only possible with the divine assistance that comes from the graces won by Christ's redemption.

The Sacrament of Baptism, which is an immediate fruit of Christ's redemption, removes the stain of Original Sin by infusing God's sanctifying grace into the soul. However, Baptism does not completely heal the inclination to sin, called concupiscence, left by Original Sin. Therefore, both grace and laborious acts of virtue are needed to overcome concupiscence. The act of conception in itself is not evil, but, because of Original Sin, every individual is conceived under a certain bondage to the Devil.

> **By our first parents' sin, the devil has acquired a certain domination over man, even though man remains free. Original sin entails "captivity under the power of him who henceforth has the power of death, that is, the devil."[68]** (CCC 407)

The Second Vatican Council document *Gaudium et Spes* describes the effect of Original Sin and the Evil One on human history:

> **"The whole of man's history has been the story of our combat with the powers of evil, stretching, so our Lord tells us, from the very dawn of history until the last day. Finding himself in the midst of the battlefield man has to struggle to do what is right, and it is at great cost to himself, and aided by God's grace, that he succeeds in achieving his own inner integrity."[69] (CCC 409)**

Nevertheless, Original Sin does not leave the human person totally corrupted.[70] By taking advantage of God's saving and healing graces, the saints have given constant witness to the transcendent goodness and spiritual beauty potentially present in the heart of every person.

CONCLUSION

God created Adam and Eve out of his great love. He gave them the world to watch over and invited them to share in his friendship. They enjoyed a state of original holiness and justice and were perfectly happy. This came to an abrupt end when Adam and Eve disobeyed God.

> **Why did God not create a world so perfect that no evil could exist in it? With infinite power God could always create something better.[71] But with infinite wisdom and goodness God freely willed to create a world "in a state of journeying" towards its ultimate perfection. In God's plan this process of becoming involves the appearance of certain beings and the disappearance of others, the existence of the more perfect alongside the less perfect, both constructive and destructive forces of nature. With physical good there exists also *physical evil* as long as creation has not reached perfection.[72] (CCC 310)**

The Fall of Adam and Eve introduced sin, suffering, and death into the world. They lost their state of original holiness and justice not only for themselves but also for all of their descendants. Thus, every human person—except the Blessed Virgin Mary—has inherited the stain of Original Sin. This sinful state, without redemption, prevents people from entering into everlasting life with God in Heaven. Without a Redeemer, every man and woman would be consigned to the slavery of sin.

However, God did not abandon his people. Since God is an infinitely loving Father, he promised a Redeemer who would defeat Satan and reconcile God with his people. Thus, out of the despair of sin, our first parents were given the hope of redemption and a renewed friendship with God.

Christ on the Cross by Velázquez.
Without a Redeemer, every man and woman would be consigned to the slavery of sin.

Creator Alme Siderum

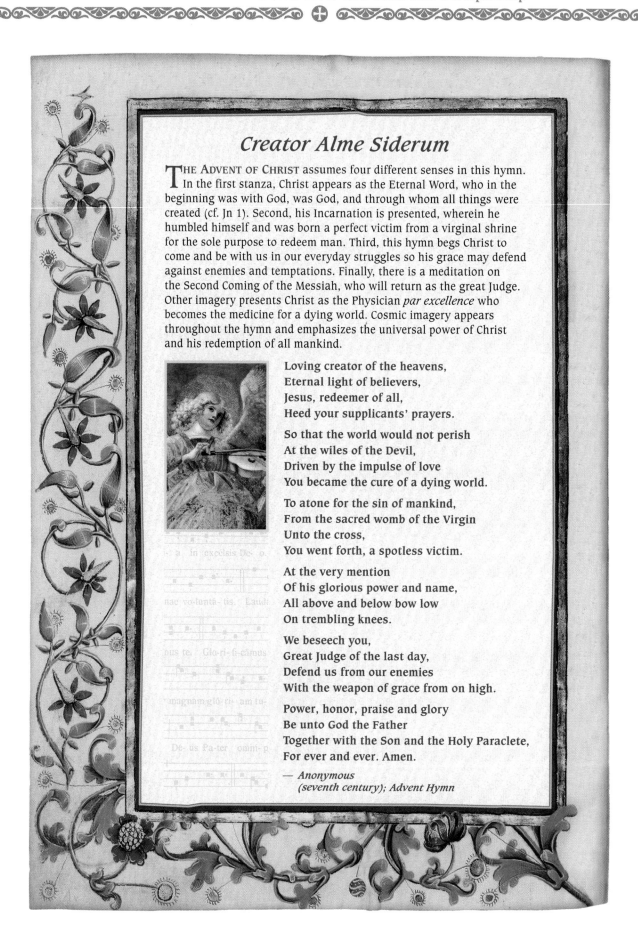

THE ADVENT OF CHRIST assumes four different senses in this hymn. In the first stanza, Christ appears as the Eternal Word, who in the beginning was with God, was God, and through whom all things were created (cf. Jn 1). Second, his Incarnation is presented, wherein he humbled himself and was born a perfect victim from a virginal shrine for the sole purpose to redeem man. Third, this hymn begs Christ to come and be with us in our everyday struggles so his grace may defend against enemies and temptations. Finally, there is a meditation on the Second Coming of the Messiah, who will return as the great Judge. Other imagery presents Christ as the Physician *par excellence* who becomes the medicine for a dying world. Cosmic imagery appears throughout the hymn and emphasizes the universal power of Christ and his redemption of all mankind.

Loving creator of the heavens,
Eternal light of believers,
Jesus, redeemer of all,
Heed your supplicants' prayers.

So that the world would not perish
At the wiles of the Devil,
Driven by the impulse of love
You became the cure of a dying world.

To atone for the sin of mankind,
From the sacred womb of the Virgin
Unto the cross,
You went forth, a spotless victim.

At the very mention
Of his glorious power and name,
All above and below bow low
On trembling knees.

We beseech you,
Great Judge of the last day,
Defend us from our enemies
With the weapon of grace from on high.

Power, honor, praise and glory
Be unto God the Father
Together with the Son and the Holy Paraclete,
For ever and ever. Amen.

— *Anonymous*
(seventh century); Advent Hymn

SUPPLEMENTARY READING

1. *Let Us Show Each Other God's Generosity*

Recognize to whom you owe the fact that you exist, that you breathe, that you understand, that you are wise, and, above all, that you know God and hope for the kingdom of heaven and the vision of glory, now darkly as in a mirror but then with greater fullness and purity. You have been made a son of God, co-heir with Christ. Where did you get all this, and from whom?

Let me turn to what is of less importance: the visible world around us. What benefactor has enabled you to look out upon the beauty of the sky, the sun in its course, the circle of the moon, the countless number of stars, with the harmony and order that are theirs, like the music of a harp? Who has blessed you with rain, with the art of husbandry, with different kinds of food, with the arts, with houses, with laws, with states, with a life of humanity and culture, with friendship and the easy familiarity of kinship?

Who has given you dominion over animals, those that are tame and those that provide you with food? Who has made you lord and master of everything on earth? In short, who has endowed you with all that makes man superior to all other living creatures?

Is it not God who asks you now in your turn to show yourself generous above all other creatures and for the sake of all other creatures? Because we have received from him so many wonderful gifts, will we not be ashamed to refuse him this one thing only, our generosity? Though he is God and Lord he is not afraid to be known as our Father. Shall we for our part repudiate those who are our kith and kin?

Brethren and friends, let us never allow ourselves to misuse what has been given us by God's gift. If we do, we shall hear Saint Peter say: *Be ashamed of yourselves for holding on to what belongs to someone else. Resolve to imitate God's justice, and no one will be poor.* Let us not labor to heap up and hoard riches while others remain in need. If we do, the prophet Amos will speak out against us with sharp and threatening words: *Come now, you that say: When will the new moon be over, so that we may start selling? When will the sabbath be over, so that we may start opening our treasures?*

Let us put into practice the supreme and primary law of God. He sends down rain on just and sinful alike, and causes the sun to rise on all without distinction. To all earth's creatures he has given the broad earth, the springs, the rivers and the forests. He has given the air to the birds, and the waters to those who live in the water. He has given abundantly to all the basic needs of life, not as a private possession, not restricted by law, not divided by boundaries, but as common to all, amply and in rich measure. His gifts are not deficient in any way, because he wanted to give equality of blessing to equality of worth, and to show the abundance of his generosity.

— St. Gregory Nazianzen

Adam Naming the Creatures
Lithography by Currier
"Out of the ground the LORD God formed every beast of the field and every bird of the air, and brought them to the man to see what he would call them; and whatever the man called every living creature, that was its name. The man gave names to all cattle, and to the birds of the air, and to every beast of the field; but for the man there was not found a helper fit for him." (Gn 2:19-20)

SUPPLEMENTARY READING Continued

2. *The Word "Angel" Denotes a Function Rather Than a Nature*

You should be aware that the word "angel" denotes a function rather than a nature. Those holy spirits of heaven have indeed always been spirits. They can only be called angels when they deliver some message. Moreover, those who deliver messages of lesser importance are called angels; and those who proclaim messages of supreme importance are called archangels. And so it was that not merely an angel but the archangel Gabriel was sent to the Virgin Mary. It was only fitting that the highest angel should come to announce the greatest of all messages.

Some angels are given proper names to denote the service they are empowered to perform. In that holy city, where perfect knowledge flows from the vision of almighty God, those who have no names may easily be known. But personal names are assigned to some, not because they could not be known without them, but rather to denote their ministry when they came among us. Thus, Michael means "Who is like God"; Gabriel is "The Strength of God"; and Raphael is "God's Remedy."

Whenever some act of wondrous power must be performed, Michael is sent, so that his action and his name may make it clear that no one can do what God does by his superior power. So also our ancient foe desired in his pride to be like God, saying: *I will ascend into heaven; I will exalt my throne above the stars of heaven; I will be like the Most High*. He will be allowed to remain in power until the end of the world when he will be destroyed in the final punishment. Then, he will fight with the archangel Michael, as we are told by John: *A battle was fought with Michael the archangel*.

So too Gabriel, who is called God's strength, was sent to Mary. He came to announce the One who appeared as a humble man to quell the cosmic powers. Thus God's strength announced the coming of the Lord of the heavenly powers, mighty in battle. Raphael means, as I have said, God's remedy, for when he touched Tobit's eyes in order to cure him, he banished the darkness of his blindness. Thus, since he is to heal, he is rightly called God's remedy.

— Pope St. Gregory the Great

3. *Adam and Christ*

The holy Apostle has told us that the human race takes its origin from two men, Adam and Christ; two men equal in body but unequal in merit, wholly alike in their physical structure but totally unlike in the very origin of their being. *The first man, Adam*, he says, *became a living soul, the last Adam a life-giving spirit.*

The first Adam was made by the last Adam, from whom he also received his soul, to give him life. The last Adam was formed by his own action; he did not have to wait for life to be given him by someone else, but was the only one who could give life to all. The first Adam was formed from valueless clay, the second Adam came forth from the precious womb of the Virgin. In the case of the first Adam, earth was changed into flesh; in the case of the second Adam, flesh was raised up to be God.

What more need be said? The second Adam stamped his image on the first Adam when he created him. That is why he took on himself the role, and the name, of the first Adam, in order that he might not lose what he had made in his own image. The first Adam, the last Adam; the first had a beginning, the last knows no end. The last Adam is indeed the first; as he himself says: *I am the first and the last*.

Now that we are reborn, as I have said, in the likeness of our Lord, and have indeed been adopted by God as his children, let us put on the complete image of our Creator so as to be wholly like him, not in the glory that he alone possesses, but in innocence, simplicity, gentleness, patience, humility, mercy, harmony, those qualities in which he chose to become, and to be, one with us.

— St. Peter Chrysologus

VOCABULARY

ADAM
The first man and our first father. Together with Eve, he committed the first sin (Original Sin). This Hebrew name refers to the particular individual or to mankind in general.

BIBLE
Sacred Scripture; the books that contain the truth of God's Revelation, which were composed by human authors under the inspiration of the Holy Spirit. The Bible contains forty-six books in the Old Testament and twenty-seven in the New.

CREATION
God's bringing forth the universe and all its inhabitants into being out of nothing. Creation is good but has been corrupted by sin.

EDEN
The name of the garden in which God placed Adam and Eve.

EMPIRICAL DATA
Information gathered from sensory observation and experimentation.

EVE
The first woman and our first mother. Eve was created from the rib of Adam, and thus woman, unlike the animals, is man's equal and complement. With Adam, she committed the first sin (Original Sin).

EVOLUTION
The scientific theory that species came to be as they are by a gradual process of change and development. Valid theories on the origin of life cannot contradict two facts: God created all matter, and the creation of human beings is a special act of the divine Creator.

IMAGE
A representation such as a statue or picture. Each human person is made in the image of God; that is, human beings are like God insofar as having intelligence, free will, and the capacity to love

INERRANT
Making no mistakes or errors. Scripture is inerrant; it always teaches truth, never falsehood.

INFALLIBLE
Incapable of error. The Bible and the Church are infallible because of a special protection by God the Holy Spirit.

INSPIRED
Guided by God; from a word meaning "breathed in." The human writers of Scripture wrote in their own words but through God's inspiration wrote what he intended them to write and nothing more.

ORIGINAL HOLINESS
The state of harmony that existed between our first parents and God before the Fall by which they participated in divine life.

ORIGINAL JUSTICE
The supernatural and preternatural gifts enjoyed by our first parents before the Fall; these include sanctifying grace and exemption from sin, suffering, death, and concupiscence.

ORIGINAL SIN
Adam and Eve's abuse of their human freedom by disobeying God's command. As a consequence, they lost the grace of original holiness and justice and became subject to death; sin became universally present in the world. Every human person except Christ and the Blessed Virgin Mary has been born with the stain of Original Sin. This sin separates mankind from God, darkens the intellect, weakens the will, and introduced into human nature an inclination toward sin.

PRETERNATURAL GIFTS
The gifts bestowed on our first parents, which include exemption from concupiscence, sickness, death, and ignorance. These gifts are distinct from the supernatural gifts by which our first parents were adopted as children of God and became partakers of divine nature. Though both preternatural and supernatural gifts were lost because of Original Sin, supernatural gifts are bestowed in the Sacrament of Baptism.

VOCABULARY Continued

SALVATION HISTORY
The story of God's plan to save man from the consequences of sin. This plan began with Creation, is unfolding now, and will continue until the end of time at the Second Coming.

SCRIPTURE
See Bible.

SERPENT
The form taken by Satan in the Garden of Eden. The Hebrew word *nahash* refers to a fearsome, murderous creature.

SOUL
The form of the body, this is an individual spiritual substance created directly by God in his image and likeness. The unity of a body and soul form a human person. The soul is immortal—it does not perish when separated from the body at death—and it will be united with a glorified body at the final resurrection.

TRANSCENDENT
Beyond the limits of ordinary human experience or knowledge.

VOID
Empty; without form; the state of the world before God gave it form and created beings to fill it.

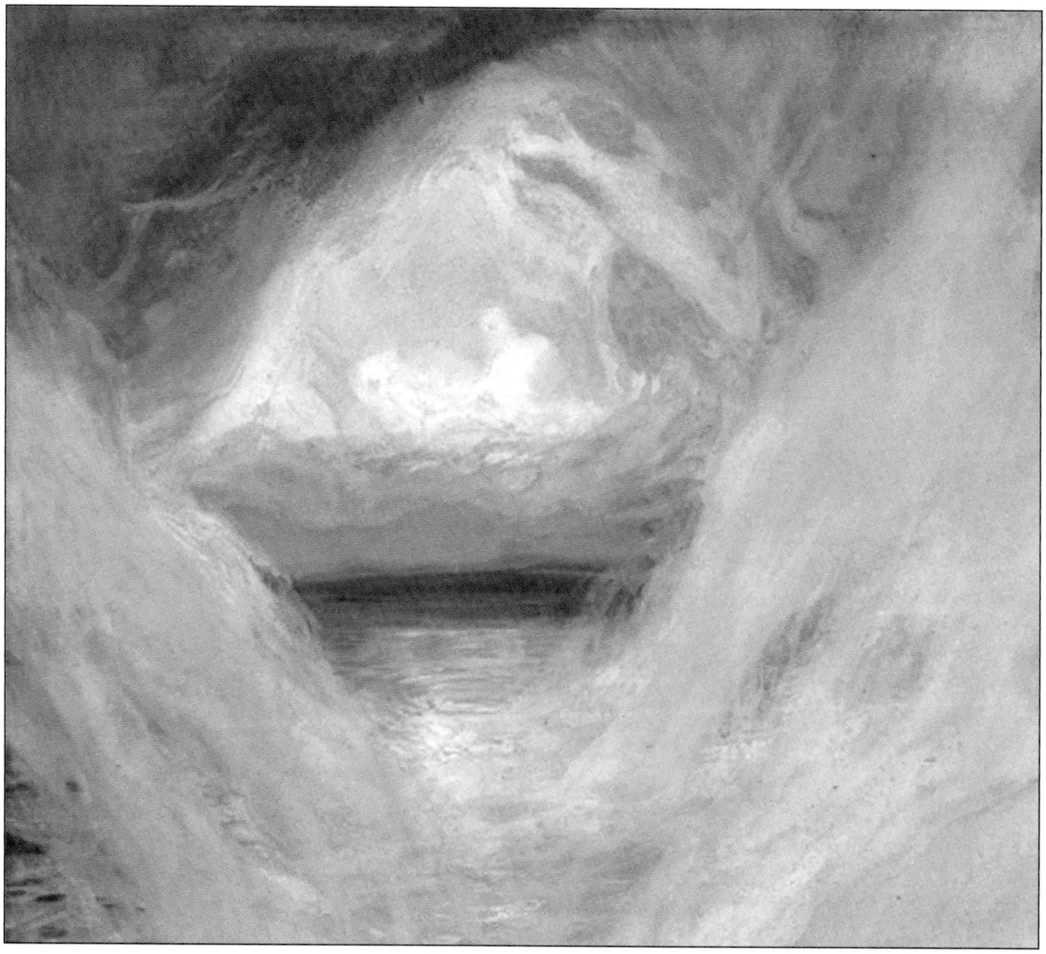

The Creation by Tissot.
"The earth was without form and void, and darkness was upon the face of the deep; and the Spirit of God was moving over the face of the waters." (Gn 1: 2)

STUDY QUESTIONS

1. According to the opening chapters of Genesis, how are man and woman unique among all visible creation?
2. What vocation, or mission, did God give Adam and Eve?
3. What concept explains the attitude people are to have toward their call to dominate creation?
4. What is salvation history?
5. What does it mean to say the Bible is inspired and inerrant?
6. Which Person or Persons of the Blessed Trinity were involved in creation?
7. How are Christ, the Holy Spirit, and the Blessed Trinity alluded to in Genesis?
8. Why did God create the universe?
9. Why was the creation of human beings a special way to reveal God's goodness and love?
10. What does it mean to possess the image and likeness of God?
11. What operations does the human soul carry out?
12. What is meant by original holiness and justice?
13. What is an angel?
14. What was the one limitation God placed on Adam and Eve's freedom in the Garden of Eden?
15. What lie did the serpent tell Eve?
16. How did Christ describe Satan?
17. How can Original Sin be described as a sin of pride?
18. What were the consequences of Original Sin for Adam and Eve?
19. What were the consequences of Original Sin for Adam and Eve's descendants?
20. What is the effect of Original Sin on your mind and will?
21. What is concupiscence?
22. How did Adam and Eve suffer for Original Sin?
23. What did banishment from the Garden of Eden symbolize?
24. In the Book of Genesis, what is the first clear sign sin had entered the world?
25. According to the Book of Genesis, what was the moral history of the world after the Fall?
26. How are the effects of Original Sin transmitted?
27. What is the difference between Adam and Eve's sin and the Original Sin their descendants inherit?
28. What is the wound of Original Sin?
29. Who are the models to overcome the effects of Original Sin?

PRACTICAL EXERCISES

1. In order to understand it properly, explain why it is important to keep in mind the Bible is ancient, religious literature.

2. God assigned Adam and Eve to fill the earth and exercise dominion over it. Despite sin, how has the human race been obedient to this divine mission?

3. "Man with all his noble qualities, with sympathy which feels for the most debased, with benevolence which extends not only to other men but to the humblest living creature, with his god-like intellect which has penetrated into the movements and constitution of the solar system—with all these exalted powers—Man still bears in his bodily frame the indelible stamp of his lowly origin." This quote from Charles Darwin's *The Descent of Man* offers one of the more striking claims of the theory of evolution: humans have evolved from lesser animals such as apes. Is this theory in accord with the creation narrative in the Book of Genesis? Can a Catholic believe in evolution? Why is it acceptable to believe in the evolution of the body but not the evolution of the soul?

4. In the Fall, the serpent tempted Adam and Eve with the chance to be like God. Adam and Eve sinned by choosing power for themselves instead of God's love. How is Original Sin like all other sins? What temptations does the Devil use today to draw young people away from God? How do these temptations relate to the one faced by Adam and Eve?

Cain Flying Before Jehovah's Curse by Corman.
"The LORD said, 'What have you done? The voice of your brother's blood is crying to me from the ground. And now you are cursed from the ground, which has opened its mouth to receive your brother's blood from your hand. When you till the ground, it shall no longer yield to you its strength; you shall be a fugitive and a wanderer on the earth.' Cain said to the LORD, 'My punishment is greater than I can bear. Behold, thou hast driven me this day away from the ground; and from thy face I shall be hidden; and I shall be a fugitive and a wanderer on the earth, and whoever finds me will slay me.' Then the LORD said to him, 'Not so! If any one slays Cain, vengeance shall be taken on him sevenfold.' And the LORD put a mark on Cain, lest any who came upon him should kill him." (Gn 4: 10-15)

FROM THE CATECHISM

135 "The Sacred Scriptures contain the Word of God and, because they are inspired they are truly the Word of God" (*DV* 24).

311 Angels and men, as intelligent and free creatures, have to journey toward their ultimate destinies by their free choice and preferential love. They can therefore go astray. Indeed, they have sinned. Thus has *moral evil*, incommensurably more harmful than physical evil, entered the world. God is in no way, directly or indirectly, the cause of moral evil.[73] He permits it, however, because he respects the freedom of his creatures and, mysteriously, knows how to derive good from it:

> For almighty God . . . , because he is supremely good, would never allow any evil whatsoever to exist in his works if he were not so all-powerful and good as to cause good to emerge from evil itself.[74]

355 "God created man in his own image, in the image of God he created him, male and female he created them."[75] Man occupies a unique place in creation: (I) he is "in the image of God"; (II) in his own nature he unites the spiritual and material worlds; (III) he is created "male and female"; (IV) God established him in his friendship.

357 Being in the image of God the human individual possesses the dignity of a person, who is not just something, but someone. He is capable of self-knowledge, of self-possession and of freely giving himself and entering into communion with other persons. And he is called by grace to a covenant with his Creator, to offer him a response of faith and love that no other creature can give in his stead.

705 Disfigured by sin and death, man remains "in the image of God," in the image of the Son, but is deprived "of the glory of God,"[76] of his " likeness." The promise made to Abraham inaugurates the economy of salvation, at the culmination of which the Son himself will assume that "image"[77] and restore it in the Father's "likeness" by giving it again its Glory, the Spirit who is "the Giver of Life."

1147 God speaks to man through the visible creation. The material cosmos is so presented to man's intelligence that he can read there traces of its Creator.[78] Light and darkness, wind and fire, water and earth, the tree and its fruit speak of God and symbolize both his greatness and his nearness.

1700 The dignity of the human person is rooted in his creation in the image and likeness of God (*article 1*); it is fulfilled in his vocation to divine beatitude (*article 2*). It is essential to a human being freely to direct himself to this fulfillment (*article 3*). By his deliberate actions (*article 4*), the human person does, or does not, conform to the good promised by God and attested by moral conscience (*article 5*). Human beings make their own contribution to their interior growth; they make their whole sentient and spiritual lives into means of this growth (*article 6*). With the help of grace they grow in virtue (*article 7*), avoid sin, and if they sin they entrust themselves as did the prodigal son[79] to the mercy of our Father in heaven (*article 8*). In this way they attain to the perfection of charity.

1704 The human person participates in the light and power of the divine Spirit. By his reason, he is capable of understanding the order of things established by the Creator. By free will, he is capable of directing himself toward his true good. He finds his perfection "in seeking and loving what is true and good."[80]

1705 By virtue of his soul and his spiritual powers of intellect and will, man is endowed with freedom, an "outstanding manifestation of the divine image."[81]

1706 By his reason, man recognizes the voice of God which urges him "to do what is good and avoid what is evil."[82] Everyone is obliged to follow this law, which makes itself heard in conscience and is fulfilled in the love of God and of neighbor. Living a moral life bears witness to the dignity of the person.

FROM THE CATECHISM Continued

2402 In the beginning God entrusted the earth and its resources to the common stewardship of mankind to take care of them, master them by labor, and enjoy their fruits.[83] The goods of creation are destined for the whole human race. However, the earth is divided up among men to assure the security of their lives, endangered by poverty and threatened by violence. The appropriation of property is legitimate for guaranteeing the freedom and dignity of persons and for helping each of them to meet his basic needs and the needs of those in his charge. It should allow for a natural solidarity to develop between men.

2566 *Man is in search of God.* In the act of creation, God calls every being from nothingness into existence. "Crowned with glory and honor," man is, after the angels, capable of acknowledging "how majestic is the name of the Lord in all the earth."[84] Even after losing through his sin his likeness to God, man remains an image of his Creator, and retains the desire for the one who calls him into existence. All religions bear witness to men's essential search for God.[85]

ENDNOTES - CHAPTER ONE

1. *Spe Salvi*, 33.
2. *Spe Salvi*, 11.
3. Is 53:11; cf. 53:12; Jn 8:34-36; Acts 3:14.
4. Cf. Gn 1:26.
5. Cf. Gn 3:17.
6. Gn 1:1.
7. Ibid.
8. Cf. *GS* 12 § 1; 24 § 3; 39 § 1.
9. Gn 2:15.
10. Gn 1:28.
11. Wis 11:24.
12. Cf. CCC 358.
13. Gn 1:28.
14. Cf. Gn 1:28-31.
15. Cf. *CA* 37-38.
16. CCC 2402.
17. Cf. *SRS* 32; *CA* 51.
18. Gn 1:3.
19. Gn 1:2.
20. Gn 2:7.
21. *DV* 11.
22. *Adv. hær.* III, 24, 1.
23. Gn 1:26.
24. Cf. CCC 291, 292.
25. *Dei Filius*, can. § 5: DS 3025.
26. St. Bonaventure, *In II Sent.* I, 2, 2, 1.
27. St. Thomas Aquinas, *Sent.* 2, Prol.
28. Gn 1:26-27.
29. Cf. Mt 16:25-26; Jn 15:13; Acts 2:41.
30. Cf. Mt 10:28; 26:38; Jn 12:27; 2 Mc 6:30.
31. Gn 2:7.
32. Cf. CCC 357.
33. Cf. Mt 19.
34. *GS* 12 § 3.
35. *GS* 24 § 3.
36. St. Thomas Aquinas, *STh* I, 114, 3, *ad* 3.
37. Mt 18:10.
38. Cf. Lk 22:43.
39. Cf. Mt 28:2-7.
40. CCC 352.
41. Cf. Council of Trent (1546): DS 1511.
42. Cf. *LG* 2.
43. Cf. CCC 376.
44. Cf. Gn 2:16-17.
45. Jn 8:44; cf. Mt 4:1-11.
46. 1 Jn 3:8.
47. Cf. Gn 3:1-5; Wis 2:24.
48. Cf. Jn 8:44; Rev 12:9.
49. Lateran Council IV (1215): DS 800.
50. Jn 8:44.
51. Sir 10:12.
52. Wis 2:23-24.
53. Rom 5:19.
54. St. Maximus, *Conf.*; cf. CCC 398.
55. Rom 5:12.
56. *GS* 13 § 1.
57. *GS* 13 § 2.
58. Cf. Gn 1:31.
59. Cf. Gn 3:7-16.
60. Cf. Gn 2:21-25.
61. Cf. Gn 3:17-18.
62. Cf. Gn 3:17, 19.
63. Gn 3:19.
64. Cf. CCC 400.
65. Cf. Council of Trent: DS 1511-1512.
66. St. Thomas Aquinas, *De Malo* 4, 1.
67. 2 Cor 5:15.
68. Council of Trent (1546): DS 1511; cf. Heb 2:14.
69. *GS* 37 § 2.
70. Cf. CCC 406.
71. Cf. St. Thomas Aquinas, *STh* I, 25, 6.
72. Cf. St. Thomas Aquinas, *SCG* III, 71.
73. Cf. St. Augustine, *De libero arbitrio* 1, 1, 2: PL 32, 1223; St. Thomas Aquinas, *STh* I-II, 79, 1.
74. St. Augustine, *Enchiridion* 3, 11: PL 40, 236.
75. Gn 1:27.
76. Rom 3:23.
77. Cf. Jn 1:14; Phil 2:7.
78. Cf. Wis 13:1; Rom 1:19f.; Acts 14:17.
79. Lk 15:11-32.
80. *GS* 15 § 2.
81. *GS* 17.
82. *GS* 16.
83. Cf. Gn 1:26-29.
84. Ps 8:5; 8:1.
85. Cf. Acts 17:27.

The Mystery of Redemption

CHAPTER 2

Preparing for the Messiah

Beginning with his promise to Adam and Eve, the Old Testament recounts God's plan of redemption, which was eventually fulfilled in the Incarnation of Jesus Christ in the New Testament.

The Mystery of Redemption

CHAPTER 2

Preparing for the Messiah

INTRODUCTION

After his fall, man was not abandoned by God. On the contrary, God calls him and in a mysterious way heralds the coming victory over evil and his restoration from his fall.[1] (CCC 410)

Adam and Eve, unlike their descendants, were created in a state of original holiness and justice. This was lost, however, when they disobeyed God's command not to eat from the tree of the knowledge of good and evil. Our first parents brought upon themselves and their descendants the disastrous effects of their choice to rebel against the Creator, who loves them infinitely. Sin soon spread over the world, leaving mankind darkened and depraved.

God, however, did not abandon humanity. After the Fall, he promised redemption for Adam and Eve and their descendants; Satan would not have the last word. More than simply threatening the demonic serpent with punishment and defeat, God assured our first parents he would send a Redeemer—one who would overcome and defeat the evil one and obtain salvation for all people.

Beginning with his promise to Adam and Eve, the Old Testament recounts God's plan of redemption, which was eventually fulfilled in the Incarnation of Jesus Christ in the New Testament. Salvation history is the story of God reaching out to save mankind from sin. His covenants with Noah, Abraham, Moses, and David served to build up the Chosen People and prepare them for the coming Messiah, Jesus Christ, and his New Law of Love.

THIS CHAPTER WILL ADDRESS SEVERAL QUESTIONS:

- What is the "happy fault"?
- What are the senses in which Sacred Scripture can be read?
- How is Original Sin at work in the Old Testament?
- What was God's plan for marriage from the beginning?
- Who are the great figures of salvation history?
- What are the covenants of the Old Testament?
- What is the significance of the Davidic Kingdom?
- What is the role of the prophets in salvation history?

Adam and Eve Banished from Paradise (detail of pulpit in Cathedral of St. Gudule, Brussels) by Verbruggen. God did not abandon humanity. After the Fall, he promised redemption for Adam and Eve and their descendants; Satan would not have the last word.

GOD'S PROMISE OF REDEMPTION

Satan instigated the Fall of our first parents, so God first revealed to him the news of his ultimate defeat. God told the demonic serpent his head would be crushed by the "seed" of the "woman":

> **"I will put enmity between you and the woman, and between your seed and her seed; he shall bruise your head and you shall bruise his heel."** (Gn 3: 15)

Hardly had Adam and Eve committed Original Sin when God made it clear the Devil would be defeated by a "woman" and her seed. From the beginning, Christian writers have called this the First Gospel (*Protoevangelium*). This is a highly appropriate term; the word *gospel* means "good news," and these words contain the first prophecy of the Messiah who would bring salvation to all people.

> **This passage in Genesis is called the *Protoevangelium* ("first gospel"): the first announcement of the Messiah and Redeemer, of a battle between the serpent and the Woman, and of the final victory of a descendant of hers.** (CCC 410)

Early Christian writers elaborated extensively on the *Protoevangelium*, applying the names of *New Adam* and *New Eve* respectively to Jesus the Messiah and the Blessed Virgin Mary, his Mother. Christ, the New Adam, made reparation for the disobedience of the first Adam, becoming "obedient unto death, even death on a cross."[2] Christ's selfless and humble obedience to the will of his Father brought about the redemption of the world.

> **The Christian tradition sees in this passage an announcement of the "New Adam" who, because he "became obedient unto death, even death on a cross," makes amends superabundantly for the disobedience of Adam.[3] Furthermore many Fathers and Doctors of the Church have seen the woman announced in the *Protoevangelium* as Mary, the mother of Christ, the "new Eve." Mary benefited first of all and uniquely from Christ's victory over sin: she was preserved from all stain of original sin and by a special grace of God committed no sin of any kind during her whole earthly life.[4]** (CCC 411)

In light of the Good News of Jesus Christ, the "woman" is none other than the Blessed Virgin Mary. Her obedience and humble "yes" to the Archangel Gabriel was the necessary condition for the Incarnation of Jesus Christ, the Savior. Only when she had accepted the invitation to be the Mother of the Savior was Christ conceived by the power of the Holy Spirit.

In radical contrast to the disobedience of Eve, who prompted Adam to bring sin into the world, the Blessed Virgin Mary, the New Eve, cooperated with God to bring about the remedy for sin and win for everyone the possibility of redemption. Her seed, Jesus Christ, crushed the head of the serpent. By taking the sins of mankind on his shoulders and obtaining a superabundance of grace for the forgiveness of

Virgin and Child (*Durán Madonna*) by Weyden.
The Blessed Virgin Mary, the New Eve, cooperated with God to bring about the remedy for sin and win for everyone the possibility of redemption.

St. Peter captures this unity among people, which is obtained through Christ:

> **You are a chosen race, a royal priesthood, a holy nation, God's own people, that you may declare the wonderful deeds of him who called you out of darkness into his marvelous light.** (1 Pt 2: 9)

True unity, therefore, does not consist in a common, pagan sinfulness but rather in a participation in Christ's life, which he gratuitously bestows on people through the merits of his Paschal Mystery.

GOD'S COVENANT WITH ABRAHAM

> **"In you all the nations of the earth shall be blessed."[21]** (CCC 59)

The history of God's Chosen People, the Jews, out of whom the Savior and Messiah, Jesus Christ, came, begins with God's calling of Abraham, whom God selected to be their father. The Book of Genesis describes Abraham as a holy man filled with a humble faith and docility to God's will. When God first called Abraham, he asked him to leave his home in Ur of the Chaldeans and to go to the land of Canaan.

> **The Lord said to Abram, "Go from your country and your kindred and your father's house to the land that I will show you. And I will make of you a great nation, and I will bless you, and make your name great, so that you will be a blessing. I will bless those who bless you, and him who curses you I will curse; and by you all the families of the earth shall bless themselves." (Gn 12: 1-3)**

In this call to Abraham (then named Abram), God promised he would become the patriarch of a mighty nation. Though his wife Sarah was barren and past the age of childbearing, God promised Abraham would have a son. Despite his uncertainty and perhaps even his consternation, Abraham never questioned God's will. Rather, he believed God with an unwavering faith.

As God had predicted, Sarah bore a son whom Abraham named Isaac, the first of a multitude of descendants. Like Adam and Noah, Abraham became the father of a chosen, divinely favored people, and his offspring first heard the Word of God.

> **Israel is the priestly people of God, "called by the name of the Lord," and "the first to hear the word of God,"[22] the people of "elder brethren" in the faith of Abraham.** (CCC 63)

Abraham, Sarah, and the Angel by Provost.
Like Adam and Noah, Abraham became the father of a chosen, divinely favored people, and his offspring first heard the Word of God.

As if believing he and Sarah could have a son in their old age was not enough, Abraham was given an even greater test of faithfulness. When Isaac was a young man, God commanded Abraham to offer Isaac as a human sacrifice. Trusting completely in God's will, Abraham proceeded to fulfill this most challenging and ostensibly inexplicable task.

Abraham and Isaac traveled to the mountains of Moriah. Abraham took with him the wood for the burnt offering. As they approached the site of the sacrifice, Abraham laid the wood of the sacrifice upon Isaac's shoulders. Nearing the altar, Isaac asked his father about the sacrificial lamb. Abraham replied, "God will provide himself the lamb for a burnt offering."[23] Abraham then bound Isaac and laid him on the altar, drawing a knife to slay his beloved son.

> **The angel of the LORD called to him from heaven, and said, "Abraham, Abraham!" And he said, "Here am I." He said, "Do not lay your hand on the lad or do anything to him; for now I know that you fear God, seeing you have not withheld your son, your only son, from me." And Abraham lifted up his eyes and looked, and behold, behind him was a ram, caught in a thicket by his horns; and Abraham went and took the ram, and offered it up as a burnt offering instead of his son. (Gn 22: 11-13)**

Because of his heroic fidelity and generosity, God blessed and loved Abraham more than anyone who had come before him.

> **The angel of the LORD called to Abraham a second time from heaven, and said, "By myself I have sworn, says the LORD, because you have done this, and have not withheld your son, your only son, I will indeed bless you, and I will multiply your descendants as the stars of heaven and as the sand which is on the seashore. And your descendants shall possess the gate of their enemies, and by your descendants shall all the nations of the earth bless themselves, because you have obeyed my voice." (Gn 22: 15-18)**

The Sacrifice of Abraham by Rembrandt.
Because of his heroic fidelity and generosity, God blessed and loved Abraham more than anyone who had come before him.

God's covenant with Abraham initiated the formation of a people who were chosen to worship the one true God. From this point on, God revealed himself and his will through the patriarchs, judges, and prophets of this Chosen People. The culmination of this Divine Revelation is the Incarnate Word, Jesus Christ.

> **The people descended from Abraham would be the trustees of the promise made to the patriarchs, the chosen people, called to prepare for that day when God would gather all his children into the unity of the Church.[24] They would be the root onto which the Gentiles would be grafted, once they came to believe.[25] (CCC 60)**

This famous Old Testament story of the sacrifice of Isaac by Abraham is very rich in redemptive symbolism, prefiguring the Passion and Death of Christ. First, Abraham and Isaac traveled to Mt. Moriah on a donkey, the same beast of burden that carried Christ into Jerusalem on his way to his sacrificial Death.

Second, Abraham was willing to offer his son as a sacrifice in accordance with God's will. God the Father offered his Only-Begotten Son, Jesus Christ, to be sacrificed for the sins of the world. Abraham promised Isaac God himself would provide the sacrificial victim; this found its ultimate fulfillment not in the ram caught in the thicket but in the Lamb of God nailed to the Cross. Finally, Isaac walked to the altar carrying the wood for his own sacrifice. Christ carried the wood of his Cross to Calvary for his own Crucifixion.

The physical sign of God's covenant with Abraham was circumcision. The blood shed by the males under the Abrahamic Covenant is a type of the Blood shed by Christ to establish the New Covenant. In this way, among many others, the Chosen People formed through Abraham prepared the way for the People of God formed in Christ.

The Annunciation by Beccafumi.
From the moment of his conception in the virginal womb of the Blessed Virgin Mary, accomplished through the power of the Holy Spirit, the redemption of man began to unfold.

THIS CHAPTER WILL ADDRESS SEVERAL QUESTIONS:

- How did God prepare the Blessed Virgin Mary and St. Joseph for their missions as Mother and foster-father of the Savior?
- What do the genealogies of Christ reveal?
- What is the significance of the Annunciation, the Visitation, the Nativity, the Presentation in the Temple, and the Finding of Christ in the Temple?
- What is the meaning of Christ's hidden years?
- Why did God become man?
- How is Christ's life redemptive?
- What is redemption?

THE ANNUNCIATION

In the sixth month the angel Gabriel was sent from God to a city of Galilee named Nazareth, to a virgin betrothed to a man whose name was Joseph, of the house of David; and the virgin's name was Mary. And he came to her and said, "Hail, full of grace, the Lord is with you!" But she was greatly troubled at the saying, and considered in her mind what sort of greeting this might be. And the angel said to her, "Do not be afraid, Mary, for you have found favor with God. And behold, you will conceive in your womb and bear a son, and you shall call his name Jesus." (Lk 1:26-31)

Annunciation by Memling.
"Hail, full of grace, the Lord is with you!."
(Lk 1:28)

For centuries, the Israelites had awaited the promised Messiah, who had been foretold in the Book of Genesis and by the prophets. These expectations of a savior were especially heightened during those periods when Israel was oppressed by her enemies and exiled to foreign lands. Israel's latest humiliation was military occupation by the Romans. Many Israelites looked for a political or military messiah who would liberate them and restore the Kingdom of Israel to its former glory. While God had been gradually preparing his people for the Messiah and the redemption according to his plan, the exact details were very much unclear to the Jews.

You, O Bethlehem Ephrathah, who are little to be among the clans of Judah, from you shall come forth for me one who is to be ruler in Israel, whose origin is from of old, from ancient days. (Mi 5:2)

The prophet Micah had foretold that the Messiah would be born in Bethlehem, the City of David, in Judah. However, the story of the *Paschal Mystery* (i.e., the redemption accomplished by the Suffering, Death, and Resurrection of Jesus Christ) begins with the *Annunciation* in Nazareth, a small town in the northern region of Israel called Galilee.

In his Gospel, St. Luke reports God sent his messenger, the Archangel Gabriel, to a virgin named Mary. He greeted her with the words, "Hail, full of grace, the Lord is with you!."[2]

To become the mother of the Savior, Mary "was enriched by God with gifts appropriate to such a role."[3] The angel Gabriel at the moment of the annunciation salutes her as "full of grace."[4] In fact, in order for Mary to be able to give the free assent of her faith to the announcement of her vocation, it was necessary that she be wholly borne by God's grace. (CCC 490)

In the Archangel Gabriel's greeting, the phrase "full of grace," (In Greek, *kecharitomene*) was used in place of a name. This particular word had never been used to address anyone in Sacred Scripture, but it stands to reason the Blessed Virgin Mary would have indeed been filled with God's grace. She had been chosen from all time to bear God himself in her womb, and, to prepare her for this unique role, she had been conceived without any stain of Original Sin.

"The most Blessed Virgin Mary...in the first instance of her conception, by a singular grace and privilege granted by Almighty God, in view of the merits of Jesus Christ, the Savior of the human race, was preserved free from all stain of original sin." (*Ineffabilis Deus*)

This perennial teaching of the Church is called the *Immaculate Conception*. Pope Bl. Pius IX solemnly declared it a dogma of the Faith in 1854. The Blessed Virgin Mary was preserved from all stain of Original Sin; this implies she was also preserved from the consequences of Original Sin, meaning she was free from concupiscence and was filled with an abundance of grace to reject any temptation to sin. It is important to emphasize her sinlessness was not due to her own merit but was a grace and privilege God had given her in anticipation of the merits Christ would gain by his redemption. It is most fitting that the Blessed Virgin Mary—the New Eve who would give birth to Christ, the New Adam—would be without sin.

> **The Fathers of the Eastern tradition call the Mother of God "the All-Holy" (*Panagia*), and celebrate her as "free from any stain of sin, as though fashioned by the Holy Spirit and formed as a new creature."[5] By the grace of God Mary remained free of every personal sin her whole life long. (CCC 493)**

The Immaculate Conception (detail) by Altomonte.
It is most fitting that the Blessed Virgin Mary—the New Eve who would give birth to Christ, the New Adam—would be without sin.

The Blessed Virgin Mary was perplexed by the greeting of the angelic messenger, "Hail, full of grace." The Archangel Gabriel, whose name means *fortitude of God*, reassured her she had "found favor with God."[6] He then explained God was calling her to a crucial role in his plan of redemption. The Son she would bear is the "Son of God";[7] he would reign over a kingdom with no end. His name would be Jesus, which means *God saves*. He would be the Savior of the world.

It is significant to note God had chosen the name of the Blessed Virgin Mary's Son. A name designated by God clearly indicates a person's calling and mission. In this case, Jesus is *the Son of God, who would save the people from their sins*.

> **Jesus means in Hebrew: "God saves." At the annunciation, the angel Gabriel gave him the name Jesus as his proper name, which expresses both his identity and his mission.[8] (CCC 430)**

The Archangel Gabriel then described Christ's role to establish the Kingdom of God in the world.

> **"He will be great, and will be called the Son of the Most High; and the Lord God will give to him the throne of his father David, and he will reign over the house of Jacob for ever; and of his kingdom there will be no end." (Lk 1:32-33)**

All of this must have been overwhelming for the young woman of Nazareth. However, she did not doubt God's word or refuse to cooperate; she simply asked how this would be "since I have no husband."[9] The child would be conceived of the Holy Spirit. For this reason, the Blessed Virgin Mary is called the Spouse of the Holy Spirit. For the first and only time in human history, a woman had conceived a child solely by divine intervention. The Blessed Virgin Mary remained a virgin because the conception was the work of God.

> **From the first formulations of her faith, the Church has confessed that Jesus was conceived solely by the power of the Holy Spirit in the womb of the Virgin Mary, affirming also the corporeal aspect of this event: Jesus was conceived "by the Holy Spirit without human seed."[10] (CCC 496)**

The Archangel Gabriel then declared a second time the child would be called the "Son of God."[11] St. Matthew, quoting the Prophet Isaiah, wrote in his Gospel, "'A virgin shall conceive and bear a son, and his name

Marriage of the Virgin (detail) by Murillo.
St. Joseph—the spouse of the Blessed Virgin Mary—was also called to play an essential role in the life of Christ. The Son of God was born into a family and educated and formed by both a father and a mother, thus sharing fully in the human experience.

shall be called Emmanuel' (which means, God with us)."[12] This description of the divine Sonship of Jesus Christ is mentioned more than once to emphasize the divinity of the child to be borne by the Blessed Virgin Mary.

In philosophical terms, Christ's divine Sonship means he is not a human person but rather a divine Person who, in addition to his divine nature, took on a human nature. Christ is a divine Person with two natures: one human and one divine. Consequently, every action and word of Christ is ascribed to God himself. Because Christ is truly Emmanuel, everything he did throughout his life took on a redemptive value for the salvation of man.

After the angelic message was delivered to the Blessed Virgin Mary, all of creation, metaphorically speaking, awaited the most important response in the history of salvation. Indeed, the redemption of the human race could only begin if she were to assent to God's plan. Her "yes" would overturn, once and for all, Eve's infamous "no" and prepare the way for God to enter into the world by becoming man.

The Blessed Virgin Mary answered:

> **"Behold, I am the handmaid of the Lord; let it be to me according to your word." (Lk 1:38)**

The Gospel of St. John expresses what happened next as a result of her consent:

> **"The Word became flesh and dwelt among us." (Jn 1:14)**

The conception of Jesus Christ, the Son of God, in the womb of the Blessed Virgin Mary is called the *Incarnation*. It is essential and fascinating to note God's plan of salvation could only occur through willing, human cooperation. While the Incarnation was the work of God, it needed the consent of a human being.

The Blessed Virgin Mary's act of faith and generous "yes" to God's will brought the Savior into the world through the power of the Holy Spirit. Never in the history of mankind was such a human response so important. Mary's *fiat* (Latin for "let it be done") serves as a model for every disciple of Christ. Through the generous acceptance of and conformity to the divine will, a person allows God to fulfill his plans for salvation through him or her.

ST. JOSEPH'S DREAM

> **When his mother Mary had been betrothed to Joseph, before they came together she was found to be with child of the Holy Spirit; and her husband Joseph, being a just man and unwilling to put her to shame, resolved to divorce her quietly. But as he considered this, behold, an angel of the Lord appeared to him in a dream, saying, "Joseph, son of David, do not fear to take Mary your wife, for that which is conceived in her is of the Holy Spirit; she will bear a son, and you shall call his name Jesus, for he will save his people from their sins." (Mt 1:18-21)**

The long-awaited Messiah came through the Blessed Virgin Mary's generous response. This indicates God counts on faith-filled, human cooperation to implement his plan of salvation. St. Joseph—the spouse of the Blessed Virgin Mary—was also called to play an essential role in the life of Christ. Scripture refers to St. Joseph as a "just man."[13] The Old Testament concept of a *just* man was a *holy* man, someone faithful to God's will.

It was God's design for his Only-Begotten Son to be born of a virgin. However, it was also God's will for Christ to have an earthly, legal father. The Son of God was born into a family and educated and formed by both a father and a mother, thus sharing fully in the human experience. As Christ, the Son of God, matured, St. Joseph played an important role in his education and training. Sometimes St. Joseph is referred to as Christ's foster-father; this does not detract from St. Joseph but clarifies Christ's divine origin. In fact, St. Joseph is the ideal father of the Holy Family and a model for all fathers.

As recorded in the Gospel of St. Matthew, St. Joseph had his own annunciation. Like the Blessed Virgin Mary, he was very holy but without the privilege of having been preserved from all stain of Original Sin. Being so close to God, St. Joseph would have sensed and valued the extraordinary sanctity and purity of his betrothed wife. Thus, her pregnancy would have been a complete mystery to him. In fact, St. Matthew's Gospel relates her being with child troubled him greatly. St. Joseph's perplexity was resolved by an angelic messenger who appeared in a dream and

Joseph's Dream, Illumination, *Pericopes of Henry II* (Pericopes are abbreviated Gospel Books) ca. 1002. God was asking him to make a heroic act of faith and give his own generous "yes" to God's plan.

The Holy Family by Gutiérrez.
The Blessed Virgin Mary and St. Joseph fully cooperated with God's plan and thus brought salvation to the world.

revealed to him this child was not the fruit of human conception.

Like the Blessed Virgin Mary, St. Joseph was being called to play an important role in God's plan of redemption. God was asking him to make a heroic act of faith and give his own generous "yes" to God's plan. He would take care of the Mother of God and serve as the foster-father of the Son of God made man. Having received the angelic message this child was the promised Messiah and the Son of God, St. Joseph wholeheartedly committed himself to God's plan for himself and for the redemption of the world.

Through these angelic annunciations, it is apparent God counts on certain individuals to collaborate in his redemptive work. The Blessed Virgin Mary and St. Joseph fully cooperated with God's plan and thus brought salvation to the world. They were called to sacrifice their lives, personal plans, preferences, and aspirations in order to serve Christ and his mission. The example of the Holy Family reveals one thing above all: corresponding to God's call involves a total gift of self. This is especially true when God's call is to serve his kingdom. Paradoxically, this self-sacrifice can be the source of profound happiness and even joy.

While Christ is the only source of redemption, he invites all people to cooperate in his work. By doing so, people are called to imitate his generosity in laying down their lives in service to God and neighbor. The persons who have best exemplified this discipleship are the saints.

THE GENEALOGY OF CHRIST

The book of the genealogy of Jesus Christ, the son of David, the son of Abraham. Abraham was the father of Isaac, and Isaac the father of Jacob, and Jacob the father of Judah and his brothers...and Jacob the father of Joseph the husband of Mary, of whom Jesus was born, who is called Christ. (Mt 1:1-2, 16)

Each of the Gospels of Sts. Matthew[14] and Luke[15] includes a genealogy of Jesus Christ. Both genealogies emphasize his role as Savior of the human race. Both share the message that God includes all people in his plan of redemption. The human ancestors of Christ listed in these genealogies include Gentiles and Jews, men and women, saints and sinners. Both also convey truths about the Person of Jesus Christ through symbolism.

The genealogy in St. Luke's Gospel begins with Christ and traces his lineage back to Adam, the first human being. This genealogy reminds the reader, although Christ's more immediate ancestors were members of the Chosen People, he is also a descendant of Adam, the father of the entire human race. In fact, Christ is called the New Adam.

By tracing his genealogy back to Adam, St. Luke stresses Christ is the Savior and Redeemer of all people. As the New Adam, Christ repaired the damage inflicted upon the world by the sin of the first Adam as well as all personal sins. His redemption, therefore, includes not only the Chosen People but also every other descendant of Adam.

St. Matthew, whose Gospel may have been written originally for Jewish Christians, begins his genealogy with Abraham, the father of the Chosen People. St. Matthew's genealogy shows Christ is a descendant of both Abraham and King David. The ancestors of Christ listed in this genealogy encapsulate all of the prophecies concerning the Messiah. Many of them were great figures in the history of the Jewish People, who played an important role in preparing the way for the Incarnation. Others, however, were horrible failures as leaders of the Chosen People.

St. Matthew employed a literary device to reveal an important truth about Christ. While the genealogy explicitly states he is a descendant of Abraham and David, St. Matthew also implicitly teaches Christ is their perfect descendant.

> **All the generations from Abraham to David were fourteen generations, and from David to the deportation to Babylon fourteen generations, and from the deportation to Babylon to the Christ fourteen generations. (Mt 1:17)**

St. Matthew's genealogy is arranged in three groups of fourteen. Three is a symbolically perfect number, and seven is another perfect number. Fourteen is twice seven, so fourteen is a doubly perfect number. In short, Christ is the perfect descendant of Abraham and David who fulfills the promises God made to them.

This genealogy shows Christ is descended from the long line of Davidic kings, which stresses his kingship. However, as he told Pontius Pilate before his Crucifixion, his "kingship is not of this world."[16] His kingdom transcends geographical space and time; it pertains to each person's soul and eternal life. His kingdom is one of peace, joy, love, and freedom. Entrance into the Kingdom of God involves spiritual healing, personal holiness, and the reward of everlasting life.

Acceptance of Christ's kingship and entrance into his kingdom are a direct consequence of having received the sanctifying grace that flows from his Death and Resurrection. In fact, the inauguration of Christ as King occurred on the Cross. Even Pilate unwittingly acknowledged Christ's kingship when he directed a parchment, "Jesus of Nazareth, the King of the Jews,"[17] be placed on the Cross in Hebrew, Greek, and Latin. These three languages represent the universality of Christ's kingship, which includes both the Chosen People and the Gentiles. The universality of Christ's redemption is also demonstrated in both genealogies by their inclusion of Christ's Gentile ancestors.

Tree of Jesse, Book of Gospels Illumination.
Jesse was the father of King David. St. Matthew's genealogy shows Christ is descended from the long line of Davidic kings, which stresses his kingship.

At the time the Gospels were written, it was customary to limit genealogies to a person's male ancestors. However, St. Matthew's genealogy includes several women. This is significant since, in both Jewish and Gentile society, women were not considered the equals of men; neither did they enjoy the same rights. Included are the faithful convert Ruth who became the grandmother of David, the prostitute Rahab, and the "wife of Uriah," who committed adultery with David. The inclusion of grievous sinners, both male and female, indicates Christ came to save all people from their sins. Moreover, in Christ, women are restored to their original dignity and equality with men.

THE VISITATION

Mary arose and went with haste into the hill country, to a city of Judah, and she entered the house of Zechariah and greeted Elizabeth. And when Elizabeth heard the greeting of Mary, the babe leaped in her womb; and Elizabeth was filled with the Holy Spirit and she exclaimed with a loud cry, "Blessed are you among women, and blessed is the fruit of your womb! And why is this granted me, that the mother of my Lord should come to me? For behold, when the voice of your greeting came to my ears, the babe in my womb leaped for joy. And blessed is she who believed that there would be a fulfillment of what was spoken to her from the Lord." And Mary said, "My soul magnifies the Lord, and my spirit rejoices in God my Savior." (Lk 1:39-47)

Mary and Elizabeth by Bloch.
"Blessed are you among women, and blessed is the fruit of your womb!" (Lk 1:42)

At the Annunciation, the Archangel Gabriel appeared to Mary and revealed to her a miracle: her cousin St. Elizabeth, who was elderly and barren, had conceived a child and was now in her sixth month of pregnancy. St. Luke relates the Blessed Virgin Mary immediately went to visit her, a journey of some seventy miles, probably on foot.

St. Luke's narrative of the Visitation is rich in symbolism and presents additional information about the nature of the child the Blessed Virgin Mary bore in her womb. The Visitation of Mary to her cousin St. Elizabeth has parallels to King David's transfer of the Ark of the Covenant to Jerusalem as related in the Second Book of Samuel.

The Ark of the Covenant was a golden chest made in accordance with God's instructions to Moses. It was kept in the tent tabernacle and carried with the Israelites as they wandered in the desert. Eventually, it was moved by King David to Jerusalem, where it resided in Solomon's Temple. The Ark is described by St. Paul in the Book of Hebrews:

Behind the second curtain stood a tent called the Holy of Holies, having the golden altar of incense and the ark of the covenant covered on all sides with gold, which contained a golden urn holding the manna, and Aaron's rod that budded, and the tables of the covenant; above it were the cherubim of glory overshadowing the mercy seat. (Heb 9:3-5)

The Ark of the Covenant signified the presence of God on earth, a presence that was surpassed by the Incarnation of Jesus Christ—God made man. Even the contents of the Ark were surpassed and perfected by Christ.

- Instead of manna, Christ is the true Bread from Heaven who gives us his Body and Blood as spiritual food and drink.
- Aaron's rod indicated his authority and leadership over the Israelites. Christ reigns over the universal and everlasting Kingdom of God. Aaron's rod was also a sign of the Aaronic priesthood, which is replaced by the Eternal High Priesthood of Jesus Christ.
- Christ is the Word of God who perfected the teachings of the Ten Commandments with his Commandment of Love.

Because the Blessed Virgin Mary carried the Son of God in her womb, she is called the Ark of the New Covenant. It seems St. Luke compared the transfer of the Ark of the Covenant into Jerusalem to the Blessed Virgin Mary's visit with her cousin St. Elizabeth.

The Ark of the Covenant	The Ark of the New Covenant
"They carried the ark of God...and brought it out of the house of Abinadab which was on the hill." (2 Sm 6: 3)	Mary went to the hill country to visit her cousin Elizabeth.
"[David] said, 'How can the ark of the LORD come to me?'" (2 Sm 6: 9)	Elizabeth greeted Mary with the words, "Why is this granted me, that the mother of my Lord should come to me?" (Lk 1: 43)
"The ark of the LORD remained in the house of Obededom the Gittite three months; and the LORD blessed Obededom and all his household." (2 Sm 6: 11)	Mary blessed the home of Sts. Zechariah and Elizabeth by staying with them for three months.
"David danced before the LORD...leaping and dancing before the LORD." (2 Sm 6: 14, 16)	St. John the Baptist "leaped for joy" in his mother's womb before the presence of the Lord. (Lk 1: 44)

The glory of the Ark was not derived from its own magnificence; rather, it reflected the majesty of what it contained: the presence of God. In like manner, the praise St. Elizabeth gave her cousin and the Blessed Virgin Mary's words, "Henceforth all generations will call me blessed,"[18] are a reflection of her maternal role as the Bearer of God in his plan of salvation. In her womb, she carried Jesus Christ, the presence of God on earth, who established the New Covenant in his Blood. For this reason, the Blessed Virgin Mary is truly the Ark of the New Covenant, and, in the Visitation, she became the instrument of an encounter with Jesus Christ and consequently the special joy experienced by her cousin.

This role of the Blessed Virgin Mary as Mother of God was acknowledged by St. Elizabeth when she called her "the mother of my Lord."[19] Because Jesus Christ is God the Son made flesh, Second Person of the Blessed Trinity, his Mother is called the Mother of God. Though the Blessed Virgin Mary gave Christ his human nature but not his divine nature, she is not the Mother of a nature but of a Person, the Person of Christ. Hence, she is the Mother of God.

The Blessed Virgin Mary's declaration, "All generations will call me blessed," has come true. By repeating the words of the Archangel Gabriel, "Hail, full of grace, the Lord is with thee," and of St. Elizabeth, "Blessed are you among women, and blessed is the fruit of your womb!" in the *Hail Mary*, people honor the Blessed Virgin Mary every day.

The Idol Broken Down Before the Ark by Tissot.
"But when they rose early on the next morning, behold, Dagon had fallen face downward on the ground before the ark of the LORD, and the head of Dagon and both his hands were lying cut off upon the threshold; only the trunk of Dagon was left to him." (1 Sm 5: 4)
The glory of the Ark was not derived from its own magnificence; rather, it reflected the majesty of what it contained: the presence of God.

The Visitation is a natural sequel to the Annunciation. The Blessed Virgin Mary's "yes" at the Annunciation brought Christ into the world, and her cooperation in the Visitation brought her Son made flesh to others. She is the paradigm of the ideal follower of Christ, who announces the Good News by her witness of holiness and spirit of service. The Blessed Virgin Mary attended to the needs of her cousin and proclaimed the truth of salvation in her *Magnificat*. The Visitation gives a foretaste of the work Christ's disciples performed once they had received the benefit of Christ's redemption and the gift of the Holy Spirit at Pentecost.

THE BIRTH OF THE REDEEMER

A decree went out from Caesar Augustus that all the world should be enrolled. This was the first enrollment, when Quirinius was governor of Syria. And all went to be enrolled, each to his own city. And Joseph also went up from Galilee, from the city of Nazareth, to Judea, to the city of David, which is called Bethlehem, because he was of the house and lineage of David, to be enrolled with Mary, his betrothed, who was with child. And while they were there, the time came for her to be delivered. And she gave birth to her firstborn son and wrapped him in swaddling cloths, and laid him in a manger, because there was no place for them in the inn. And in that region there were shepherds out in the field, keeping watch over their flock by night. And an angel of the Lord appeared to them, and the glory of the Lord shone around them, and they were filled with fear. And the angel said to them, "Be not afraid; for behold, I bring you good news of a great joy which will come to all the people; for to you is born this day in the city of David a Savior, who is Christ the Lord. And this will be a sign for you: you will find a babe wrapped in swaddling cloths and lying in a manger." And suddenly there was with the angel a multitude of the heavenly host praising God and saying, "Glory to God in the highest, and on earth peace among men with whom he is pleased!" (Lk 2:1-14)

The circumstances surrounding the Birth of Christ richly illustrate the universal nature of his salvation. The manifestation of his Birth to various groups of people clearly demonstrates Christ came for the rich and the poor, for the Gentile and the Jew.

The first people to receive the Good News of Christ's Birth were the shepherds watching their flocks in the fields surrounding Bethlehem. These shepherds might have been in the very same pastures out of which God had called David as he was tending his father's flock.

At first glance, shepherds would seem like unlikely candidates to receive news about a new King of the Jews having been born. In Jewish society at the time of Christ, shepherds were generally poor and ignorant. They were from the lower strata of society and would not have been the first to receive news of a royal birth in any earthly kingdom. In any event, the angelic announcement of Christ's Birth to the shepherds signifies Christ had come precisely for the poor and humble. In fact, it is fitting shepherds should be the first to receive the Good News since this child would become the "Good Shepherd" of all mankind.

The angels told the shepherds the child had been born in the City of David, thus implying this child was the Messiah foretold by the prophet Micah. Next, they announced this child is the Christ—in Hebrew, *Messiah*—explicitly indicating Christ is the one foretold by the prophets in the Old Testament. This child would reestablish the everlasting Kingdom of David. Lastly, they referred to Christ as Lord, a term normally reserved for God. This title was fitting because Christ is the Son of God.

The Annunciation to the Shepherds, Illumination by Boucicaut Master. The angelic announcement of Christ's Birth to the shepherds signifies Christ had come precisely for the poor and humble.

The Adoration of the Magi by Massys.
Whereas the shepherds were poor Jews, the "wise men from the East" were wealthy Gentiles.
Christ had come not only for Jews but for all people.

The angels then gave the shepherds two signs by which they could recognize the Christ child:

> **"This will be a sign for you: you will find a babe wrapped in swaddling cloths and lying in a manger." (Lk 2: 12)**

It was common at the time to wrap newborns in swaddling cloths, so this would not have seemed at all unusual. However, to find the promised Messiah, the newborn King of the Jews, lying in a manger—an animal trough—would have been shocking. The manger, nevertheless, underlines the poverty of Christ; he had come to share fully in the human condition. Christ experienced poverty, and, throughout his public ministry, he continually reached out to the poor, stressing he had come for them. As Christ proclaimed about himself, quoting Isaiah:

> **"The Spirit of the Lord is upon me, because he has anointed me to preach good news to the poor." (Lk 4: 18)**

In his account of the Nativity, St. Matthew reports other very unlikely visitors who came to pay homage to the King of the Jews. Whereas the shepherds were poor Jews, the "wise men from the East"[20] were wealthy Gentiles. Christ had come not only for Jews but for all people.

"Magi" is the scriptural term for these wise men, suggesting they were astrologers. Christian tradition has assumed there were three of them because they brought three gifts; these three are generally described as Persians named Gaspar (or Caspar), Melchior, and Balthasar. Their homage to the newborn King of the Jews—gold, frankincense, and myrrh—represent Christ's kingship, divinity, and eventual Crucifixion.

The circumstances surrounding the Birth of Christ foreshadow his future Passion and Death. The cave or stable is a type of the cave that would serve as Jesus' tomb. The wooden manger prefigures the Cross, and the swaddling cloths hint at the shroud that would envelop his Body after Death. The poverty, humility, and discomfort of Christ's Birth foreshadow the terrible circumstances of his Death on the Cross.

It is interesting to note Bethlehem means "house of bread," and the manger was a trough from which animals ate. Both Bethlehem and the manger point to the Holy Eucharist, the spiritual food of Christians. Through his work of redemption, Christ became the Bread of Life. "The bread of God is that which comes down from heaven, and gives life to the world."[21]

The Adoration of the Shepherds by Tiepolo.
The newborn Christ was surrounded by poorly clad shepherds and barnyard animals.

DETACHMENT AND POVERTY

Every aspect of Christ's life is an occasion to teach about the way that leads to eternal life. His extreme poverty is particularly striking. Artistic images of the Nativity seem to capture this material destitution. There was no crib; the Son of God had to settle for a manger. The newborn Christ was surrounded by poorly clad shepherds and barnyard animals.

God our Creator was born in a stable; this is clearly a mystery: *God became a defenseless baby lying in the poverty of a manger.* Christ's Birth also presaged the absolute poverty of his Passion and Death. On the Cross, Christ was stripped of his garments, abandoned by many of his followers, and executed like a common criminal.

Christ's poverty portrays an aspect of his work of redemption: a radical detachment from worldly possessions, which must be imitated in order to develop a deep relationship with him. Though it involves *not having*, *doing without*, *denying oneself*, and *giving up* good things, Christian poverty, properly understood, is not negative. Detachment means freedom from undue attachment to material things. This freedom allows a person to put the good things of creation in their proper perspective so God is placed first in his or her life. Christian poverty is begun by renouncing luxury and superfluous possessions; the benefit is an even greater share in the graces of the redemption by generously and cheerfully accepting the hardships encountered in life. Things can be had and used—indeed, life is impossible without material possessions—but they do not become gods.

Practically speaking, poverty is necessary to stay focused on Christ, whether in prayer or works of charity. The human heart easily becomes attached to material goods that can suffocate friendship with Christ. The deceptive attractions of the partial goods of this world can never satisfy the longings of the human heart and instead separate people from Christ, who is the real goal.

In order to unite oneself with Christ, he or she needs to renounce attachment to material things and learn to lead a simple and sober life. This teaching of Christ is illustrated in the story of the rich young man, who impressively lived all the Commandments. Christ, nevertheless, told the young man he needed one more thing in order to become perfect:

> **"If you would be perfect, go, sell what you possess and give to the poor, and you will have treasure in heaven; and come, follow me." (Mt 19:21)**

Poverty makes room in the human heart for an intimate relationship with Christ, which in turn helps the whole person be his witnesses in the world. Poverty allows the Holy Spirit to fill the heart completely with Christ and prepares it to play a role in the Church's evangelization—a role the rich young man unfortunately declined because of his "great possessions."[22]

> **The kingdom belongs *to the poor and lowly*, which means those who have accepted it with humble hearts. Jesus is sent to "preach good news to the poor";[23] he declares them blessed, for "theirs is the kingdom of heaven."[24] To them—the "little ones"—the Father is pleased to reveal what remains hidden from the wise and the learned.[25] Jesus shares the life of the poor, from the cradle to the cross; he experiences hunger, thirst, and privation.[26] Jesus identifies himself with the poor of every kind and makes active love toward them the condition for entering his kingdom.[27] (CCC 544)**

THE PRESENTATION

> **At the end of eight days, when he was circumcised, he was called Jesus, the name given by the angel before he was conceived in the womb. And when the time came for their purification according to the law of Moses, they brought him up to Jerusalem to present him to the Lord (as it is written in the law of the Lord, "Every male that opens the womb shall be called holy to the Lord") and to offer a sacrifice according to what is said in the law of the Lord, "a pair of turtledoves, or two young pigeons." (Lk 2:21-24)**

The next event related by St. Luke in the infancy narrative of our Lord is the Presentation of Christ in the Temple. This Jewish ritual served a dual purpose under the Mosaic Law. First, a woman who had given birth was considered ritually "unclean." Some weeks after childbirth, she was required to go to the Temple to offer a sacrifice for her purification. Secondly, every firstborn male belonged to God by virtue of the Passover. For this reason, the Law required parents to present their firstborn male to God in the Temple and then "redeem," or buy back, the child.

The Presentation of Christ (detail) by Broederlam.
The Law required parents to present their firstborn male to God in the Temple and then "redeem," or buy back, the child.

These laws and their fulfillment are particularly meaningful in the case of the Blessed Virgin Mary and Christ. The doctrine of the Virgin Birth teaches Christ was conceived by the power of the Holy Spirit. Furthermore, because of her Immaculate Conception, which preserved her from all stain of Original Sin, the Blessed Virgin Mary was sinless and in no need of purification. She, nevertheless, showed herself obedient to the Law by offering a sacrifice for purification. Similarly, Christ, the God-man, had no need of being redeemed since he himself is the Redeemer. His parents, nonetheless, presented him to the Father in the Temple in obedience to the Law.

When the Blessed Virgin Mary and St. Joseph entered the Temple with the infant Christ, they were greeted by a righteous man named St. Simeon, who recognized Christ as the Savior. While the causal passerby would have seen an ordinary child, St. Simeon, through the inspiration of the Holy Spirit, understood the reality of Jesus as the Messiah. In the same way, the Holy Spirit enables every Christian to see God's presence in the Scriptures, the sacraments, the Church, and in the ordinary events of life.

Before leaving the Temple, the Blessed Virgin Mary and St. Joseph encountered a prophetess named St. Anna, who also recognized Jesus as the promised Messiah. St. Anna never left the Temple and prayed and fasted day and night. Likewise—through participation in the liturgies of the Church, especially the Holy Mass, and through prayer and fasting—Christians are given the grace to perceive the presence of Christ in the world.

As with all of the *Joyful Mysteries* of Christ's infancy, the Presentation contains prophetic references to the Cross. Christ, the firstborn Son, was offered to God according to Jewish Law; however, in addition to this ritual act commemorating the first Passover and the liberation of the Hebrews from slavery in Egypt, the true Paschal Lamb was offered in the Temple. This offering, which was initiated in the Temple, reached its fulfillment on the Cross. Indeed, St. Simeon told the Blessed Virgin Mary this child is a sign of contradiction and her soul would also be pierced. In this way, the Presentation officially initiates Christ's journey to Calvary to redeem the world.

Simeon's Song of Praise (detail) by Rembrandt.
St. Simeon, through the inspiration of the Holy Spirit, understood the reality of Jesus as the Messiah.

THE FINDING IN THE TEMPLE AND CHRIST'S OBEDIENCE

The child grew and became strong, filled with wisdom; and the favor of God was upon him. Now his parents went to Jerusalem every year at the feast of the Passover. And when he was twelve years old, they went up according to custom; and when the feast was ended, as they were returning, the boy Jesus stayed behind in Jerusalem. His parents did not know it, but supposing him to be in the company they went a day's journey, and they sought him among their kinsfolk and acquaintances; and when they did not find him, they returned to Jerusalem, seeking him. (Lk 2: 40-45)

The final event of Christ's early life described in the Gospel of St. Luke occurred when he was twelve years old. Christ, the Blessed Virgin Mary, and St. Joseph had traveled to Jerusalem for the feast of the Passover. This was the greatest feast of the Jewish year, and people gathered from all over the country and even foreign lands to attend the celebrations in Jerusalem. Christ was twelve years old, so he would have been able to accompany St. Joseph to the part of the Temple reserved for men.

The Holy Family traveled to Jerusalem with a large group of family and friends. It was customary on these journeys for the men to travel in one group and the women in another, and the children would have been going back and forth between the two groups. For this reason, his Mother and foster-father did not notice Christ was missing for one full day after having left Jerusalem. Immediately, they went back to the city, where they searched for him.

> **After three days they found him in the temple, sitting among the teachers, listening to them and asking them questions; and all who heard him were amazed at his understanding and his answers.** (Lk 2: 46-47)

Disputation with the Doctors (detail) by Duccio.
St. Luke's account of the Finding of Christ in the Temple is filled with redemptive significance.

The Blessed Virgin Mary asked Christ why he had done this to them. His response marks his first recorded words in the New Testament:

> **"How is it that you sought me? Did you not know that I must be in my Father's house?"** (Lk 2: 49)

While Christ's words, at first glance, might seem disrespectful, we know this could not have been the case. Christ, as God the Son, fulfilled the Commandments perfectly and, therefore, would have given perfect honor to his parents. This reply indicates Christ clearly understood his divinity; furthermore, he knew his mission, above all else, involved obedience to his heavenly Father. However, as if to emphasize Christ must also be obedient to his earthly parents, St. Luke continues:

> **[Jesus] went down with them and came to Nazareth, and was obedient to them; and his mother kept all these things in her heart. And Jesus increased in wisdom and in stature, and in favor with God and man.** (Lk 2: 51-52)

These few words sum up the next eighteen years of Jesus' life. He lived with his parents in Nazareth and was obedient to them. In his childhood and adolescent years, Christ's conformity to the will of his Father in Heaven took the form of obedience to the Blessed Virgin Mary and St. Joseph. Faithful obedience in all things is the hallmark of Christ's life from his infancy to the Cross.

Jesus' obedience to his mother and legal father fulfills the fourth commandment perfectly and was the temporal image of his filial obedience to his Father in heaven. The everyday obedience of Jesus to Joseph and Mary both announced and anticipated the obedience of Holy Thursday: "Not my will..."[28] The obedience of Christ in the daily routine of his hidden life was already inaugurating his work of restoring what the disobedience of Adam has destroyed.[29] (CCC 532)

Christ Returning to His Parents by Martini.
As he was "lost" to his parents, he was "lost" to his disciples after the Crucifixion.

At the heart of Christ's redemption is his constant obedience to the will of his Father. Obedience essentially involves submitting one's actions to the will of another and, in many instances, entails renouncing one's own particular desires and preferences in deference to someone else's. As related by St. Paul, Christ's obedience atoned for Adam's disobedience:

As by one man's disobedience many were made sinners, so by one man's obedience many will be made righteous. (Rom 5: 19)

St. Luke's account of the Finding of Christ in the Temple is filled with redemptive significance. Jerusalem was his ultimate destination, where he died on the Cross in reparation for the sins of mankind. His three days in the Temple prefigures the three days that he spent in the tomb. As he was "lost" to his parents, he was "lost" to his disciples after the Crucifixion. Even the pain and sorrow of the Blessed Virgin Mary and St. Joseph were echoed in the pain suffered by Christ's followers at the Cross. In the Temple, Christ insisted he must be about his Father's business; through his obedience unto death, he perfectly fulfilled his Father's "business" of redemption.

WHY THE WORD BECAME FLESH

St. John's opens his Gospel by declaring Jesus Christ is God:

In the beginning was the Word, and the Word was with God, and the Word was God;...all things were made through him. (Jn 1: 1, 3)

The Second Person of the Blessed Trinity, God the Son, the Word through whom all things were created, became man and lived among us. Since the creation of the world, including the creation of man, was accomplished through God the Son, it is fitting the re-creation of man, through the healing graces of the redemption, was entrusted to God the Son as well.

In a manifestation of God's infinite love and wisdom, "the Word became flesh."[30] God loves the pinnacle of his creation so much that he took on their nature to suffer and die on the Cross—the high price for sins. Through his suffering, Death, and Resurrection, Christ merited for every person a share in his life and the attainment of everlasting life.

Among others, there are four particular reasons the Word became flesh:

- to make expiation for sins, reconcile man with God, and restore human nature lost by sin.
- to manifest the infinite depth of God's love.
- to offer a model of holiness.
- to allow people to share in his divine life.

THE WORD BECAME FLESH FOR EXPIATION, RECONCILIATION, AND RESTORATION

God became man first of all to reconcile all people with himself by making expiation for sins. What does this mean?

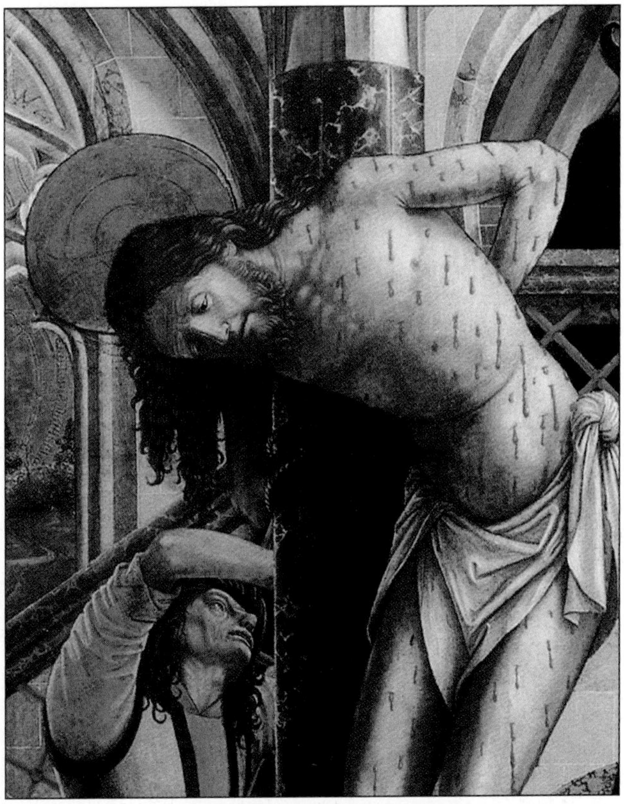

Flagellation (detail) by Pacher.
Since man brought sin into the world, justice demanded a man should offer the atonement for sin.

The Fall of our first parents created a rift between God and the human race. In creation, God had lavished Adam and Eve with wondrous blessings, the greatest of which was their intimacy with him. They had complete freedom, with only one commandment: the prohibition against eating the fruit of the tree of the knowledge of good and evil. They succumbed to the serpent's deceitful promise: they would become "like God"; they violated God's command and sinned.

It is important to ask how serious sin is. The severity of an offense can be gauged by the dignity of the one offended. For instance, if a twelve-year-old boy were to strike his younger sister, he would have committed a sin against charity and justice. However, if the same twelve-year-old boy were to strike his elderly grandmother, his misdeed would be far worse given the respect owed to her dignity. The offended party in the case of Original Sin was God himself, whose dignity is infinite. Original Sin involved an outright rejection of God's goodness and his will by our first parents. It was a sin of rebellion and an attempt to usurp God's authority and glory. The logical conclusion: Original Sin is infinitely serious since it offended the infinite dignity of God. Because the seriousness of sin is infinite, reparation could not have been made by any finite being, i.e., by anyone less than the infinite God.

Human beings, on their own, could never have repaired the damage caused by the sin of Adam and Eve. No human effort—in the form of prayer, sacrifice, or good moral behavior—could ever have bridged the rift between God and man created by Original Sin or repaired the staggering damage caused by personal sins. Any sacrifice, regardless of the value of the offering or the dignity of sacrificial victim, would have been insufficient. The only sacrifice capable of reconciling man with God has to be of infinite value.

Why was a *sacrifice* necessary to repair the damage caused by sin? After all, God created the universe by a mere word; why could he not have forgiven people simply by desiring it to be so? The answer lies in God's perfection, which demands perfect justice. Since man brought sin into the world, justice demanded a man should offer the atonement for sin. However, no human being could pay the infinite debt for sin, no matter how great the sacrifice. The only possibility would be for the man offering the sacrifice to be, at the same time, God.

Thus, there is the need for a savior who possesses the natures of both God and man. Only Christ, the God-man, could fulfill this necessary condition for redemption; only he is a divine Person with a divine nature and a human nature.

> **Jesus Christ is true God and true man, in the unity of his divine person; for this reason he is the one and only mediator between God and men. (CCC 480)**

Christ Falls on the Way to Calvary (detail) by Raphael.
The sacrifice of Christ is so valuable it repairs and atones not only for Original Sin but also the actual (personal) sins of every person, past, present, and future.

God, in his infinite wisdom, offered the human race a solution to reconcile all people to himself. Jesus Christ, God made man, is the sacrificial victim for the expiation of all sins. Christ is both God and man, which gives his sacrifice on the Cross an infinite value; this is more than enough to pay the crushing debt incurred by sin. In fact, the sacrifice of Christ is so valuable it repairs and atones not only for Original Sin but also the actual (personal) sins of every person, past, present, and future.

> **No man, not even the holiest, was ever able to take on himself the sins of all men and offer himself as a sacrifice for all. The existence in Christ of the divine person of the Son, who at once surpasses and embraces all human persons and constitutes himself as the Head of all mankind, makes possible his redemptive sacrifice *for all*.** (CCC 616)

What exactly was the redemptive sacrifice offered by Christ? Salvation comes above all through the sacrifice of Christ on the Cross. However, as the *Catechism* summarizes:

> **Christ's whole life is a mystery of *redemption*. Redemption comes to us above all through the blood of his cross,[31] but this mystery is at work throughout Christ's entire life:**
>
> - **already in his Incarnation through which by becoming poor he enriches us with his poverty;[32]**
> - **in his hidden life which by his submission atones for our disobedience;[33]**
> - **in his word which purifies its hearers;[34]**
> - **in his healings and exorcisms by which "he took our infirmities and bore our diseases";[35]**
> - **and in his Resurrection by which he justifies us.[36]** (CCC 517)

Every action of Christ from his Incarnation to his Ascension into Heaven carries an infinite value, thereby winning for human beings a superabundance of grace. The reality of Christ's divinity gives an infinite value and merit to everything he did, whether it was working as a carpenter or dying on the Cross. As the *Catechism* teaches:

> **From the first moment of his Incarnation the Son embraces the Father's plan of divine salvation in his redemptive mission.** (CCC 606)

Thus, the first reason God became man is so people could be redeemed. Reparation for sin was necessary. Every person has the capacity to commit an infinitely evil offense, but not even the holiest person has the ability to offer an infinitely worthy sacrifice. Only God could do this through a human nature, so he became man to reconcile people with himself by making expiation for sins. He did this not only by his Passion and Death but also by everything he did during his time on earth.

THE WORD BECAME FLESH TO MANIFEST GOD'S LOVE

Good Friday by Tissot.
God displayed the immensity of his love for man so people might serve him not out of fear but out of love.

God became man to show all people how much he loves them.

God displayed the immensity of his love for man so people might serve him not out of fear but out of love. Since God is absolutely perfect, he has no need of anything and, therefore, did not need to create anything. He does not need the love of human beings or their service. God is infinitely happy as God and has no need of anything more to enhance or maintain his happiness. Nonetheless, as a manifestation of his infinite love, he freely deigned to create man and woman so they could share in his goodness and eternal happiness.

Even when Adam and Eve sinned, God did not give up on them but devised his plan of redemption. Part of this plan was to reveal his infinite love. He became man and shared in the human experience. In his humanity, God actually bore the burden and suffered for the sins of all people. This radical love was demonstrated above all else by his Passion and Death on the Cross.

Among the array of possible redemptive plans, God chose to suffer and die as the means to save man. By doing so, he demonstrated his love for his creatures knows no bounds. Thus, one of the effects of his Passion, so intimately linked to atonement for sin, was to show the great depth of his love.

"Greater love has no man than this, that a man lay down his life for his friends." (Jn 15: 13)

On a purely human level, true love is never measured simply by nice words; neither is it gauged only by the intensity of sentiment. The quality of love is determined by how much a person is willing to sacrifice for his or her beloved. Christ's sacrifice both demonstrates the seriousness of sins—by the exorbitant price required for redemption—and offers overwhelming testimony of the extent of God's love.

God is omnipotent, but, at the moment of his Passion, he did not display his power even when tempted to do so. The crowds taunted, "If you are the King of the Jews, save yourself";[37] this is reminiscent of Satan's temptation in the desert: "If you are the Son of God, command these stones to become loaves of bread."[38]

Christ chose to drink from the cup that had been prepared for him by his Father. He submitted himself to the terrible humiliation and unbearable physical and moral pain heaped on him by his executioners.

Through his suffering, Christ made himself radically accessible and vulnerable, imploring compassion. The downtrodden, the sick, the lonely, and especially the sinner can find a loving home in the heart of Christ. His physical sufferings say, "I love you," in a way words never can.

These sufferings were offered for each and every individual. For this reason, St. Paul was both moved and inspired to say:

> **The life I now live in the flesh I live by faith in the Son of God, who loved me and gave himself for me. (Gal 2: 20)**

It is incredible to consider Christ's executioners slapped, mocked, and spit on the one who created the universe. Christ, as he hung naked and thirsty on the Cross, allowed himself the same ill treatment meted out to the most heinous criminals.

For his followers, it seemed like a catastrophic ending in light of Christ's promises of an eternal kingdom. What a sense of disillusionment the Passion must have produced in their hearts as they sadly recalled the Master's unqualified statement, "I am the way, and the truth, and the life."[39] In a final humiliation, intended to advertise the apparent failure of his Messianic mission, Pilate had Christ's "crime" affixed to the Cross: "This is the King of the Jews."[40]

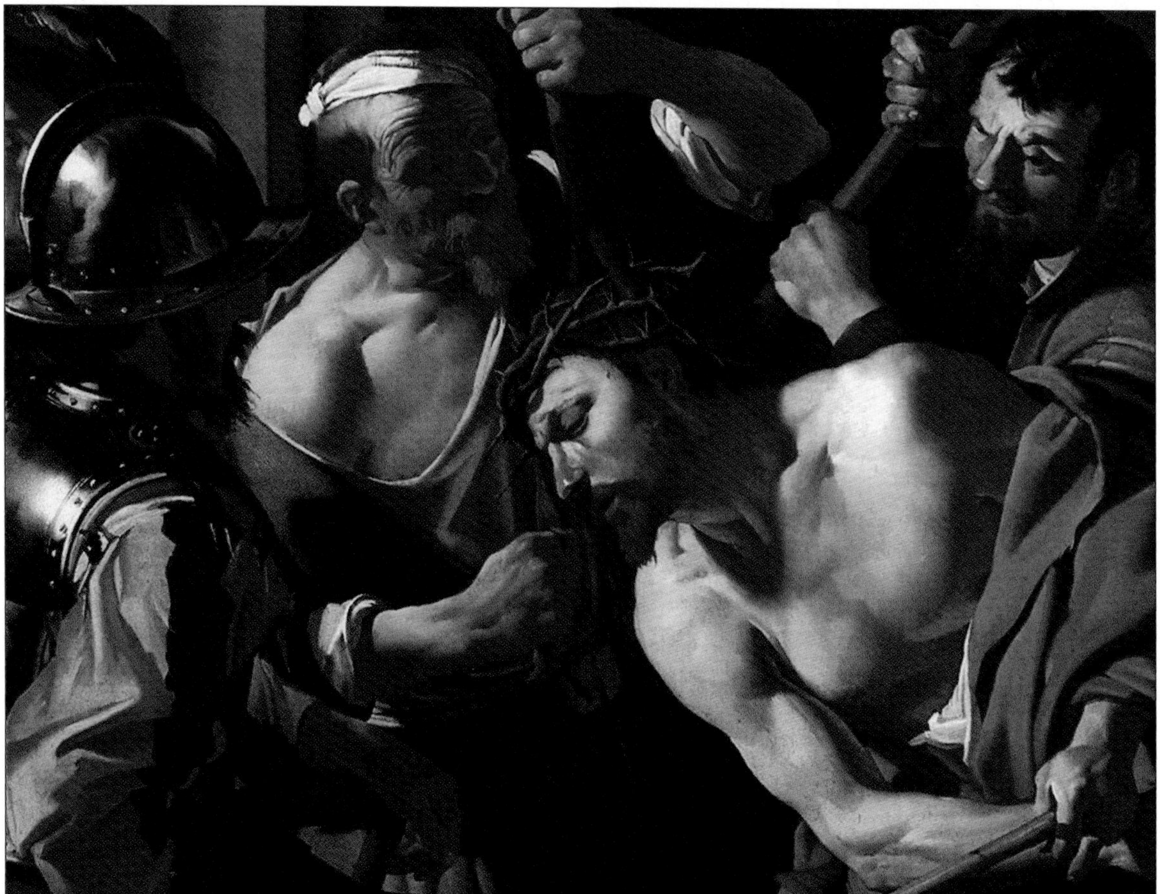

The Crowning with Thorns by Baburen.
His physical sufferings say, "I love you," in a way words never can.

Every facet of Christ's suffering is an invitation to approach God confidently, who shows, in a most touching way, how much the pinnacle of his creation is worth to him. Many are intimidated by someone mounted on a golden throne surrounded by the rich and the powerful, but who cannot be drawn to a God who, in his humanity, suffered terrible indignities and Crucifixion?

By his actions, God tells every person who suffers he has infinite compassion. For those who are lonely and misunderstood, his Passion and Death are a marvelous reminder he is not indifferent to their plight. Lastly, those who are exhausted by overwork or afflicted by failure or tragedy can find ample room in the God who suffered for and redeemed him or her. This revelation of God's love is certainly one of the reasons Adam's sin is truly *felix culpa*.

THE WORD BECAME FLESH TO OFFER A MODEL OF HOLINESS

God became incarnate to offer an example of holiness and show forth the dignity of the human person. He gave an example of how, with grace, a person can overcome the temptations of the world, the Devil, and the flesh.

The life and words of Christ can be an inexhaustible source of inspiration for every human being. By his life, Christ shows the potential greatness of the human person. In fact, without the example of Christ's life to imitate, people would certainly fail to meet their true spiritual and moral calling.

In the Sermon on the Mount, Christ gave his disciples the Beatitudes, a kind of manual to reach true spiritual greatness. These compelling words have moved generations of men and women to aspire to the high standards preached by Christ. The life and words of Christ, which are found in the Gospels, are not simply intended to be studied or analyzed in a purely academic sense; they are meant to be lived.

Because of the incredible spiritual nourishment within Christ's life and words, it is greatly beneficial to read the Gospels in a prayerful manner. Christian tradition has developed two important methods of mental prayer: meditation and contemplation.

The Sermon on the Mount by Bloch.
In the Sermon on the Mount, Christ gave his disciples the Beatitudes, a kind of manual to reach true spiritual greatness.

> **Meditation is a prayerful quest engaging thought, imagination, emotion, and desire. Its goal is to make our own in faith the subject considered, by confronting it with the reality of our own life. (CCC 2723)**
>
> **Contemplative prayer is the simple expression of the mystery of prayer. It is a gaze of faith fixed on Jesus, an attentiveness to the Word of God, a silent love. It achieves real union with the prayer of Christ to the extent that it makes us share in his mystery. (CCC 2724)**

In the presence of God, the words of the Gospel can be taken to heart in a meditative and contemplative way. Prayer then leads to resolutions that can be implemented in daily life. In this way, with the help of grace, the Word of God, Jesus Christ, becomes incarnate within his people.

Washing of the Feet by Palma.
Christ washed the feet of his Apostles and taught them his followers would be known by their humble service and selfless love.

One of the objectives of Christ's preaching was to instruct his followers how to live saintly lives. His life and his teachings coincide with the goal of holiness of life. They are designed to challenge the Christian to work toward heroic sanctity by putting his words and example into practice.

> **In all of his life Jesus presents himself as *our model*. He is the "perfect man,"[41] who invites us to become his disciples and follow him. In humbling himself, he has given us an example to imitate, through his prayer he draws us to pray, and by his poverty he calls us to accept freely the privation and persecutions that may come our way.[42]** (CCC 520)

One example of Christ's call to imitate him arose during the Last Supper. Christ washed the feet of his Apostles and taught them his followers would be known by their humble service and selfless love.

> **"If I then, your Lord and Teacher, have washed your feet, you also ought to wash one another's feet."** (Jn 13: 14)

> **"By this all men will know that you are my disciples, if you have love for one another."** (Jn 13: 35)

Christ also called his disciples to imitate him in sacrifice.

> **"If any man would come after me, let him deny himself and take up his cross daily and follow me."** (Lk 9: 23)

For centuries, it has been a traditional devotional practice to meditate on the details of Christ's suffering and Death. The saints have found Christ's Passion is his most moving and inspiring sermon despite having said little during those awful hours.

The Passion of Christ, first of all, teaches *charity*. The reason behind Christ's suffering is his tremendous love. He desires to save all people from the ravages of sin and bring them to eternal life.

The Passion also teaches *humility*, a virtue Christ displayed especially during the events leading up to and including the Crucifixion. The mockery, humiliating abuse, and shameful Death are the standard of humility required by a saintly life.

Additionally, the Passion teaches *obedience*. The first Adam alienated himself from God through disobedience to the divine will as expressed by the one commandment. In contrast to Adam and Eve, Christ was completely obedient to God's plan for salvation though it involved unbearable pain, intense sorrow, and a slow agonizing death. The virtue of obedience requires sacrifice of the will in terms of preferences and personal autonomy. It means to pursue a course of action that requires internal suffering and, at times, physical pain.

Christ in the Garden of Gethsemane by Conca. Throughout his terrifying ordeal, Christ was immersed in prayer. He prepared for the culminating event of his life by praying in the Garden of Gethsemane.

Finally, the Passion teaches *prayer*. Throughout his terrifying ordeal, Christ was immersed in prayer. He prepared for the culminating event of his life by praying in the Garden of Gethsemane. In this prayer, filled with anguish, he saw the whole panorama of sin and evil before his eyes. He intensely prayed his Father would grant him the strength to finish this most foreboding part of his redemptive mission. This hour of prayer was so agonizing Christ's sweat became like great drops of blood. By word and example, Christ taught prayer is at the heart of discipleship. Prayer is absolutely necessary to obtain the strength to imitate Christ in his sufferings.

Many saints have manifested this power of prayer through their heroic lives. For example, Bl. Teresa of Calcutta (Mother Teresa) performed incredible deeds out of devotion to the poorest of the poor. She and her Missionaries of Charity worked with the sick and the dying, always with smiles and tremendous compassion. Their secret was imitation of Christ centered on a life of prayer, which gave them the strength for a truly sacrificial love.

As the saints have manifested, meditation on the life of Christ and imitation of his holiness is at the heart of the spiritual life. Through prayer, a person slowly discovers a part of him- or herself in every person in the Gospels and the Lord is addressing him or her personally. At the same time, the aim of the Christian life is to emulate the life of the main character of the Gospels, the Redeemer and Savior, Jesus Christ. He is the way to the Father, and, by meditating on his life and teachings in the Gospels, each person can discover and rediscover God's will through the sacred humanity of Christ.

In many and various ways God spoke of old to our fathers by the prophets, but in these last days he has spoken to us by a Son. (Heb 1:1-2)

ST. CHARLES BORROMEO

St. Charles Borromeo was born into a noble Italian family in 1538. He received the tonsure at age twelve and began his theological studies. Because of his family connections, he was named a cardinal deacon in 1560 and appointed secretary of state of the papal states under his uncle, Pope Pius IV. In this position, St. Charles oversaw the final sessions of the Council of Trent, the purpose of which was to clarify the doctrines of the Faith under attack from Protestant Reformers and to reform the life of the Church by removing abuses. Largely through St. Charles' efforts, the Council completed its work.

Notwithstanding his important work for the Church, St. Charles lived a worldly life. Not until the death of his older brother did he resolve to give himself over to more spiritual matters. In 1563, he received the Sacrament of Holy Orders and three months later was consecrated a bishop. He immediately devoted himself to the production of a new catechism that embodied the teachings of the Council of Trent, and he worked on the revision of the Roman Missal for the celebration of Mass as well as the reform of Church music. St. Charles' catechism became the basis of Catholic instruction for some four hundred years.

When St. Charles was appointed Archbishop of Milan, he implemented the Tridentine reforms in that diocese. Milan was one of the most important archdioceses outside of Rome but had not had a resident bishop for more than eighty years. For this reason, the diocese was beset with many problems and in great need of reform. Many of its clergy were ignorant or ill equipped to fulfill their pastoral duties, and the laity, consequently, were deprived of the guidance and direction they needed to lead good, Christian lives.

St. Charles was a remarkable man; his personal example brought about effective reform. While in Milan, he established three seminaries to train clergy and required annual retreats for all clerics to help develop their spiritual lives. He made regular visits to his parishes and utilized the reforming orders such as the Jesuits. St. Charles also founded the Confraternity of Christian Doctrine, which had 2000 teachers to instruct the children of Milan in 740 schools. His reforms became a pattern for other dioceses throughout Europe.

However, resistance to reform in Milan was strong, and not everyone welcomed these changes. Many sought to block his authority, and even some religious communities opposed him. There was even an assassination attempt on his life.

During the summer of 1578, plague raged throughout Milan. St. Charles continued his work in the city and personally helped provide food for the poor and care for the sick and dying. His personal example and strong determination helped make Milan an exemplary archdiocese and demonstrated the effectiveness of the Tridentine reforms.

St. Charles died in 1584. His feast day is November 4.

Illustration: *St. Carlo Borromeo* by Borgianni. Devotion to the Holy Trinity and a pious, charitable heart are the symbolic elements of this portrait.

THE WORD BECAME FLESH TO ALLOW A SHARE IN DIVINE LIFE

God became man, perhaps surprisingly, because he wanted to experience his own divine life. The Gospels call people to share in God's divine life through Jesus Christ by the power of the Holy Spirit. Participation in the life of God is made possible by the sanctifying graces Christ obtained through his redemption.

> Sanctifying grace is an habitual gift, a stable and supernatural disposition that perfects the soul itself to enable it to live with God, to act by his love. *Habitual grace*, the permanent disposition to live and act in keeping with God's call, is distinguished from *actual graces* which refer to God's interventions, whether at the beginning of conversion or in the course of the work of sanctification. (CCC 2000)

Christ instituted the Seven Sacraments as the primary means of receiving his sanctifying grace as well as actual graces. The first sacrament necessary to participate in his divine life is Baptism. Through the Sacrament of Baptism, a person is cleansed of all sin, Original and personal; is incorporated into the Mystical Body of Christ, the Church; and becomes a temple of the Holy Spirit. In Baptism, the merits of Christ's redemption are applied to the soul through sanctifying grace.

> Baptism not only purifies from all sins, but also makes the neophyte, "a new creature," an adopted son of God, who has become a "partaker of the divine nature,"[43] member of Christ and co-heir with him,[44] and a temple of the Holy Spirit.[45] (CCC 1265)

Through the sanctifying grace received in Baptism, a person truly shares in the life of Christ. As he or she struggles to put Christ's teachings into practice, the Holy Spirit gives actual grace so Christ's life increasingly animates the soul.

The indwelling of the Blessed Trinity in the soul is a gratuitous gift of God at Baptism, but, at the same time, this intimacy requires conforming one's life to the words and actions of Christ. At the Last Supper, Christ told his Apostles their intimate relationship with God would depend, with the help of grace, on their effort to live the Good News.

> **"He who has my commandments and keeps them, he it is who loves me; and he who loves me will be loved by my Father, and I will love him and manifest myself to him."** (Jn 14: 21)

It is essential to keep in mind a person cannot become Christlike by his or her effort alone but only through the transforming grace won by Christ's redemption. Christ made it clear to his Apostles their fruitfulness would be dependent on being united to him.

Baptism of Christ by Veronese.
Through the sanctifying grace received in Baptism, a person truly shares in the life of Christ.

> **"As the branch cannot bear fruit by itself, unless it abides in the vine, neither can you, unless you abide in me."** (Jn 15: 4)

Incorporation into the life of Christ enables a person to love his or her neighbor with Christ's own love. Christ's New Commandment states, "Love one another as I have loved you."[46] This reflection of the heart of

Christ makes Christians "the light of the world."[47] Jesus Christ is the only Light of the World, but, by sharing in his life and his love, every Christian is enabled to reflect his light to others.

The early Church had a keen awareness of this participation; as St. Peter declared, through Christ, Christians "become partakers of the divine nature."[48] This does not mean they become omnipotent, omniscient, eternal, and the like; rather, the power of grace transforms them into adopted children of God in union with Jesus Christ by the power of the Holy Spirit.

> **The Word became flesh to make us "*partakers of the divine nature*":[49] "For this is why the Word became man, and the Son of God became the Son of man: so that man, by entering into communion with the Word and thus receiving divine sonship, might become a son of God."[50] "For the Son of God became man so that we might become God."[51] "The only-begotten Son of God, wanting to make us sharers in his divinity, assumed our nature, so that he, made man, might make men gods."[52] (CCC 460)**

Sacred Heart of Jesus by Chambers.
Jesus Christ is the only Light of the World, but, by sharing in his life and his love, every Christian is enabled to reflect his light to others.

Christ's redemption gives everyone the capacity to become like God. This participation in God's divine nature through Jesus Christ is in direct opposition to what Adam and Eve desired upon eating the forbidden fruit. Our first parents hoped to acquire God's knowledge and glory independently of him. By contrast, the divinization brought about by sanctifying grace makes Christians participants in the life of the Blessed Trinity. People's desire to be *like God* has been fulfilled in Christ, who offers every person the opportunity to share in God's own life.

In union with Jesus Christ, his followers are children of God and can, therefore, call upon God as *our Father*. By incorporation into Christ through Baptism, the faithful enter into an entirely new relationship with God the Father. No longer simply made in the image and likeness of God, they become his sons and daughters.

The sanctifying grace bestowed on Christians through Baptism enables them to reflect the life of Christ not just by imitation but by inclusion into his very life. Sharing in the life of Christ leads to the realization people are called to live a full life in him.

The seed of Christ's life, which was planted at Baptism, is meant to grow to maturity through deeds of faith inspired by charity. The more one follows Christ through prayer, union with the Cross, deeds of charity, and the like, the more Christlike he or she becomes. Every Christian should strive to be able to say, as St. Paul, "I have been crucified with Christ; it is no longer I who live, but Christ who lives in me."[53] The *Catechism* summarizes these ideas:

> **Christ enables us *to live in him* all that he himself lived, and *he lives it in us*. "By his Incarnation, he, the Son of God, has in a certain way united himself with each man."[54] We are called only to become one with him, for he enables us as the members of his Body to share in what he lived for us in his flesh as our model:**
>
>> **We must continue to accomplish in ourselves the stages of Jesus' life and his mysteries and often to beg him to perfect and realize them in us and in his whole Church.... For it is the plan of the Son of God to make us and the whole Church partake in his mysteries and to extend them to and continue them in us and in his whole Church. This is his plan for fulfilling his mysteries in us.[55] (CCC 521)**

CHRIST'S LIFE WAS FOR REDEMPTION

A mystery is a reality that can never be fully comprehended by human reason. The mystery of the redemption begins with the Incarnation and spans Christ's entire life through his Ascension into Heaven.

However, the intervention of Jesus Christ, the Word of God, in the world begins at creation. The opening verses of St. John's Gospel identifies Christ with the Word of God who has existed with the Father for all eternity; through the Word all things were created.

> **In the beginning was the Word, and the Word was with God, and the Word was God. He was in the beginning with God; all things were made through him, and without him was not anything made that was made. (Jn 1:1-3)**

A few verses later, speaking of the mystery of the Incarnation, St. John reveals:

> **The Word became flesh and dwelt among us, full of grace and truth. (Jn 1:14)**

The Incarnation is a fascinating mystery that can never be completely understood. The Creator of the universe, who is eternal and omnipotent, entered into his creation as a human being. God became visible by taking on a human nature. He spoke in human language; he lived in a family, obeyed his parents, prayed and worshiped, studied religion, and worked, just like every person. God the Son participated fully in the human experience and was like all people in all things but sin.

> **By His incarnation the Son of God has united Himself in some fashion with every man. He worked with human hands, He thought with a human mind, acted by human choice[56] and loved with a human heart. Born of the Virgin Mary, He has truly been made one of us, like us in all things except sin.[57] (*Gaudium et Spes*, 22)**

Christ and the Good Thief by Titian.
Though he was the one offended by sin, God the Son became a man to take upon himself the debt of human sins as if he had sinned.

Because of the mystery of the Incarnation, everything Christ did was at the service of redemption and salvation. Though he was the one offended by sin, God the Son became a man to take upon himself the debt of human sins. By means of the sacred humanity of Jesus Christ—God made man—a human person can share in the life of all of the Persons of the Blessed Trinity, who bestow the grace of salvation. In this manner, the human nature of Christ is God's instrument of redemption.

> **From the swaddling clothes of his birth to the vinegar of his Passion and the shroud of his Resurrection, everything in Jesus' life was a sign of his mystery.[58] His deeds, miracles and words all revealed that "in him the whole fullness of deity dwells bodily."[59] His humanity appeared as "sacrament," that is, the sign and instrument, of his divinity and of the salvation he brings: what was visible in his earthly life leads to the invisible mystery of his divine sonship and redemptive mission. (CCC 515)**

THE REDEMPTIVE VALUE OF CHRIST'S HIDDEN LIFE

Ordinary daily life was an important part of Christ's plan of redemption. It is interesting to note the greater part of Christ's redemptive work was spent as an ordinary person. He lived with his family, worked at a trade, and had a circle of friends. His daily routine during this period of his life was much the same as anyone else's.

Jesus and His Mother at the Fountain by Tissot. Christ spent the better part of his life in mundane affairs; this indicates each person's ordinary life is a means of union with him.

Christ spent the better part of his life in mundane affairs; this indicates each person's ordinary life is a means of union with him. Christ redeemed man by engaging in everyday affairs; this reveals each person can find Christ through everyday activities. For example, mowing a lawn or writing an essay, if done for love of God with as much human perfection possible, can be turned into prayer.

During the greater part of his life Jesus shared the condition of the vast majority of human beings: a daily life spent without evident greatness, a life of manual labor. His religious life was that of a Jew obedient to the law of God,[60] a life in the community. From this whole period it is revealed to us that Jesus was "obedient" to his parents and that he "increased in wisdom and in stature, and in favor with God and man."[61] (CCC 531)

The great majority of people are called to follow Christ's example by offering the ordinary activities of each day to God, which makes them sources of grace. The command to love as Christ loved can be fulfilled first at home and then among friends, classmates, and colleagues. Dedication to Christ amid ordinary activities involves being a good friend, helping those in need, visiting the sick, participating in charitable activities, and the like. A kind greeting, a display of genuine interest, a phone call, or a birthday card are just a few ways a person can imitate Christ's hidden life and live his commandment of charity.

THE POWER OF CHRIST'S WORDS

As evidenced in St. Paul's Letter to the Hebrews, the early Church clearly understood the tremendous power of Christ's words.

> **The word of God is living and active, sharper than any two-edged sword, piercing to the division of soul and spirit, of joints and marrow, and discerning the thoughts and intentions of the heart. (Heb 4: 12)**

The words of Christ are redemptive and have the power to purify consciences. These words are especially purifying and sanctifying when they form part of the sacraments. For example, through the repetition of Christ's words at the Last Supper, bread and wine become his Body and Blood in the Sacrament of the Eucharist.

Sermon on the Mount (detail), Altarpiece by Olrik.
The words of Christ are intended to grow within and mature, bearing fruits of humility, wisdom, and charity.

In addition to their significance in the liturgy, Christ's words are an effective means to provoke conversion. For example, through Christ's words it is discovered people are called to love their enemies, be detached from material possessions, embrace their crosses, and forgive others.

Throughout the Gospels, Christ's words prompt examinations of conscience. As a person meditates on Christ's words, he or she is able to examine his or her conscience, and, noticing discrepancies between his or her conduct and Christ's teachings, he or she is moved to contrition and conversion.

St. Augustine was drawn to conversion through the preaching of St. Ambrose and the words of Scripture. Many people have repented and converted upon hearing the words of Christ explained through preaching. It is sufficient to reflect on the huge crowds of people moved by Christ's words at papal gatherings and Masses around the world. This phenomenon has been especially apparent at World Youth Days, which often draw over 1,000,000 young people.

The Word of God, as Christ taught, functions as a tiny seed destined to grow and bear fruit.[62] The seed, which represents the teachings of Christ, is not meant simply to be heard but to be converted into action. For those words to take effect, however, the hearer must make a serious effort and persevere to put Christ's teachings into practice.

> **Jesus' invitation to enter his kingdom comes in the form of parables, a characteristic feature of his teaching.[63] Through his parables he invites people to the feast of the kingdom, but he also asks for a radical choice: to gain the kingdom, one must give everything.[64] Words are not enough; deeds are required.[65] The parables are like mirrors for man: will he be hard soil or good earth for the word?[66] (CCC 546)**

As Christ's words are taken to heart, the listener is affected in an unexpected way. The two-step process—bringing the Gospel texts to prayer and striving to put them into practice—transforms the person into another Christ. The words of Christ are intended to grow within and mature, bearing fruits of humility, wisdom, and charity. This fruitfulness also helps a person witness effectively the life of Christ to others.

THE DIVINE MERCY OF CHRIST

Among the many attractive features of Christ's personality, one that has moved the hearts of many is his compassion. In Jesus Christ, God became man to reveal the love of the Father. This love is revealed through the Redeemer's compassion toward the sick, the downtrodden, the sorrowful, and the sinful.

> **When he saw the crowds, he had compassion for them, because they were harassed and helpless, like sheep without a shepherd.** (Mt 9: 36)

Compassion is a special kind of love in which a person identifies with the sufferings of another with a desire to relieve his or her pain. Christ was never indifferent to anyone's pain and sorrow. The whole Gospel, in a sense, is a narrative of Christ's compassion for everyone, especially the suffering and the poor.

The words of the Gospel are eternal and thus apply to every circumstance, every culture, and every age. Moreover, everyone is an object of Christ's compassion; he is never indifferent to anyone's pain or sorrow. Being infinitely compassionate, he does not will hardship for anyone; rather, he desires spiritual purification and healing.

When a person experiences compassion for the plight of a neighbor, often he or she can go no further than to give heartfelt sympathy. Jesus Christ, however, not only identifies with suffering but also offers a remedy.

The robust healing ministry of Christ is also an allegory of how our Lord treats spiritual infirmities. For example, though he cured lepers physically, these healings symbolize the removal of sin, a kind of spiritual leprosy. The restoration of sight and hearing signify Christ's power to give the light of faith and the ability to see and hear the truth and to understand and penetrate the Word of God.

Jesus Healing the Blind of Jericho (detail) by Poussin.
The restoration of sight and hearing signify Christ's power to give the light of faith and the ability to see and hear the truth and to understand and penetrate the Word of God.

People suffer in many ways: physical illness, financial troubles, professional failure, psychological problems, loneliness, and in other ways. Suffering can produce feelings of helplessness and a sense of dread. However, turning to Christ amid adversity brings peace and security to the soul as one remembers God is in control. Through personal suffering, a person can unite him- or herself to the Passion of Christ, which brings joy and peace together with a saintly life. Many experience the truth of these consoling words:

> **"Come to me, all who labor and are heavy laden, and I will give you rest. Take my yoke upon you, and learn from me; for I am gentle and lowly in heart; and you will find rest for your souls. For my yoke is easy, and my burden is light."** (Mt 11: 28-30)

Lastly, Christ's compassion heals the wounds of sin. His work of redemption is designed not so much to remove hardship and suffering as it is to bring forgiveness of sins, which leads to everlasting life.

> **By freeing some individuals from the earthly evils of hunger, injustice, illness and death,[67] Jesus performed messianic signs. Nevertheless he did not come to abolish all evils here below,[68] but to free men from the gravest slavery, sin, which thwarts them in their vocation as God's sons and causes all forms of human bondage.[69]** (CCC 549)

LIBERATION IN CHRIST

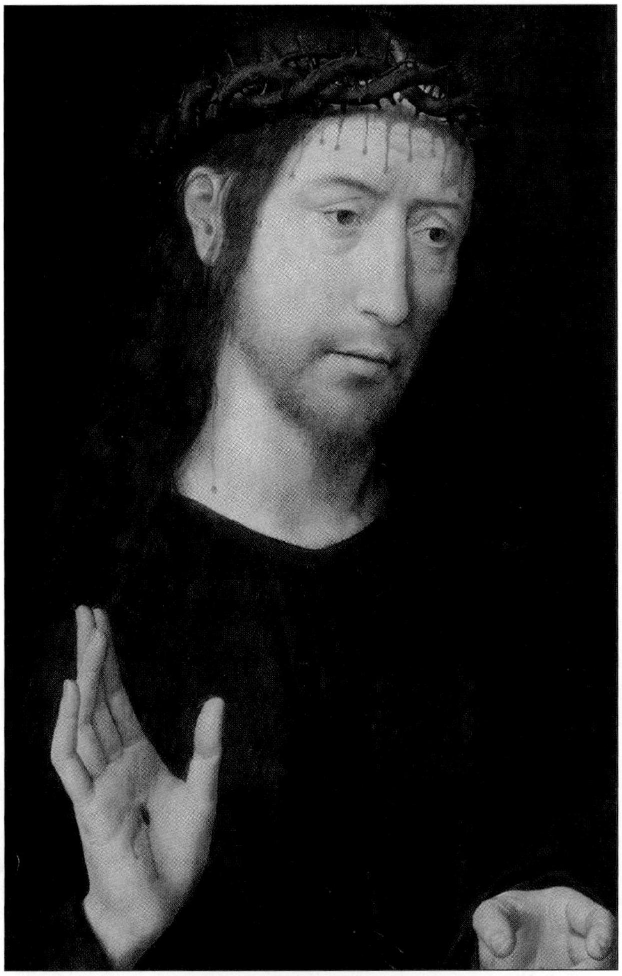

Man of Sorrows by Memling.
Through justification, Christ not only makes the necessary reparation for sin but also transforms the soul by sanctifying grace.

God created man in a state of original justice. Through the sin of Adam and the subsequent personal sins committed by all people, the human race incurred a debt for which just reparation could never have been made by man alone. Only Jesus Christ, who has both a divine and human nature, could reconcile man with God through his Death and Resurrection. This worthy sacrifice offered for the sins of mankind is called *justification*.

Redemption atones for all sin and renews the soul. The superabundant graces Christ won by the redemption cleanse the soul from sin and make it pleasing to God. Beginning with Baptism, the soul receives sanctifying grace; the infused virtues of faith, hope, and charity; and the gifts of the Holy Spirit.

Through justification, Christ not only makes the necessary reparation for sin but also transforms the soul by sanctifying grace. The graces won by the redemption produce a profound change in the soul of the human person.

> **Justification *detaches man from sin* which contradicts the love of God, and purifies his heart of sin. Justification follows upon God's merciful initiative of offering forgiveness. It reconciles man with God. It frees from the enslavement to sin, and it heals. (CCC 1990)**

The grace of justification is meant not only to forgive sins but also to lead a person to holiness. The grace of justification received in Baptism is completely unmerited and obtained only through God's merciful love. Sanctifying grace, which brings about an intimate union with the Blessed Trinity, is meant to grow through struggle and conform one's life to the teachings of Christ. God, in his infinite mercy, bestows an increase of sanctifying grace in response to desires and actions to imitate the life of Christ faithfully.

> **Justification establishes *cooperation between God's grace and man's freedom*. On man's part it is expressed by the assent of faith to the Word of God, which invites him to conversion, and in the cooperation of charity with the prompting of the Holy Spirit who precedes and preserves his assent. (CCC 1993)**

CONCLUSION

Why is Christianity attractive? The answer is simple: Christ is attractive. God entered the world by taking on a human nature. He spoke directly and identified with human labors, hardships, and sufferings out of love. Not only did he enter humanity but he made himself completely accessible as an infant lying in a manger. His entire life was a display of radical love coupled with a desire to redeem man. The Crucifixion is indeed a mystery of the love God has for his children. In the end, the Son of God died on the Cross for each and every person. There is one explanation for this extraordinary sacrifice: "God is love."[70] He created man to be happy and share in his divine life, and true happiness is found only in him.

Magnificat

Luke 1: 46-55; Vespers

The *Magnificat*, also known as *Mary's Song*, praises God for having selected the Blessed Virgin Mary to be Mother of God as well as his divine mercy and sympathy. It expresses her joyous exaltation and gratitude for her own personal blessings. She proclaims God's sovereignty and special love for the lowly and his particular mercy to Israel.

The Blessed Virgin Mary's sublime prayer draws from the Old Testament (cf. 1 Sam 2: 1-10) and the New Testament (cf. Lk 1: 46-55). It can be divided into three stanzas. The first praises a mighty and merciful God who has overlooked the humble state of his handmaiden and has bestowed upon her the incomparable privilege to become the Mother of God, whereby all generations will call her blessed (cf. Lk 1: 46-50). The second reflects on God's divine justice, which exalts and assists the meek and lowly while thwarting the efforts of the proud and powerful (cf. Lk 1: 51-53). The third stanza recalls God's fidelity and mercy toward his Chosen People (cf. Lk 1: 54-55).

My soul magnifies the Lord,
and my spirit rejoices in God my Savior,
for he has regarded the low estate of
his handmaiden.
For behold, henceforth all generations
will call me blessed;
for he who is mighty has done great things
for me,
and holy is his name.
And his mercy is on those who fear him
from generation to generation.
He has shown strength with his arm,
he has scattered the proud in the
imagination of their hearts,
he has put down the mighty from their thrones,
and exalted those of low degree;
he has filled the hungry with good things,
and the rich he has sent empty away.
He has helped his servant Israel,
in remembrance of his mercy,
as he spoke to our fathers,
to Abraham and to his posterity for ever.

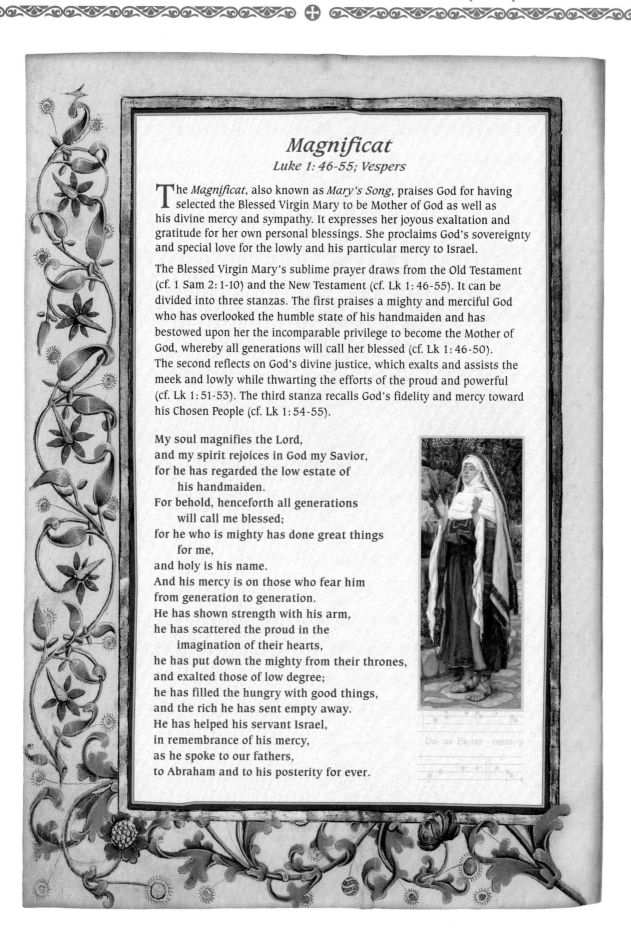

SUPPLEMENTARY READING

1. *The Example of Nazareth*

Nazareth is a kind of school where we may begin to discover what Christ's life was like and even to understand his Gospel. Here we can observe and ponder the simple appeal of the way God's Son came to be known, profound yet full of hidden meaning. And gradually we may even learn to imitate him.

Here we can learn to realize who Christ really is. And here we can sense and take account of the conditions and circumstances that surrounded and affected his life on earth: the places, the tenor of the times, the culture, the language, religious customs, in brief, everything which Jesus used to make himself known to the world. Here everything speaks to us, everything has meaning. Here we can learn the importance of spiritual discipline for all who wish to follow Christ and to live by the teachings of his Gospel.

First, we learn from its silence....The silence of Nazareth should teach us how to meditate in peace and quiet, to reflect on the deeply spiritual, and to be open to the voice of God's inner wisdom and the counsel of his true teachers. Nazareth can teach us the value of study and preparation, of meditation, of a well-ordered personal spiritual life, and of silent prayer that is known only to God.

Second, we learn about family life. May Nazareth serve as a model of what the family should be. May it show us the family's holy and enduring character and exemplify its basic function in society: a community of love and sharing, beautiful for the problems it poses and the rewards it brings, in sum, the perfect setting for rearing children—and for this there is no substitute.

Finally, in Nazareth, the home of a craftsman's son, we learn about work and the discipline it entails. I would especially like to recognize its value—demanding yet redeeming—and to give it proper respect. I would remind everyone that work has its own dignity. On the other hand, it is not an end in itself. Its value and free character, however, derive not only from its place in the economic system, as they say, but rather from the purpose it serves.

—Pope Paul VI

2. *The Wonder of the Incarnation*

The very Son of God, older than the ages, the invisible, the incomprehensible, the incorporeal, the beginning of beginning, the light of light, the fountain of life and immortality, the image of the archetype, the immovable seal, the perfect likeness, the definition and word of the Father: he it is who comes to his own image and takes our nature for the good of our nature, and unites himself to an intelligent soul for the good of my soul, to purify like by like. He takes to himself all that is human, except for sin. He was conceived by the Virgin Mary, who had been first prepared in soul and body by the Spirit; his coming to birth had to be treated with honor, virginity had to receive new honor. He comes forth as God, in the human nature he has taken, one being, made of two contrary elements, flesh and spirit. Spirit gave divinity, flesh received it.

He who makes rich is made poor; he takes on the poverty of my flesh, that I may gain the riches of his divinity. He who is full is made empty; he is emptied for a brief space of his glory, that I may share in his fullness. What is this wealth of goodness? What is this mystery that surrounds me? I received the likeness of God, but failed to keep it. He takes on my flesh, to bring salvation to the image, immortality to the flesh. He enters into a second union with us, a union far more wonderful than the first.

Holiness had to be brought to man by the humanity assumed by one who was God, so that God might overcome the tyrant by force and so deliver us and lead us back to himself through the mediation of his Son. The Son arranged this for the honor of the Father, to whom the Son is clearly obedient in all things.

—St. Gregory Nazianzen

SUPPLEMENTARY READING Continued

3. *Eve and Mary*

The Lord, coming into his own creation in visible form, was sustained by his own creation which he himself sustains in being. His obedience on the tree of the cross reversed the disobedience at the tree in Eden; the good news of the truth announced by an angel to Mary, a virgin subject to a husband, undid the evil lie that seduced Eve, a virgin espoused to a husband.

As Eve was seduced by the word of an angel and so fled from God after disobeying his word, Mary in her turn was given the good news by the word of an angel, and bore God in obedience to his word. As Eve was seduced into disobedience to God, so Mary was persuaded into obedience to God; thus the Virgin Mary became the advocate of the virgin Eve.

Christ gathered all things into one, by gathering them into himself. He declared war against our enemy, crushed him who at the beginning had taken us captive in Adam, and trampled on his head, in accordance with God's words to the serpent in Genesis: *I will put enmity between you and the woman, and between your seed and her seed; he shall lie in wait for your head, and you shall lie in wait for his heel.*

The one lying in wait for the serpent's head is the one who was born in the likeness of Adam from the woman, the Virgin. This is the seed spoken of by Paul in the letter to the Galatians: *The law of works was in force until the seed should come to whom the promise was made.*

He shows this even more clearly in the same letter when he says: *When the fullness of time had come, God sent his Son, born of a woman.* The enemy would not have been defeated fairly if his vanquisher had not been born of a woman, because it was through a woman that he had gained mastery over man in the beginning, and set himself up as man's adversary.

That is why the Lord proclaims himself the Son of Man, the one who renews in himself that first man from whom the race born of woman was formed; as by a man's defeat our race fell into the bondage of death, so by a man's victory we were to rise again to life.

— St. Irenæus, *Against Heresies*

Annunciation by Pittoni.
"As Eve was seduced by the word of an angel and so fled from God after disobeying his word, Mary in her turn was given the good news by the word of an angel, and bore God in obedience to his word." — St. Irenæus, *Against Heresies*

SUPPLEMENTARY READING Continued

4. *The Mystery of Our Reconciliation with God*

To speak of our Lord, the son of the Blessed Virgin Mary, as true and perfect man is of no value to us if we do not believe that he is descended from the line of ancestors set out in the Gospel.

Matthew's gospel begins by setting out *the genealogy of Jesus Christ, son of David, son of Abraham*, and then traces his human descent by bringing his ancestral line down to his mother's husband, Joseph. On the other hand, Luke traces his parentage backward step by step to the actual father of mankind, to show that both the first and the last Adam share the same nature.

No doubt the Son of God in his omnipotence could have taught and sanctified men by appearing to them in a semblance of human form as he did to the patriarchs and prophets, when for instance he engaged in a wrestling contest or entered into conversation with them, or when he accepted their hospitality and even ate the food they set before him. But these appearances were only types, signs that mysteriously foretold the coming of one who would take a true human nature from the stock of the patriarchs who had gone before him. No mere figure, then, fulfilled the mystery of our reconciliation with God, ordained from all eternity. The Holy Spirit had not yet come upon the Virgin nor had the power of the Most High overshadowed her, so that within her spotless womb Wisdom might build itself a house and the Word become flesh. The divine nature and the nature of a servant were to be united in one person so that the Creator of time might be born in time, and he through whom all things were made might be brought forth in their midst.

— Pope St. Leo the Great

5. *The Whole World Awaits Mary's Reply*

You have heard, O Virgin, that you will conceive and bear a son; you have heard that it will not be by man but by the Holy Spirit. The angel awaits an answer; it is time for him to return to God who sent him. We too are waiting, O Lady, for your word of compassion; the sentence of condemnation weighs heavily upon us.

The price of our salvation is offered to you. We shall be set free at once if you consent. In the eternal Word of God we all came to be, and behold, we die. In your brief response we are to be remade in order to be recalled to life.

Tearful Adam with his sorrowing family begs this of you, O loving Virgin, in their exile from Paradise. Abraham begs it, David begs it. All the other holy patriarchs, your ancestors, ask it of you, as they dwell in the country of the shadow of death. This is what the whole earth waits for, prostrate at your feet. It is right in doing so, for on your word depends comfort for the wretched, ransom for the captive, freedom for the condemned, indeed, salvation for all the sons of Adam, the whole of your race.

Answer quickly, O Virgin. Reply in haste to the angel, or rather through the angel to the Lord. Answer with a word, receive the Word of God. Speak your own word, conceive the divine Word. Breathe a passing word, embrace the eternal Word.

Why do you delay, why are you afraid? Believe, give praise, and receive. Let humility be bold, let modesty be confident. This is no time for virginal simplicity to forget prudence. In this matter alone, O prudent Virgin, do not fear to be presumptuous. Though modest silence is pleasing, dutiful speech is now more necessary. Open your heart to faith, O blessed Virgin, your lips to praise, your womb to the Creator. See, the desired of all nations is at your door, knocking to enter. If he should pass by because of your delay, in sorrow you would begin to seek him afresh, the One whom your soul loves. Arise, hasten, open. Arise in faith, hasten in devotion, open in praise and thanksgiving. *Behold the handmaid of the Lord*, she says, *be it done to me according to your word.*

— St. Bernard

SUPPLEMENTARY READING Continued

6. *The Faithful Foster-Father and Guardian*

There is a general rule concerning all special graces granted to any human being. Whenever the divine favor chooses someone to receive a special grace, or to accept a lofty vocation, God adorns the person chosen with all the gifts of the Spirit needed to fulfill the task at hand.

This general rule is especially verified in the case of Saint Joseph, the foster-father of our Lord and the husband of the Queen of our world, enthroned above the angels. He was chosen by the eternal Father as the trustworthy guardian and protector of his greatest treasures, namely, his divine Son and Mary, Joseph's wife. He carried out this vocation with complete fidelity until at last God called him, saying: "Good and faithful servant enter into the joy of your Lord."

What then is Joseph's position in the whole Church of Christ? Is he not a man chosen and set apart? Through him and, yes, under him, Christ was fittingly and honorably introduced into the world. Holy Church in its entirety is indebted to the Virgin Mother because through her it was judged worthy to receive Christ. But after her we undoubtedly owe special gratitude and reverence to Saint Joseph.

In him the Old Testament finds its fitting close. He brought the noble line of patriarchs and prophets to its promised fulfillment. What the divine goodness had offered as a promise to them, he held in his arms.

Obviously, Christ does not now deny to Joseph that intimacy, reverence and very high honor which he gave him on earth, as a son to his father. Rather we must say that in heaven Christ completes and perfects all that he gave at Nazareth.

Now we can see how the last summoning words of the Lord appropriately apply to Saint Joseph: "Enter into the joy of your Lord." In fact, although the joy of eternal happiness enters into the soul of a man, the Lord preferred to say to Joseph: "Enter into joy." His intention was that the words should have a hidden spiritual meaning for us. They convey not only that this holy man possesses an inward joy, but also that it surrounds him and engulfs him like an infinite abyss.

Remember us, Saint Joseph, and plead for us to your foster-child. Ask your most holy bride, the Virgin Mary, to look kindly upon us, since she is the mother of him who with the Father and the Holy Spirit lives and reigns eternally. Amen.

— St. Bernardine of Siena

Childhood of Christ by Honthorst.
"He [St. Joseph] was chosen by the eternal Father as the trustworthy guardian and protector of his greatest treasures, namely, his divine Son and Mary, Joseph's wife." — St. Bernardine of Siena

VOCABULARY

ANNA
The prophetess who recognized Jesus as the Messiah when he was presented in the Temple. Anna, or Ann, is also the name of the mother of the Blessed Virgin Mary.

ANNUNCIATION
The visit of the Archangel Gabriel to the Blessed Virgin Mary to inform her she would be the Mother of the Savior, commemorated on March 25. Having given her consent to God's word, the Blessed Virgin Mary became the Mother of God the Son by the power of the Holy Spirit.

ATONEMENT
Reparation for an offense through a voluntary action that expiates the injustice done.

ELIZABETH
The wife of St. Zechariah, mother of St. John the Baptist, and kinswoman of the Blessed Virgin Mary.

FINDING IN THE TEMPLE
Described in Luke 2: 41-52, Christ and his parents went to Jerusalem for the Feast of the Passover. On the return journey, the Blessed Virgin Mary and St. Joseph discovered Christ was not with them and, after three days, found him in the Temple, discoursing with the teachers of the Law.

FIAT
Latin for "let it be done." This was the Blessed Virgin Mary's response to God's plan of redemption; it was her consent to become the Mother of God (Lk 1: 38).

GABRIEL
One of the Archangels named in Sacred Scripture and the special messenger of God to the Blessed Virgin Mary at the Annunciation (cf. Dn 9: 21; Lk 1: 19, 26).

GENEALOGY
From the Greek for "tracing of descent"; the study of ancestry or a list of someone's ancestors. Sts. Matthew and Luke contain genealogies of Christ in their Gospels.

IMMACULATE CONCEPTION
In light of God's free choice of the Blessed Virgin Mary from all eternity to be the Mother of his Son, it was ordained, from the first moment of her conception, she—by a singular grace of God and by virtue of the foreseen merits of Jesus Christ—was preserved from all stain of Original Sin. Believed from antiquity, this dogma was formally defined by Pope Bl. Pius IX in 1854.

INCARNATION
From the Latin for "to become flesh"; the mystery of the hypostatic union of the divine and human natures in the one divine Person of the Word, Jesus Christ. To bring about man's salvation, the Son of God was made flesh (cf. Jn 1: 14) and became man.

INDWELLING OF THE BLESSED TRINITY
The Blessed Trinity—Father, Son, and Holy Spirit—are present in the soul from the moment of Baptism and remain as long as that soul is in a state of grace.

JUSTIFICATION
Being made right with God. It is a free and undeserved gift of God through the sacrifice of Jesus Christ.

MAGI
The wise men described in Matthew 2. They came from the East (likely Persia) to adore the newborn King of the Jews and brought him gifts of gold, frankincense, and myrrh. Tradition has given them the names Gaspar, Melchior, and Balthasar.

MARY
The Mother of Jesus. The Blessed Virgin Mary's greatest privilege is her divine Motherhood and, hence, her title Bearer of God, or Mother of God.

NATIVITY
The Birth of our Lord Jesus Christ in Bethlehem as well as the events surrounding his Birth.

VOCABULARY Continued

PASCHAL MYSTERY
Christ's work of redemption accomplished by his Passion, Death, Resurrection, and Ascension, whereby, "dying he destroyed our death, rising he restored our life" (CCC 1067; cf. 654). The Paschal Mystery is celebrated and made present in the liturgies of the Church, and its saving effects are communicated especially through the Sacrament of the Eucharist, which renews the Paschal Sacrifice of Christ as the sacrifice offered by the Church (CCC 571, 1362-1372).

PRESENTATION
The Presentation of Christ in the Temple (Lk 2: 22-40) was performed in obedience to the Mosaic Law, which required the offering of the firstborn male, as well as the ritual purification of the mother, forty days after childbirth. Commemorated February 2, it is sometimes called Candlemas and, in the extraordinary form of the Latin Rite, marks the end of the Christmas season.

REDEMPTION
Jesus Christ, through his sacrificial Death on the Cross, set man free from the slavery of sin.

SANCTIFYING GRACE
The free and unmerited favor of God dispensed through the sacraments. This grace heals human nature, which has been wounded by sin, giving man a share in the divine life, which is infused into the soul by the Holy Spirit.

SIMEON
St. Simeon recognized Jesus as the Christ at the Presentation in the Temple.

VIRGIN BIRTH
The Blessed Virgin Mary conceived Christ by the power of the Holy Spirit. She, therefore, was a virgin when she gave birth to Jesus Christ. The Virgin Birth is also an implicit proclamation of the divinity of Jesus Christ.

VISITATION
The Blessed Virgin Mary visited her kinswoman St. Elizabeth (cf. Lk 1: 39-80). St. Elizabeth's greeting, "Blessed are you among women, and blessed is the fruit of your womb!" forms part of the Hail Mary. St. Elizabeth went on to call the Blessed Virgin Mary "mother of my Lord."

The Ascension by Copley.
The Paschal Mystery is Christ's work of redemption accomplished by his Passion, Death, Resurrection, and Ascension, whereby, "dying he destroyed our death, rising he restored our life" (CCC 1067; cf. 654).

STUDY QUESTIONS

1. What is the relationship between the Archangel Gabriel's greeting, "full of grace," and the dogma of the Immaculate Conception?
2. What is the significance of the name God, through the Archangel Gabriel, gave the child?
3. What is the Virgin Birth?
4. What is the Incarnation?
5. How do the Blessed Virgin Mary's and St. Joseph's cooperation indicate people's role in salvation?
6. What was St. Joseph's "annunciation"?
7. What is the chief difference between Sts. Luke's and Matthew's genealogies of Christ?
8. What is the purpose of St. Luke's genealogy?
9. How does St. Matthew's genealogy support Christ's kingship?
10. How does St. Matthew's genealogy imply Christ is the perfect Son of David and Abraham?
11. Why is the Blessed Virgin Mary called the Ark of the New Covenant?
12. How did St. Elizabeth acknowledge the Blessed Virgin Mary is the Mother of God?
13. Who first received the Good News of Christ's Birth?
14. What is the significance of the privilege given to the shepherds?
15. What is the significance of the visit from the Magi?
16. What is Christian poverty?
17. How is the encounter with the rich young man a warning about attachment to material possessions?
18. At the Presentation, the Holy Family carried out the precepts of the Mosaic Law. What conclusion can be drawn from this?
19. What did Sts. Simeon and Anna recognize in the infant Christ?
20. How was the Finding in the Temple a revelation of Christ's divinity?
21. What virtue seems to be most important in Christ's hidden life, and why might it have been so important?
22. What interior dispositions does obedience demand?
23. Of the Persons of the Blessed Trinity, why is it appropriate for God the Son to have been entrusted with the redemption of the world?
24. What four reasons are presented in this chapter as to why God became man?
25. Why was the Incarnation necessary for man to have been reconciled with God?
26. What redemptive sacrifice was offered by Christ?
27. How does the act of creation demonstrate God's love?
28. How does God's plan of redemption show his love?
29. How is Christ's Passion part of Adam's *felix culpa*?
30. How can a person make Christ incarnate in his or her life by reading the Gospels?
31. What is meditation?
32. What is contemplation?
33. Why is Christ a model to imitate?
34. What is sanctifying grace?
35. What is actual grace?

STUDY QUESTIONS Continued

36. How does God primarily give both sanctifying and actual graces?

37. Which sacrament establishes sanctifying grace in the soul?

38. What is the indwelling of the Blessed Trinity?

39. How does sanctifying grace change a person's relationship with God the Father?

40. What portion of Christ's life is the mystery of redemption?

41. What does it mean to say Christ is like us in all ways but sin?

42. What does it mean to say Christ's human nature is a sacrament?

43. What are some examples of Christ's ordinary life?

44. What are some ordinary activities that can be means of union with Christ?

45. How can ordinary activities be turned into prayer?

46. What is an example of the power of Christ's words in the sacraments?

47. How do Christ's words help people examine their consciences?

48. How is Christ's healing ministry not only physical but also spiritual?

49. Why did Christ not abolish all suffering from the earth?

50. What is justification?

51. What does redemption give the soul in addition to forgiveness of sins?

PRACTICAL EXERCISES

1. In St. Luke's Gospel, an angel appears to the Blessed Virgin Mary; in St. Matthew's Gospel, an angel appears to St. Joseph. Create a graphic organizer comparing these two "annunciations" to see the parallels between them. Possible categories include the following.

- to whom the announcement was made
- who made the announcement
- the role of fear
- the message of the announcement
- how the person responded

2. When the Blessed Virgin Mary first saw her cousin St. Elizabeth, both St. Elizabeth and her unborn child "recognized" she was carrying "my Lord" inside her. The Blessed Virgin Mary uttered her poetic prayer, *Magnificat*. Read Luke 1: 46-55 and identify the ideas presented in this prayer in a bullet-point list.

3. Search the Internet for a Catholic religious order. Write a brief paragraph about how that order lives the evangelical counsels of chastity, poverty, and obedience.

4. St. Paul wrote "In my flesh I complete what is lacking in Christ's afflictions." (Col 1: 24) Brainstorm ten ways a student can make reparation for the sins of the world; limit these to ordinary, nondramatic ways.

5. Select a Passion narrative from one of the four Gospels and list every suffering endured by Christ the Evangelist records.

6. Search the Internet for and read the life of a Catholic saint. Write a paragraph about how that saint's life reflected one of the four reasons God became man.

FROM THE CATECHISM

423 We believe and confess that Jesus of Nazareth, born a Jew of a daughter of Israel at Bethlehem at the time of King Herod the Great and the emperor Caesar Augustus, a carpenter by trade, who died crucified in Jerusalem under the procurator Pontius Pilate during the reign of the emperor Tiberius, is the eternal Son of God made man. He "came from God,"[71] "descended from heaven,"[72] and "came in the flesh."[73] For "the Word became flesh and dwelt among us, full of grace and truth; we have beheld his glory, glory as of the only Son from the Father... And from his fullness have we all received, grace upon grace."[74]

436 The word "Christ" comes from the Greek translation of the Hebrew *Messiah*, which means "anointed." It became the name proper to Jesus only because he accomplished perfectly the divine mission that "Christ" signifies. In effect, in Israel those consecrated to God for a mission that he gave were anointed in his name. This was the case for kings, for priests and, in rare instances, for prophets.[75] This had to be the case all the more so for the Messiah whom God would send to inaugurate his kingdom definitively.[76] It was necessary that the Messiah be anointed by the Spirit of the Lord at once as king and priest, and also as prophet.[77] Jesus fulfilled the messianic hope of Israel in his threefold office of priest, prophet, and king.

489 Throughout the Old Covenant the mission of many holy women *prepared* for that of Mary. At the very beginning there was Eve; despite her disobedience, she receives the promise of a posterity that will be victorious over the evil one, as well as the promise that she will be the mother of all the living.[78] By virtue of this promise, Sarah conceives a son in spite of her old age.[79] Against all human expectation God chooses those who were considered powerless and weak to show forth his faithfulness to his promises: Hannah, the mother of Samuel; Deborah; Ruth; Judith and Esther; and many other women.[80] Mary "stands out among the poor and humble of the Lord, who confidently hope for and receive salvation from him. After a long period of waiting the times are fulfilled in her, the exalted Daughter of Sion, and the new plan of salvation is established."[81]

524 When the Church celebrates *the liturgy of Advent* each year, she makes present this ancient expectancy of the Messiah, for by sharing in the long preparation for the Savior's first coming, the faithful renew their ardent desire for his second coming.[82] By celebrating the precursor's birth and martyrdom, the Church unites herself to his desire: "He must increase, but I must decrease."[83]

527 Jesus' *circumcision*, on the eighth day after his birth,[84] is the sign of his incorporation into Abraham's descendants, into the people of the covenant. It is the sign of his submission to the Law[85] and his deputation to Israel's worship, in which he will participate throughout his life. This sign prefigures that "circumcision of Christ" which is Baptism.[86]

530 The *flight into Egypt* and the massacre of the innocents[87] make manifest the opposition of darkness to the light: "He came to his own home, and his own people received him not."[88] Christ's whole life was lived under the sign of persecution. His own share it with him.[89] Jesus' departure from Egypt recalls the exodus and presents him as the definitive liberator of God's people.[90]

534 The *finding of Jesus in the temple* is the only event that breaks the silence of the Gospels about the hidden years of Jesus.[91] Here Jesus lets us catch a glimpse of the mystery of his total consecration to a mission that flows from his divine sonship: "Did you not know that I must be about my Father's work?"[92] Mary and Joseph did not understand these words, but they accepted them in faith. Mary "kept all these things in her heart" during the years Jesus remained hidden in the silence of an ordinary life.

Adoration of the Shepherds (detail) by Giorgione.
The manger underlines the poverty of Christ; he had come to share fully in the human condition.

ENDNOTES - CHAPTER THREE

1. Is 7:14.
2. Lk 1:28.
3. *LG* 56.
4. Lk 1:28.
5. *LG* 56.
6. Lk 1:30.
7. Lk 1:35.
8. Cf. Lk 1:31.
9. Lk 1:34.
10. Council of the Lateran (649): DS 503; cf. DS 10-64.
11. Lk 1:35.
12. Mt 1:23.
13. Mt 1:19.
14. Cf. Mt 1:1-17.
15. Cf. Lk 3:23-38.
16. Jn 18:36.
17. Jn 19:19.
18. Lk 1:48.
19. Lk 1:43.
20. Mt 2:1.
21. Jn 6:33.
22. Cf. Mt 19:22.
23. Lk 4:18; cf. 7:22.
24. Mt 5:3.
25. Cf. Mt 11:25.
26. Cf. Mt 21:18; Mk 2:23-26; Jn 4:6-7; 19:28; Lk 9:58.
27. Cf. Mt 25:31-46.
28. Lk 22:42.
29. Cf. Rom 5:19.
30. Jn 1:14.
31. Cf. Eph 1:7; Col 1:13-14; 1 Pt 1:18-19.
32. Cf. 2 Cor 8:9.
33. Cf. Lk 2:51.
34. Cf. Jn 15:3.
35. Mt 8:17; cf. Is 53:4.
36. Cf. Rom 4:25.
37. Lk 23:37.
38. Mt 4:3.
39. Jn 14:6.
40. Lk 23:38.
41. *GS* 38; cf. Rom 15:5; Phil 2:5.
42. Cf. Jn 13:15; Lk 11:1; Mt 5:11-12.
43. 2 Cor 5:17; 2 Pt 1:4; cf. Gal 4:5-7.
44. Cf. 1 Cor 6:15; 12:27; Rom 8:17.
45. Cf. 1 Cor 6:19.
46. Jn 15:12.
47. Mt 5:14.
48. 2 Pt 1:4.
49. Ibid.
50. St. Irenæus, *Adv. hæres.* 3, 19, 1: PG 7/1, 939.
51. St. Athanasius, *De inc.* 54, 3: PG 25, 192B.
52. St. Thomas Aquinas, *Opusc.* 57:1-4.
53. Gal 2:20.
54. *GS* 22 § 2.
55. St. John Eudes, *LH*, Week 33, Friday, OR.
56. Cf. Third *Council of Constantinople*: "and so His human will, though deified, is not destroyed": Denzinger 291 (556).
57. Cf. Heb 4:15.
58. Cf. Lk 2:7; Mt 27:48; Jn 20:7.
59. Col 2:9.
60. Cf. Gal 4:4.
61. Lk 2:51-52.
62. Cf. Lk 8:4-15.
63. Cf. Mk 4:33-34.
64. Cf. Mt 13:44-45; 22:1-14.
65. Cf. Mt 21:28-32.
66. Cf. Mt 13:3-9.
67. Cf. Jn 6:5-15; Lk 19:8; Mt 11:5.
68. Cf. Lk 12:13-14; Jn 18:36.
69. Cf. Jn 8:34-36.
70. 1 Jn 4:8.
71. Jn 13:3.
72. Jn 3:13; 6:33.
73. 1 Jn 4:2.
74. Jn 1:14, 16.
75. Cf. Ex 29:7; Lv 8:12; 1 Sm 9:16; 10:1; 16:1, 12-13; 1 Kgs 1:39; 19:16.
76. Cf. Ps 2:2; Acts 4:26-27.
77. Cf. Is 11:2; 61:1; Zec 4:14; 6:13; Lk 4:16-21.
78. Cf. Gn 3:15, 20.
79. Cf. Gn 18:10-14; 21:1-2.
80. Cf. 1 Cor 1:17; 1 Sm 1.
81. *LG* 55.
82. Cf. Rev 22:17.
83. Jn 3:30.
84. Cf. Lk 2:21.
85. Cf. Gal 4:4.
86. Cf. Col 2:11-13.
87. Cf. Mt 2:13-18.
88. Jn 1:11.
89. Cf. Jn 15:20.
90. Cf. Mt 2:15; Hos 11:1.
91. Cf. Lk 2:41-52.
92. Lk 2:49 alt.

The Mystery of Redemption

CHAPTER 4

Redemption and the Paschal Mystery

From Christ's Paschal Mystery, people have learned to appreciate the great evil of sin and the even greater love of God.

The Mystery of Redemption

CHAPTER 4

Redemption and the Paschal Mystery

INTRODUCTION

Christianity begins with a fact: "The Word was made flesh and dwelt among us."[1] God became man to reveal the fullness of truth and suffer and die for man's salvation; this was confirmed by the Resurrection of Jesus Christ. The living Christ, who conquered sin and death, is the reason for people's faith as well as for their hope and joy. As St. Paul stated in his First Letter to the Corinthians:

If Christ has not been raised, then our preaching is in vain and your faith is in vain. (1 Cor 15: 14)

From the earliest Christian era, the Passion, Death, and Resurrection of Jesus Christ have been called the Paschal Mystery. These events are the culmination of Christ's redemptive mission—a mission that began at the moment of his conception. As God-made-man, every word and action of Christ has infinite redemptive value and merits a superabundance of grace. In God's infinite providence, however, Christ's redemptive work on earth culminated in his suffering and Death on the Cross, after which he rose again, thus manifesting his victory over death.

The Paschal Mystery cannot be understood outside the first Passover, which occasioned the liberation of the Chosen People from their slavery in Egypt. The Israelites, who had been in Egypt for over four centuries, were only allowed to leave because of the death of every firstborn male of the Egyptians. The firstborn males of the Israelites, however, were spared this punishment through the sacrifice of the paschal lamb, a lamb whose blood had been placed on the doorposts and lintels of their homes.

The paschal lamb, whose blood had saved the Israelites from slavery in Egypt, was a type, or prefigurement, of Jesus Christ, the Lamb of God whose Blood saved all people from the slavery of sin.[2] The events leading up to and culminating in Christ's Death on the Cross and his glorious Resurrection are a mystery because it can never be fully comprehended by human reason how Christ, being both God and man, could die for sins and rise from the dead.

The events of Christ's Passion (i.e., his suffering), Death, and Resurrection are a manifestation of God's infinite love that achieved redemption. Love is measured by self-sacrifice; the love that prompted Jesus Christ, true God and true man, to suffer and die in atonement for sins is unparalleled. Thus, the Passion of Christ is testimony of God's infinite love for each and every person.

God Inviting Christ to Sit on the Throne at His Right Hand by Grebber.
Seated at the right hand of the Father, Christ intercedes continuously on behalf of his people.

The glorification of Christ through his Resurrection from the dead and his Ascension into Heaven serves as the ultimate sign of the victory of his redemption. Seated at the right hand of the Father, Christ intercedes continuously on behalf of his people. He and the Father sent the Holy Spirit, who bestows the graces of his redemption on the Apostles and all of the followers of Christ.

THIS CHAPTER WILL ADDRESS SEVERAL QUESTIONS:

- Why was Christ baptized?
- What temptations did Christ experience?
- What is the significance of the Transfiguration?
- What is the New Commandment, and how does it relate to the Decalogue?
- What is the significance of the Eucharist?
- What is the Paschal Mystery?
- What is the meaning of the Passion?
- What is the significance of the Resurrection, and did it really occur?

Baptism of Christ by Murillo.
The Baptism of Christ by St. John is a powerful sign of his solidarity with every human person born in sin.

THE BAPTISM OF CHRIST

Jesus came from Galilee to the Jordan to John, to be baptized by him. John would have prevented him, saying, "I need to be baptized by you, and do you come to me?" But Jesus answered him, "Let it be so now; for thus it is fitting for us to fulfill all righteousness." Then he consented. And when Jesus was baptized, he went up immediately from the water, and behold, the heavens were opened and he saw the Spirit of God descending like a dove, and alighting on him; and lo, a voice from heaven, saying, "This is my beloved Son, with whom I am well pleased." (Mt 3:13-17)

Jesus Christ began his public ministry and his road to the Cross when he was about thirty years old. He appeared at the River Jordan, where St. John the Baptist, who had been chosen by God to prepare the hearts of men and women for the Messiah, was preaching and baptizing for the forgiveness of sins.

As Christ approached, St. John the Baptist saw him from a distance and declared:

"Behold, the Lamb of God, who takes away the sin of the world!" (Jn 1:29)

Through the eyes of faith, St. John the Baptist recognized the Person for whom he had been preparing the way. These words of St. John are repeated by the priest at each Mass. Like St. John, each person is called to recognize, through the eyes of faith, the presence of Christ, who comes in the Eucharist.

Upon hearing Christ's request for baptism, St. John the Baptist, recognizing his own unworthiness, refused. Even so, Christ insisted, telling him it was necessary "to fulfill all righteousness."[3]

The baptism offered by St. John was a baptism of repentance. Since Christ had committed no sins—indeed, as God, was free from all stain of Original Sin—and had no need of repentance, why did he request a baptism of repentance? The *Catechism* answers this question: the Baptism of Christ by St. John indicates Christ's acceptance of his mission and an anticipation of his own Death and Resurrection.

The baptism of Jesus is on his part the acceptance and inauguration of his mission as God's suffering Servant. He allows himself to be numbered among sinners; he is already "the Lamb of God, who takes away the sin of the world."[4] Already he is anticipating the "baptism" of his bloody death.[5] Already he is coming to "fulfill all righteousness," that is, he is submitting himself entirely to his Father's will: out of love he consents to this baptism of death for the remission of our sins.[6] (CCC 536)

Though sinless, Christ identified himself fully with sinners as part of his plan of redemption. The Baptism of Christ by St. John is a powerful sign of his solidarity with every human person born in sin. Since he mercifully and generously chose to take upon himself the entire burden of sin, it was fitting he allowed himself to be baptized with sinners.

The Crucifixion (detail) by Grünewald.
Through the eyes of faith, St. John the Baptist recognized the Person for whom he had been preparing the way.

In the Sacrament of Baptism, Christians become identified with Christ's Paschal Mystery. The symbolism of this spiritual reality is particularly strong through Baptism by immersion, whereby a person enters into Christ's Death and rises anew with him in his Resurrection.

Having emerged from the waters of the River Jordan, the Holy Spirit descended upon Christ in the form of a dove, and a voice from Heaven spoke, saying, "This is my beloved Son, with whom I am well pleased."[7] Thus, the Baptism of Christ was also a manifestation of the Blessed Trinity.

The Baptism of Christ by St. John marked the beginning of his public ministry. From this moment on, Christ moved steadily toward the Cross.

> Jesus' Baptism anticipated his death on the Cross, and the heavenly voice proclaimed an anticipation of the Resurrection. These anticipations have now become reality. John's baptism with water has received its full meaning through the Baptism of Jesus' own life and death. To accept the invitation to be baptized now means to go to the place of Jesus' Baptism. It is to go where he identifies himself with us and to receive there our identification with him. The point where he anticipates death has now become the point where we anticipate rising again with him. (Pope Benedict XVI, *Jesus of Nazareth* [New York, New York: Doubleday, 2007], 18)

THE WEDDING AT CANA

> **On the third day there was a marriage at Cana in Galilee, and the mother of Jesus was there; Jesus also was invited to the marriage, with his disciples. (Jn 2: 1-2)**

Following the Baptism of Christ, he proceeded with his disciples, whom he had just called, to a wedding in the village of Cana. St. John the Evangelist specifically mentions Christ's Mother was also in attendance. This was one of her last appearances in the Gospel until her appearance at the foot of the Cross. These two seemingly unrelated events—Cana and the Cross—are closely linked in St. John's Gospel.

At some point during the wedding celebration, which at that time probably lasted several days, the hosts ran out of wine. The Blessed Virgin Mary approached Christ and informed him, "They have no wine."[8] He answered her, saying,

> **"O woman, what have you to do with me? My hour has not yet come." (Jn 2: 4)**

The Wedding at Cana by Murillo.
The miracle at Cana is rich in symbolism. The water became wine, which evokes Christ having shed Blood and water on the Cross.

It might seem strange, at first glance, for Christ to refer to his Mother as "woman." This hearkens back to the *Protoevangelium*, in which God revealed Satan would be defeated by the seed of the *woman*. By calling his mother "woman," Christ implied a public miracle, at this point, would publicly mark the beginning of his Redemptive mission—a mission that culminated on the Cross. Indeed, the next time Christ referred to his Mother as "woman," he was on the Cross, when his Death occasioned the defeat of Satan.

Following Christ's reply, the Blessed Virgin Mary did not hesitate. She turned to the servants, telling them, "Do whatever he tells you."[9] This is wonderful advice from the Mother of God, and it beautifully illustrates her role in the life of the Church. She always intercedes for and points people to her Son, counseling, "Do whatever he tells you."

The miracle at Cana is rich in symbolism. The water became wine, which evokes Christ having shed Blood and water on the Cross. It also refers to the Eucharist, in which wine becomes the Blood of Christ, which is the re-presentation of the Paschal Mystery. It is the second Luminous Mystery of the Rosary.

CHRIST'S TEMPTATION BY SATAN

Temptations in the Desert

> **Jesus was led up by the Spirit into the wilderness to be tempted by the devil. And he fasted forty days and forty nights, and afterward he was hungry.** (Mt 4: 1-2)

The Gospel of St. Matthew records, after his baptism by St. John, Christ went into the wilderness, where he prayed and fasted for forty days. The number forty indicates a period of trial and preparation. Indeed, these forty days were both a preparation for Christ's public ministry and a time of temptation. The forty days Christ spent praying and fasting are the prototype of the forty days of Lent, which ready Christians to experience anew the events of Christ's Passion, Death, and Resurrection.

Temptation of Christ in the Wilderness (detail) by Juan de Flandes.
"...command this stone to become bread."

During his time in the wilderness, Christ prepared for the establishment of his kingdom and his public ministry, which climaxed with his Death on the Cross. Sharing fully in the human experience, Christ suffered intensely from hunger and the harsh climate. At that moment, when Christ was at his weakest, Satan came to tempt him.

From the moment God had foretold his defeat in the *Protoevangelium*, Satan had probably been waiting to discover the identity of the woman and her Son so as to engage them in supernatural battle. Coming to tempt Christ, he was determined to find out if he truly is the Son of God, the promised Messiah.

Satan began by tempting Christ in the flesh. This tactic had worked well throughout human history; one consequence of Original Sin is the body is no longer completely subject to the will. It often rebels, leading to sin.

> **The devil said to him, "If you are the Son of God, command this stone to become bread."** (Lk 4: 3)

Satan's first temptation was to make Christ's self-sacrifice, in this case fasting, seem unreasonable. He tried to entice Christ to pursue what yielded pleasure and comfort. However, this temptation of the flesh had absolutely no effect. Christ simply answered:

> **"Man shall not live by bread alone, but by every word that proceeds from the mouth of God." (Mt 4: 4)**

Christ's response clearly indicates the flesh does not truly and completely satisfy, but obedience to the will of God does. Christ's response is also intriguing since he himself is the Word of God and the Bread from Heaven. He satisfies man's hunger with the Word of the Gospel and the spiritual food of the Eucharist.

Having failed in his first effort, Satan tempted Christ a second time. He took Christ to the top of the Temple in Jerusalem and told him to throw himself off, claiming, if Christ is truly the Son of God, the angels would surely rescue him.

> **The devil took him to the holy city, and set him on the pinnacle of the temple, and said to him, "If you are the Son of God, throw yourself down; for it is written, 'He will give his angels charge of you,' and 'On their hands they will bear you up, lest you strike your foot against a stone.'" (Mt 4: 5-6)**

Jesus Carried Up to a Pinnacle of the Temple by Tissot. Satan often tempts people the same way. While it is natural to desire the glory of the Kingdom of God, people often resist the sacrifice required to enter it.

This particular temptation was for Christ to perform a great miracle in front of all the religious leaders of Israel. They would immediately proclaim him the promised Messiah "without the Cross." Though this second temptation is open to several interpretations, it is certain Satan tempted Christ to believe, as the Son of God, he should be immune to suffering. The Devil also implied the Passion, which Christ was called to suffer, was evidence of God's indifference and a life of self-sacrifice is without meaning.

Satan often tempts people the same way. While it is natural to desire the glory of the Kingdom of God, people often resist the sacrifice required to enter it. As Thomas à Kempis wrote:

> **Jesus hath many lovers of His heavenly kingdom, but few bearers of his cross.**[10]

Christ understood perfectly the nature of his mission. In order to redeem the world, he had to suffer and die on the Cross. He chose to fulfill this redemptive mission out of his infinite love for people, and he calls every person to do the same.

> **"If any man would come after me, let him deny himself and take up his cross daily and follow me." (Lk 9: 23)**

Having failed a second time, Satan tempted Christ once more. The last temptation promised Christ tremendous worldly success and power. He offered everything in the world if Christ would only worship him.

> **The devil took him to a very high mountain, and showed him all the kingdoms of the world and the glory of them; and he said to him, "All these I will give you, if you will fall down and worship me." (Mt 4: 8-9)**

Many Jews at the time of Christ expected a political or military messiah who would defeat the Roman occupiers and restore the temporal glory of the Davidic Kingdom. Had Christ come in this manner, he

Temptation on the Mount by Duccio. The last temptation promised Christ tremendous worldly success and power. Satan offered everything in the world if Christ would only worship him.

would have been proclaimed the messiah immediately. They would have gathered around him, and he would have established an earthly kingdom encompassing all nations—a kingdom that would have surpassed even David's.

While Jesus Christ is the rightful King of all peoples, his kingdom is not of this world and was obtained through his self-giving sacrifice on the Cross. Through his obedience to the Father, Christ defeated Satan.

Having failed a third time, Satan left Christ.

> **Jesus has emerged victorious from his battle with Satan. To the tempter's lying divinization of power and prosperity, to his lying promise of a future that offers all things to all men through power and through wealth—he responds with the fact that God is God, that God is man's true Good.** (Pope Benedict XVI, *Jesus of Nazareth*, p. 45)

The *Catechism* gives a summary of the role these demonic temptations played in Christ's work of redemption.

> **Jesus fulfills Israel's vocation perfectly: in contrast to those who had once provoked God during forty years in the desert, Christ reveals himself as God's Servant, totally obedient to the divine will. In this, Jesus is the devil's conqueror: "he binds the strong man" to take back his plunder.[11] Jesus' victory over the tempter in the desert anticipates victory at the Passion, the supreme act of obedience of his filial love for the Father.** (CCC 539)

By his prompt rejection of the Satan's temptations, Christ, the New Adam, counteracted the disobedience of the first Adam, who had surrendered to Satan's temptation to eat of the forbidden fruit and rebel against God's authority.

> **The evangelists indicate the salvific meaning of this mysterious event: Jesus is the new Adam who remained faithful just where the first Adam had given into temptation.** (CCC 539)

Get Thee Behind Me, Satan by Tissot.
It is clear St. Peter was speaking out of his great love for his Master. Nevertheless, he was trying to dissuade Christ from carrying out God's redemptive plan to save the human race.

The Temptation to Avoid Suffering

In the desert, Satan tempted Christ to establish his kingdom without the Cross. This temptation is repeated throughout the Gospels. Christ's wisdom and miracles often prompted crowds of people to declare him king, but he always managed to slip away.

Though Christ would not undergo the Passion for another three years, it is implied he would be beset with at least one more temptation to shun the Cross. According to St. Luke,

> **When the devil ended every temptation, he departed from him until an opportune time.** (Lk 4: 13)

When his Passion came near, Christ spoke to his Apostles about his imminent Passion and Death. St. Peter protested and tried to dissuade him from going to Jerusalem. In response, Christ severely reproached St. Peter, identifying him with Satan himself.

> **Peter took him and began to rebuke him, saying, "God forbid, Lord! This shall never happen to you." But he turned and said to Peter, "Get behind me, Satan! You are a hindrance to me; for you are not on the side of God, but of men."** (Mt 16: 22-23)

It is clear St. Peter was speaking out of his great love for his Master. Nevertheless, he was trying to dissuade Christ from carrying out God's redemptive plan to save the human race—a plan that requires the Cross. By doing so, St. Peter echoed Satan's temptation for Christ to reject the Cross. St. Peter invoked human logic: suffering and death are to be avoided at all costs; conversely, in God's logic, these constitute the only hope of salvation. This is why Christ referred to St. Peter as Satan—the name of the evil one who sought to undermine Christ's redemptive work.

It requires a deep faith to accept the value and the power of the Cross. On a human level, self-sacrifice does not make sense; neither does the willing acceptance of pain and anguish seem reasonable. After all, human beings have an instinct for self-preservation and are naturally inclined to seek pleasure and avoid pain. By this reasoning, the Passion seemed to be a colossal failure. Even most of Christ's followers abandoned him at the Cross, losing hope in him and his mission. However, it was precisely his sacrificial offering on the Cross that redeemed mankind. God's logic, in which humility overcomes pride and suffering heals, is reflected in the Blessed Virgin Mary's *Magnificat*:

> **He has shown strength with his arm,**
> **he has scattered the proud in the imagination of their hearts,**
> **he has put down the mighty from their thrones,**
> **and exalted those of low degree;**
> **he has filled the hungry with good things,**
> **and the rich he has sent empty away.** (Lk 1:51-53)

A Liar and a Murderer

In the Scriptures, the temptations of the Devil seem to come in two forms: distortion of the truth and fear. The ultimate and tragic consequence of surrendering to his temptations is the destruction of the soul. Christ sheds light on the lies of Satan and their consequences:

> **"He was a murderer from the beginning, and has nothing to do with the truth, because there is no truth in him. When he lies, he speaks according to his own nature, for he is a liar and the father of lies."** (Jn 8:44)

One of the Apostles, Judas, fell under the influence of Satan. In this instance, Satan's lies destroyed Judas himself.

> **After the morsel, Satan entered into [Judas]. Jesus said to him, "What you are going to do, do quickly."** (Jn 13:27)

Judas' reasons for betraying Christ are not entirely known. Some scholars suggest he was motivated by greed, evidenced by the money he received. Others argue he had become disenchanted with the other-worldly kingdom preached by Christ, preferring a military or political messiah instead. Whatever his motive, Judas succumbed to a lie: something good could come to him or the world by betraying Christ to his enemies. At the provocation of Satan, he betrayed Jesus with a kiss.

At the insistance of the Father of Lies,[12] Judas betrayed Christ, who is the source, origin, and reality of truth itself. After his betrayal, Judas dreadfully succumbed to another lie: there was no hope or mercy left for him. Despairing, Judas took his own life.

The Capture of Christ (detail) by Cimabue.
At the insistance of the Father of Lies, Judas betrayed Christ, who is the source, origin, and reality of truth itself.

Sadly, Judas was not the only one to fail Christ. Christ had predicted St. Peter would deny him three times.

> **"Simon, Simon, behold, Satan demanded to have you, that he might sift you like wheat, but I have prayed for you that your faith may not fail; and when you have turned again, strengthen your brethren." And he said to him, "Lord, I am ready to go with you to prison and to death." He said, "I tell you, Peter, the cock will not crow this day, until you three times deny that you know me."** (Lk 22:31-34)

Following Christ's arrest, St. Peter fulfilled this prophecy.[13] His denials sprang out of a fear of suffering and failure to believe in the power of Christ's redemptive suffering.

Pontius Pilate was also tempted to reject the truth of Christ's innocence. Fearing a riot, Pilate ordered the Crucifixion against his better judgment and the admonition of his wife. Had Pilate sought the truth and acted out of justice, Christ's life would have been spared.

These illustrations from the Gospel accounts of the Passion show how Satan used accomplices to kill the Savior and to denigrate his message of truth. Almost every person mentioned in the account of the Passion was acting as an agent of the Devil. Nevertheless, God used this grave injustice as the means of redemption. The ignominious Cross was converted into a glorious sign of redemption.

CHRIST MANIFESTS HIS DIVINITY

In the desert, Satan had tempted Christ to reveal his divinity in a dramatic way. Throughout his hidden years and public life, Christ's divinity was veiled by his humanity. For thirty years, he had blended into the village culture of Nazareth. His life had seemed ordinary and uneventful; he surprised his fellow townsmen during his first public appearance in the synagogue. St. Matthew records the reaction of the astonished assembly:

> **"Where did this man get this wisdom and these mighty works? Is not this the carpenter's son? Is not his mother called Mary?" (Mt 13: 54-55)**

Jesus Wept (detail) by Tissot.
While his words and deeds were extraordinary, he was still very much a man like any other.

After the Baptism of Christ and temptation in the desert, he began to unfold his teachings about the Kingdom of God on his own authority. While his words and deeds were extraordinary, he was still very much a man like any other. He became tired and hungry; he wept; and, at times, he was righteously angry. While his poverty, spirit of service, and humility made him especially attractive and very approachable, Christ's divinity, apart from his miracles, passed unnoticed, obscured by his human nature. The divinity of Christ seemed especially hidden during his Passion and Death.

While Christ worked numerous miracles during his public ministry, the Cross was the culmination of his redemptive mission. In fact, the Cross and the subsequent Resurrection is the ultimate sign of his divinity. For this reason, Christ told his Apostles it was necessary for him to go to Jerusalem where he would suffer death.

> **Jesus began to show his disciples that he must go to Jerusalem and suffer many things from the elders and chief priests and scribes, and be killed, and on the third day be raised. (Mt 16: 21)**

Christ wanted his disciples to understand his Crucifixion and Death were indispensable for the salvation of the world. However, he assured them his Death would be followed by a glorious Resurrection. Nevertheless, as we saw, St. Peter and the Apostles could not reconcile themselves to the fact that atonement for the sins of the world must involve Christ's Death.

> **Peter scorns this prediction, nor do the others understand it any better than he.[14] In this context the mysterious episode of Jesus' Transfiguration takes place on a high mountain,[15] before three witnesses chosen by himself: Peter, James, and John. (CCC 554)**

The Transfiguration by Bloch.
The dazzling light radiating from Christ manifested his divine nature. Sts. Peter, James, and John saw Christ as a man not like any other.

Transfiguration by Fra Angelico.
To add to this extraordinary scene, Moses and Elijah appeared, speaking with Christ about his imminent Death.

In order to inspire his Apostles' confidence in his Passion and Death and to show us a foretaste of his glory and people's future happiness in Heaven, Christ worked an unprecedented miracle to manifest directly his divine nature. This miracle, in which Christ was seen in his glorified state, is called the *Transfiguration* (in Greek, *Metamorphosis*). His divine nature emerged through a sudden and startling change in appearance.

> **He was transfigured before them, and his face shone like the sun, and his garments became white as light. And behold there appeared to them Moses and Elijah, talking with him.** (Mt 17: 2-3)

In an earlier scene in St. Matthew's Gospel, St. Peter had expressed faith in Christ's divinity.

> **Simon Peter replied, "You are the Christ, the Son of the living God."** (Mt 16: 16)

St. Peter's declaration implied the Apostles were beginning to realize the divinity of Christ. However, without special grace to reinforce their faith and hope, Christ's disciples might have become scandalized by the seeming failure and humiliation of the Cross. Recollection of the Transfiguration reassured the Apostles of Christ's triumphant Resurrection from the dead and bolstered their hope and optimism in the power of the Cross.

The Transfiguration took place on Mt. Tabor; similarly, Moses' meetings with God took place on a mountain, Mt. Sinai. The dazzling light radiating from Christ manifested his divine nature. Sts. Peter, James, and John saw Christ as a man not like any other. To add to this extraordinary scene, Moses and Elijah appeared, speaking with Christ about his imminent Death.

Moses represents the Law, and Elijah the prophets. The Law and the prophets had prepared the Chosen People for the coming of the Messiah and, ultimately, the Paschal Mystery itself. The Law and the prophets found their fulfillment in the Paschal Mystery of Christ.

Through the Transfiguration, three Apostles understood the Cross would be crowned by the Resurrection. The presence of Moses and Elijah endorsed the importance and efficacy of the Lord's redemptive sacrifice on Calvary. This strengthened them with a foretaste of Heaven before Christ's Passion.

> **For a moment Jesus discloses his divine glory, confirming Peter's confession. He also reveals that he will have to go by the way of the cross at Jerusalem in order to "enter into his glory."[16] Moses and Elijah had seen God's glory on the Mountain; the Law and the Prophets had announced the Messiah's sufferings.[17]** (CCC 555)

Sts. Peter, James, and John, in a sense, underwent an interior transformation as they gazed upon their Master radiating the light of his divinity. Their own deep joy and spirit of contemplation served as an anticipation of their future glory united to Christ in his Resurrection. They were reminded the Cross would invariably result in the everlasting joy of the Kingdom of God.

Another aspect of the Transfiguration was the manifestation of the Persons of the Blessed Trinity. God the Father was present in the voice, the Son in his humanity, and the Holy Spirit in the cloud.

Transfiguration (detail) by Previtali.
"This is my beloved Son, my Chosen; listen to him!"

> **Christ's Passion is the will of the Father: the Son acts as God's servant;[18] the cloud indicates the presence of the Holy Spirit. "The whole Trinity appeared: the Father in the voice; the Son in the man; the Spirit in the shining cloud."[19]** (CCC 555)

The presence of the cloud hearkened to the Exodus wherein God spoke directly to Moses. Something similar occurred during the Transfiguration, whereby God the Father spoke directly to the Apostles, instructing them to heed Christ's words.

> **A cloud came and overshadowed them; and they were afraid as they entered the cloud. And a voice came out of the cloud saying, "This is my beloved Son, my Chosen; listen to him!" (Lk 9: 34-35)**

The Transfiguration reveals what awaits every follower of Christ: the hopeful prospect of a transformation in Christ and a share in his Resurrection. Moreover, by uniting human sufferings with those of Christ, people are destined for a transformation into the very life of Christ. The Apostles' extraordinary holiness, following the descent of the Holy Spirit at Pentecost, is a testimony to our capacity for personal transformation through the power of the Cross and Resurrection.

> **The Transfiguration gives us a foretaste of Christ's glorious coming, when he "will change our lowly body to be like his glorious body."[20] But it also recalls that "it is through many persecutions that we must enter the kingdom of God."[21]** (CCC 556)

The Last Supper by Pourbus.
The Last Supper, charged with the emotion of someone bidding final farewell to his loved ones, is the setting for our Lord's greatest legacy, the Holy Eucharist.

THE LAST SUPPER

The Last Supper is the final episode in Christ's life before his Passion and Death. The Last Supper, charged with the emotion of someone bidding final farewell to his loved ones, is the setting for our Lord's greatest legacy, the Holy Eucharist. Throughout the evening, Christ gave a tremendous amount of spiritual and theological teaching to his Apostles. In fact, the words and teaching of Holy Thursday are so important that a significant portion of Catholic doctrine—including the priesthood, the Eucharist, and Christ's New Commandment of Love—is derived from this touching scene.

Though no description can do justice to the depth and scope of the Last Supper, it is accurate to say Christ's message describes the principal consequences of redemption. One of the chief effects of the Paschal Mystery is the creation of an intimate union with Christ. This union is not simply a moral union, consisting in a desire and effort to imitate Christ, but an indwelling of Christ in the soul.

An important teaching of Christ on Holy Thursday is the allegory of the vine and the branches. Christ emphatically stressed, in order for his disciples to be fruitful, they must be united to him as a branch to its vine. In this context, to be *fruitful* means to spread the Kingdom of God to others as a witness to Christ.

> **"I am the vine, you are the branches. He who abides in me, and I in him, he it is that bears much fruit, for apart from me you can do nothing."** (Jn 15: 5)

Conformity with the heart of Christ is a vital condition for leading others to Christ. Essentially, the disciple of Christ is called to center his or her life on Christ in the Eucharist, the source and summit of the Christian life. The graces flowing from the Eucharist are the spiritual food and drink of Catholics.

As our Lord explained, this new life in him is made possible when the Third Person of the Blessed Trinity, the Holy Spirit, descends upon a person. This same infusion of the Holy Spirit gave the Apostles the gifts needed to be effective witnesses and teachers of the Gospel.

In a sense, Holy Thursday details the requirements for a full life in Christ. The perfection and hallmark of the Christian life is marked by a replication of Christ's charity, drawn from the graces of the Holy Eucharist. This mature Christian discipleship consists in an intimate union with Christ by which the person exhibits a peace and joy the world cannot give. This faithful reflection of Christ's wisdom and love is crucial to the work of evangelization; it is summed up by Christ: "Apart from me you can do nothing."[22]

The Last Supper narrative in the Gospel of St. John contains five chapters of teaching and meditation directed exclusively to the Apostles. Christ began his radical teachings on charity by giving a startling example and then issuing his New Commandment: his disciples must love as he loves.

> **"A new commandment I give to you, that you love one another; even as I have loved you, that you also love one another." (Jn 13: 34)**

Before he gave his New Commandment, Christ did something that shocked his Apostles. He took upon himself the role of a servant and washed their feet. By this he showed his New Commandment of Love should be displayed in humble service.

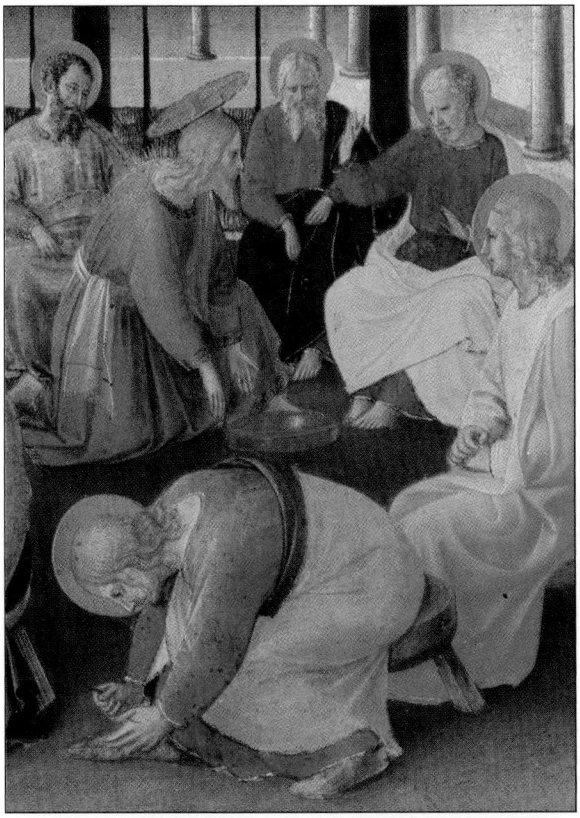

Christ Washing the Feet of the Apostles (detail) by Fra Angelico. By this he showed his New Commandment of Love should be displayed in humble service.

> **"If I then, your Lord and Teacher, have washed your feet, you also ought to wash one another's feet. For I have given you an example, that you also should do as I have done to you." (Jn 13: 14-15)**

Washing the Apostles' feet was a concrete manifestation of what it means to be a true disciple of Christ. The radical demand to love one another as God loves is a proximate preparation for Christ's supreme act of love on Calvary. The Crucifixion, in which Christ laid down his life for the redemption of every human being, is the greatest display of charity. This ability for such great love is communicated to anyone who wishes to follow him through the graces merited by the redemption.

Though free cooperation is vital, Christ's Law of Love would be impossible to live without the grace of his redemptive sacrifice. His New Commandment is possible only by uniting one's heart with Christ.

The grace to love as Christ loved is initially given in Baptism and through union with him in the Holy Eucharist, the sacramental manifestation of the Paschal Mystery instituted at the Last Supper. Christ's words at the Last Supper indicate he would offer his Body and shed his Blood for everyone.

> **"At the Last Supper, on the night he was betrayed, our Savior instituted the Eucharistic sacrifice of his Body and Blood. This he did in order to perpetuate the sacrifice of the cross throughout the ages until he should come again, and so to entrust to his beloved Spouse, the Church, a memorial of his death and resurrection: a sacrament of love, a sign of unity, a bond of charity, a Paschal banquet 'in which Christ is consumed, the mind is filled with grace, and a pledge of future glory is given to us.'"[23] (CCC 1323)**

This first Mass, celebrated by Christ in the Cenacle during the Last Supper, was an anticipation of his redemptive sacrifice. In both the Last Supper and in his Passion, Christ offered his very self to the Father. During the Last Supper, Christ offered himself in an unbloody manner, whereas the next day he would offer

The Last Supper by Juanes.
The first Mass, celebrated by Christ with his Apostles at the Last Supper, is re-presented in every age and in every place, thus enabling the faithful to share in the Paschal Mystery directly through the Liturgy of the Holy Mass.

himself in the sacrifice of the Cross. In the Last Supper, bread and wine became his Body and Blood. The Holy Eucharist is, therefore, God's greatest gift to the Church and to mankind since it is nothing less than the Real Presence of Jesus Christ in both his divinity and humanity under the appearance of bread and wine. The Eucharist is the greatest gift possible because it is God the Son himself.

By his sacrificial Death and Resurrection, Christ established the New Covenant in his Blood, thereby fulfilling and replacing the Old Covenant. The Old Covenant had been communicated to the Jewish People through Moses and consisted in the mandate to keep the Ten Commandments. In the New Covenant, the faithful are able to live the life of Christ revealed in the Gospels. St. Ignatius of Antioch, who was likely a disciple of St. John the Evangelist, explained how one can live Christ's life:

> **Every time this mystery [of the Eucharist] is celebrated, "the work of our redemption is carried on" and we "break the one bread that provides the medicine of immortality, the antidote for death, and the food that makes us live for ever in Jesus Christ."[24] (CCC 1405)**

The Law of the Old Covenant, the New Law of Love, and the Eucharist are intimately connected. The New Commandment to love others as Christ has loved not only sums up but also perfects the Ten Commandments. The Eucharist provides the grace to live the New Commandment of Love, thereby perfectly fulfilling the Old Covenant. This is how the New Covenant replaces the Old.

At the Last Supper, Christ commanded the Eucharistic sacrifice be perpetuated until the end of time. To this end, he instituted the priesthood and bestowed on his Apostles—and their successors—the sacred power and authority to act in his stead (*in persona Christi*: in the Person of Christ). Priests of the New Covenant receive the power to offer the Eucharistic sacrifice in Christ's name. Each time a priest repeats the words of consecration, the same sacrifice of Calvary is re-presented on the altar in a sacramental, unbloody manner. The first Mass, celebrated by Christ with his Apostles at the Last Supper, is re-presented in every age and in every place, thus enabling the faithful to share in the Paschal Mystery directly through the Liturgy of the Holy Mass.

THE AGONY IN THE GARDEN

> **Jesus went with them to a place called Gethsemane, and he said to his disciples, "Sit here, while I go yonder and pray." (Mt 26: 36)**

The first stage of Christ's Passion began with his Agony in the Garden of Gethsemane. After the Last Supper, Christ left the Upper Room with three of his disciples for the Garden of Gethsemane on the Mount of Olives. Christ frequently went to pray there. On this occasion, Christ was put to a much sterner test than the Devil's temptations in the wilderness.

Christ's Agony in the Garden was unique because of the burden weighing on his mind and heart. He had come to pray for strength to endure his Passion. As both man and God, Christ had a profound knowledge of every human heart.

> **He knew all men and needed no one to bear witness of man; for he himself knew what was in man. (Jn 2: 25)**

As he spoke to his Father, he realized, in spite of his sacrifice, his loving gift of redemption would be rejected by many. His deeds of loving service and self-sacrifice would prove futile for so many who would insist on refusing his friendship and mercy. This knowledge added dramatically to his terrible suffering.

In contrast to the father in the Parable of the Prodigal Son, whose sinful child repented and returned to him, Jesus Christ grieved for the many prodigal sons and daughters who would refuse his gift of forgiveness and salvation. His sorrow caused him horrendous agony; St. Luke records his sweat became like drops of blood. Though rare, *hematohidrosis* is a medical condition in which a person who is undergoing very intense anxiety literally sweats blood. The capillaries around the sweat glands, under severe stress, actually burst, causing blood to mingle with sweat. This sweating of blood powerfully attests to the intensity of Christ's agony.

Prayer in the Garden by Ricci.
He had come to pray for strength to endure his Passion. As both man and God, Christ had a profound knowledge of every human heart.

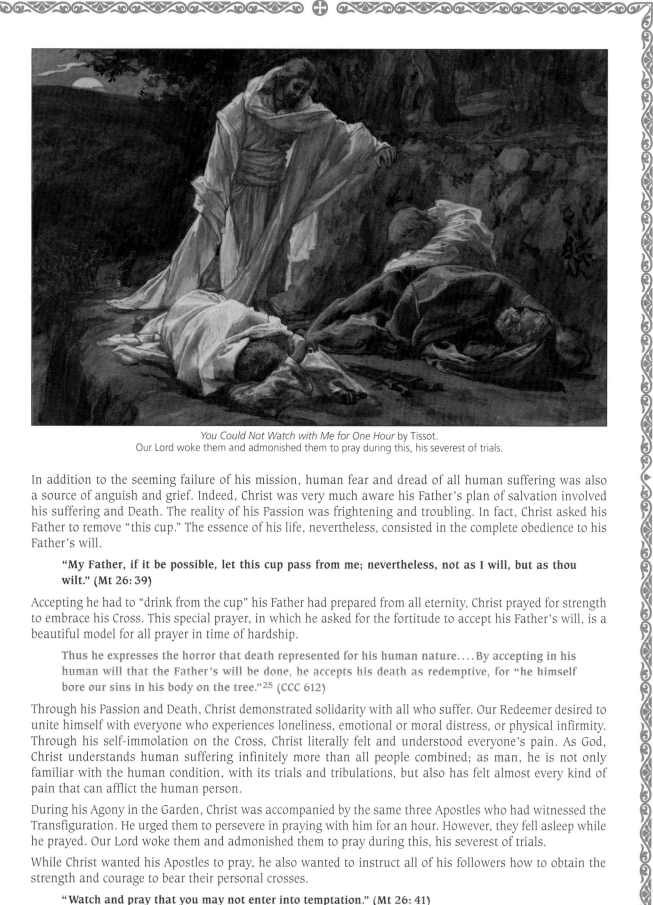

You Could Not Watch with Me for One Hour by Tissot.
Our Lord woke them and admonished them to pray during this, his severest of trials.

In addition to the seeming failure of his mission, human fear and dread of all human suffering was also a source of anguish and grief. Indeed, Christ was very much aware his Father's plan of salvation involved his suffering and Death. The reality of his Passion was frightening and troubling. In fact, Christ asked his Father to remove "this cup." The essence of his life, nevertheless, consisted in the complete obedience to his Father's will.

> **"My Father, if it be possible, let this cup pass from me; nevertheless, not as I will, but as thou wilt." (Mt 26: 39)**

Accepting he had to "drink from the cup" his Father had prepared from all eternity, Christ prayed for strength to embrace his Cross. This special prayer, in which he asked for the fortitude to accept his Father's will, is a beautiful model for all prayer in time of hardship.

> **Thus he expresses the horror that death represented for his human nature.... By accepting in his human will that the Father's will be done, he accepts his death as redemptive, for "he himself bore our sins in his body on the tree."[25] (CCC 612)**

Through his Passion and Death, Christ demonstrated solidarity with all who suffer. Our Redeemer desired to unite himself with everyone who experiences loneliness, emotional or moral distress, or physical infirmity. Through his self-immolation on the Cross, Christ literally felt and understood everyone's pain. As God, Christ understands human suffering infinitely more than all people combined; as man, he is not only familiar with the human condition, with its trials and tribulations, but also has felt almost every kind of pain that can afflict the human person.

During his Agony in the Garden, Christ was accompanied by the same three Apostles who had witnessed the Transfiguration. He urged them to persevere in praying with him for an hour. However, they fell asleep while he prayed. Our Lord woke them and admonished them to pray during this, his severest of trials.

While Christ wanted his Apostles to pray, he also wanted to instruct all of his followers how to obtain the strength and courage to bear their personal crosses.

> **"Watch and pray that you may not enter into temptation." (Mt 26: 41)**

In this instance, Christ referred to the temptation to doubt the power of the Cross and subsequently reject it. This temptation to falter in the exercise of the Faith includes the fear of suffering and death. Only with prayer can a follower of Christ believe in the power of the Cross and have the strength to shun the deceptions of Satan, who tempts people to avoid self-sacrifice.

This is a simple but telling remark; only when a person "watches and prays" can he or she follow Christ closely. Throughout the centuries, those who stay united to Christ with generous prayer are capable of living a life of heroic sacrifice and, if the occasion arises, enduring martyrdom. This martyrdom offered out of love of Christ includes the many men, women, and children who have chosen a life of self-sacrifice, often while leading ordinary lives.

The Final Temptation

The Passion (detail) by Holbein.
Christ asked his Father, provided that it was his will, for a reprieve from the suffering he was called to undergo.

In the Garden of Gethsemane, Satan again attempted to convince Christ to reject the Cross. He tempted Christ to reject his Father's plan and opt for something easier. Furthermore, given the many people who have rejected God's redemptive mercy throughout the ages, the Devil most likely tried to persuade Christ this suffering and Death would amount to very little. During that moment, Christ asked his Father, provided that it was his will, for a reprieve from the suffering he was called to undergo.

"Father, if thou art willing, remove this cup from me; nevertheless not my will, but thine, be done." (Lk 22: 42)

As Christ hung on the Cross amid the barrage of insults and taunts, a final temptation was leveled at him.

"If you are the Son of God, come down from the cross." (Mt 27: 40)

This temptation again urged Christ to abandon the Cross. He could have used his divine power to demonstrate he is God. His kingdom, however, is not of this world and could only be established by his Death on Calvary.

Christ's words on the Cross, "*Eli, Eli, lama sabachthani?*" that is, "My God, my God why hast thou forsaken me?"[26] might, at first glance, seem to indicate he felt abandoned by his Father, in this, his hour of greatest need. These words, however, come from the beginning of Psalm 22 and foretell a suffering messiah who will establish a glorious kingdom. Thus, Christ's words from the Cross actually illustrate his complete obedience to the will of his Father. Because of this servant's obedient suffering,

> **All the ends of the earth shall remember**
> **and turn to the LORD;**
> **and all the families of the nations**
> **shall worship before him.**
> **For dominion belongs to the LORD,**
> **and he rules over the nations.**
> **Yea, to him shall all the proud of the earth bow down;**
> **before him shall bow all who go down to the dust,**
> **and he who cannot keep himself alive.**
> **Posterity shall serve him;**
> **men shall tell of the Lord to the coming generation,**
> **and proclaim his deliverance to a people yet unborn,**
> **that he has wrought it. (Ps 22: 27-31)**

Satan, the perpetrator of deceit, betrayal, and murder, suffered permanent defeat through Christ's supreme act of sacrificial love. Earlier in the Gospels, Christ had proclaimed his ultimate victory over the evil one, telling his disciples:

> **"Now is the judgment of this world, now shall the ruler of this world be cast out; and I, when I a lifted up from the earth, will draw all men to myself."** (Jn 12: 31-32)

The Devil remains active, unleashing his deceitful temptations in the hopes of leaving a trail of destroyed consciences and human lives. In spite of all the wiles of the prince of darkness, union with Christ renders him powerless. For this reason,

> **Jesus' temptation reveals the way in which the Son of God is Messiah, contrary to the way Satan proposes to him and the way men wish to attribute to him.[27] This is why Christ vanquished the Tempter *for us*: "For we have not a high priest who is unable to sympathize with our weaknesses, but one who in every respect has been tested as we are, yet without sinning."[28]** (CCC 540)

THE SUFFERING SERVANT

Christ as the Man of Sorrows by Coter.
While he was spared personal moral guilt, he took upon himself everyone's guilt and experienced the full extent of the ugliness and evil of sin.

One traditional description of Christ is a Suffering Servant (cf. Isaiah 53). His willingness to serve by making satisfaction for sins extends even to his Passion and Death on the Cross.

In his sacred humanity, Christ underwent the most severe physical, psychological, and moral suffering. His entire body was covered with bruises and lacerations. He was exhausted, thirsty, and wracked with pains that nearly exceeded the limits of human endurance. Psychologically, our Lord suffered from the fear of impending suffering and death, loneliness and abandonment, witnessing the sorrow of his loved ones—especially his Mother—and outrage at the injustices being inflicted upon him. Perhaps most of all, Christ experienced moral suffering. While he was spared personal moral guilt, he took upon himself everyone's guilt and experienced the full extent of the ugliness and evil of sin. This is why Christ deserves the title Man of Sorrows.[29] He is the Suffering Servant foreseen by the Prophet Isaiah.

The immediate reason for this supreme sacrifice of his life was God's great love and his desire to atone for the sins of and redeem every human being. He wanted people to be able to recover the perfect happiness for which they had been created. In perfect obedience to his Father and out of an infinite love, Christ willingly laid down his life in a most painful manner.

> **Out of love for his Father and for men, whom the Father wants to save, Jesus freely accepted his Passion and death: "No one takes [my life] from me, but I lay it down of my own accord."[30] Hence the sovereign freedom of God's Son as he went out to his death.[31]** (CCC 609)

Consequently, every person can encounter Jesus Christ, the Suffering Servant, through personal difficulties and painful situations. Under these circumstances, he or she can join the Lord in his redemptive suffering and thus experience the greatest joy of the Resurrection.

THE PASSION OF CHRIST

All the chief priests and the elders of the people took counsel against Jesus to put him to death; and they bound him and led him away and delivered him to Pilate the governor. (Mt 27: 1-2)

He handed him over to them to be crucified. So they took Jesus, and he went out, bearing his own cross, to the place called the place of a skull, which is called in Hebrew Golgotha. (Jn 19: 16-17)

After Christ's hour in Gethsemane, Judas betrayed him with a kiss. Christ was arrested and put on trial before the Sanhedrin, the ruling council of the Jews, where he was falsely accused of blasphemy. During the interrogations, he did not aggressively proclaim his divinity but did acknowledge it when asked. Indeed, claiming to be the Son of God would have been blasphemy, a crime punishable by death under the Mosaic Law, were it not true.

The Jewish authorities brought Christ before Pontius Pilate, the Roman procurator of Judea. Knowing the charge of blasphemy carried no weight under Roman law, the Jewish authorities told Pilate he had claimed to be a king, which was a usurpation of the emperor's authority; the high priest claimed, if Christ were set free, Pilate would be no friend of Caesar. This shrewd tactic placed Pilate in a difficult position: he was torn between political ambition and his conscience, which indicated unequivocally Christ was not guilty of their accusations.

Though he preferred not to enter into what he considered a religious squabble, Pilate was obligated to come face-to-face with Christ to see for himself if he was guilty of any crime. After interrogating Christ, Pilate felt compelled to release him and looked for a way out of the situation.

Flagellation by Duccio.
Hoping to placate the crowd, Pilate ordered Christ be scourged. This consists of a brutal flogging with a whip of cords that has sharp pieces of bone or metal at the ends.

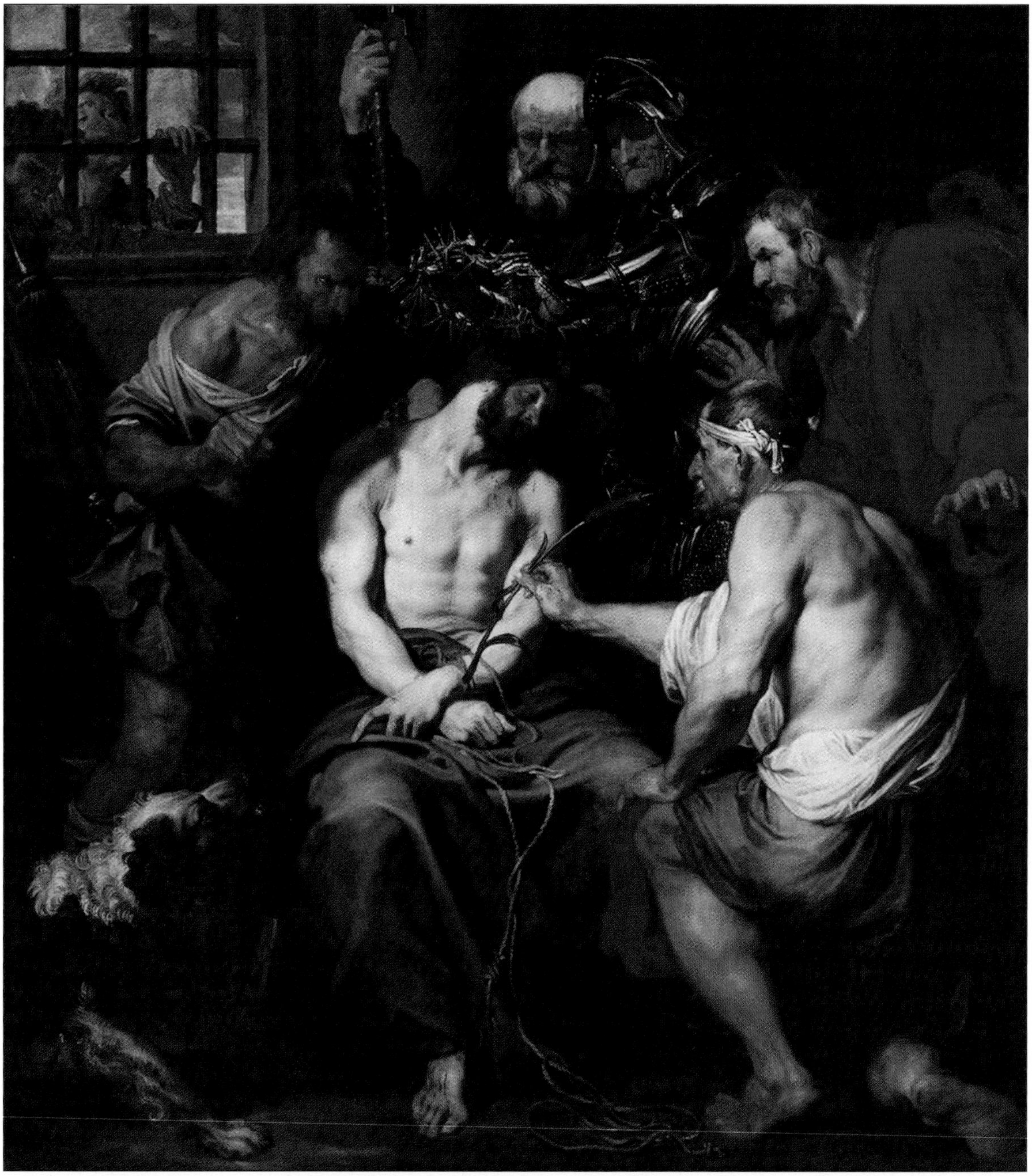

Crowning with Thorns by Van Dyck.
After the horrendous scourging, the Roman soldiers proceeded to ridicule, mock, and taunt Christ.

Pilate thought he had found a solution to this dilemma upon learning Christ came from Nazareth and, therefore, was under the jurisdiction of King Herod, the Roman tetrarch of Galilee. He sent Christ to Herod, who was in Jerusalem for the Passover. A sadistic brute, Herod had looked forward to interrogating Christ but soon grew bored when Christ would not answer him. As a joke, he dressed Christ in regal apparel and returned him to Pilate.

While Pilate wrestled with the fateful verdict, his wife sent him word about a disturbing dream that indicated he should not be a party to Christ's condemnation.

> **"Have nothing to do with that righteous man, for I have suffered much over him today in a dream."** (Mt 27: 19)

In an attempt to escape his predicament, Pilate invoked the Passover custom to release a condemned prisoner. Pilate gave the agitated crowd a choice: Barabbas, a man guilty of murder and sedition, or Jesus of Nazareth, the King of the Jews. The crowd, stirred up by the Jewish authorities, bellowed, "Barabbas!"[32]

> **Pilate then said to them, "Then what shall I do with Jesus called Messiah?" They all said, "Let him be crucified!"** (Mt 27: 22)

Pilate again desperately looked for a way to avoid condemning an innocent man to a cruel death. Hoping to placate the crowd, he ordered Christ be scourged. This consists of a brutal flogging with a whip of cords that has sharp pieces of bone or metal at the ends. Scourging tears flesh, muscle, damaged nerves, and internal organs. Many victims of this traumatic ordeal die from loss of blood or internal injury.

After the horrendous scourging, the Roman soldiers proceeded to ridicule, mock, and taunt Christ. They slapped him and spit in his face. Mockingly, the Roman legionaries dressed him as a king and crowned him with thorns. Christians should never get used to our Lord's extravagance of love by allowing himself to undergo this ordeal; it is always important to bear in mind the Person suffering is God the Son, who deserves infinite homage and adoration.

Having been scourged and crowned with thorns, Christ was the epitome of a Man of Sorrows. Pilate himself was, on some level at least, moved with pity by the pathetic site of Christ; he made one last effort to appeal to the crowd. He presented them with the bloody Christ, brutally scourged and crowned with thorns. Pilate shouted a phrase that has remained engrained in the consciousness of Christian posterity:

> **"Behold the man!"** (Jn 19: 5)

Ecce Homo by Bosch.
The image of Christ bathed in blood; crowned with thorns; and covered in welts, bruises, and gashes reveals a God of infinite love.

Despite this, the mob was not satisfied and clamored for his Crucifixion all the more. The risk to his political career proved too much for Pilate, and he finally sentenced Christ to death. In a feeble attempt to deny responsibility for the deed, he washed his hands, saying, "I am innocent of this man's blood. Look to it yourselves."[33]

The image of Christ bathed in blood; crowned with thorns; and covered in welts, bruises, and gashes reveals a God of infinite love. "Behold the man!" The battered and broken Christ is a symbol of man's violent rejection of God's loving offer of forgiveness of sin and everlasting life. It is an allegory of people's attitude and treatment of God and his laws. Nevertheless, God awaits every person's change of heart.

Christ Leaving the Prætorium (detail) by Doré.
After Pilate's sentence of death by Crucifixion, Christ embarked upon what tradition calls the *Way of the Cross.*

Jesus Meets His Mother by Tissot.
This part of Christ's Passion, marked by our Lord's superhuman effort to reach the place of his execution, is a powerful reminder that Christ is intimately familiar with pain and exhaustion.

THE CRUCIFIXION AND DEATH OF THE REDEEMER

They brought him to the place called Golgotha (which means the place of a skull). And they offered him wine mingled with myrrh; but he did not take it. And they crucified him, and divided his garments among them, casting lots for them, to decide what each should take. And it was the third hour, when they crucified him. (Mk 15: 22-25)

After Pilate's sentence of death by Crucifixion, Christ embarked upon what tradition calls *the Way of the Cross.* Christ was forced to carry his heavy Cross from Pilate's *prætorium* to Golgotha, also called Calvary (from Hebrew and Latin, respectively, for *Place of the Skull*). Given his weakened condition, loss of blood, physical shock, and trauma, this last journey was excruciating.

According to the Stations of the Cross, Christ fell three times as he summoned every ounce of strength to carry the Cross to his place of his Crucifixion. Seeing Christ could not continue on his own power, Roman soldiers forced a bystander, St. Simon of Cyrene, to help carry the Cross. This encounter between Christ and St. Simon teaches, like him, every Christian must be willing to help Christ carry his Cross.

This part of Christ's Passion, marked by our Lord's superhuman effort to reach the place of his execution, is a powerful reminder that Christ is intimately familiar with pain and exhaustion. Everyone who suffers from the burdens and cares of life will find compassion from the one who carried his Cross while suffering from punishing fatigue and excruciating pain.

The Raising of the Cross by Van Dyck.
Affixed to the Cross with his arms outstretched in a symbolic embrace of the whole human race, Christ became the icon *par excellence* of charity and mercy.

Christ's Passion reached its climax in the Crucifixion. He was nailed to the Cross through his hands and feet. Hardly had he been lifted up on the Cross when he made a heartfelt appeal to his Father.

"Father, forgive them; for they know not what they do." (Lk 23: 34)

Affixed to the Cross with his arms outstretched in a symbolic embrace of the whole human race, Christ became the icon *par excellence* of charity and mercy. Crucifixion kills the victim by slow asphyxiation. Christ's every breath became increasingly labored, causing him terrible and terrifying suffering.

Christ on the Cross Between the Two Thieves (detail) by Rubens.
Christ's consoling words to the repentant thief reveals the gates of Heaven were on the verge of being opened.

Along with Christ, two other men, called thieves or robbers, were crucified on Calvary that day. As Christ slowly suffocated amid the excruciating pain of the nails and the loss of blood, he spoke with the man on his right, assuring him of God's mercy. This man, traditionally called St. Dismas, begged God for mercy and forgiveness as he admitted his own sinfulness and Christ's sinlessness; for this reason, he is called as the "Good Thief."

> **[The Good Thief] said, "Jesus, remember me when you come into your kingdom." And he said to him, "Truly, I say to you, today you will be with me in Paradise."** (Lk 23: 42-43)

Christ's consoling words to the repentant thief reveals the gates of Heaven were on the verge of being opened.

With the words, "It is finished,"[34] Christ died.

> It is love "to the end"[35] that confers on Christ's sacrifice its value as redemption and reparation, as atonement and satisfaction. He knew and loved us all when he offered his life.[36] Now "the love of Christ controls us, because we are convinced that one has died for all; therefore all have died."[37] No man, not even the holiest, was ever able to take on himself the sins of all men and offer himself as a sacrifice for all. The existence in Christ of the divine person of the Son, who at once surpasses and embraces all human persons, and constitutes himself as the Head of all mankind, makes possible his redemptive sacrifice *for all*. (CCC 616)

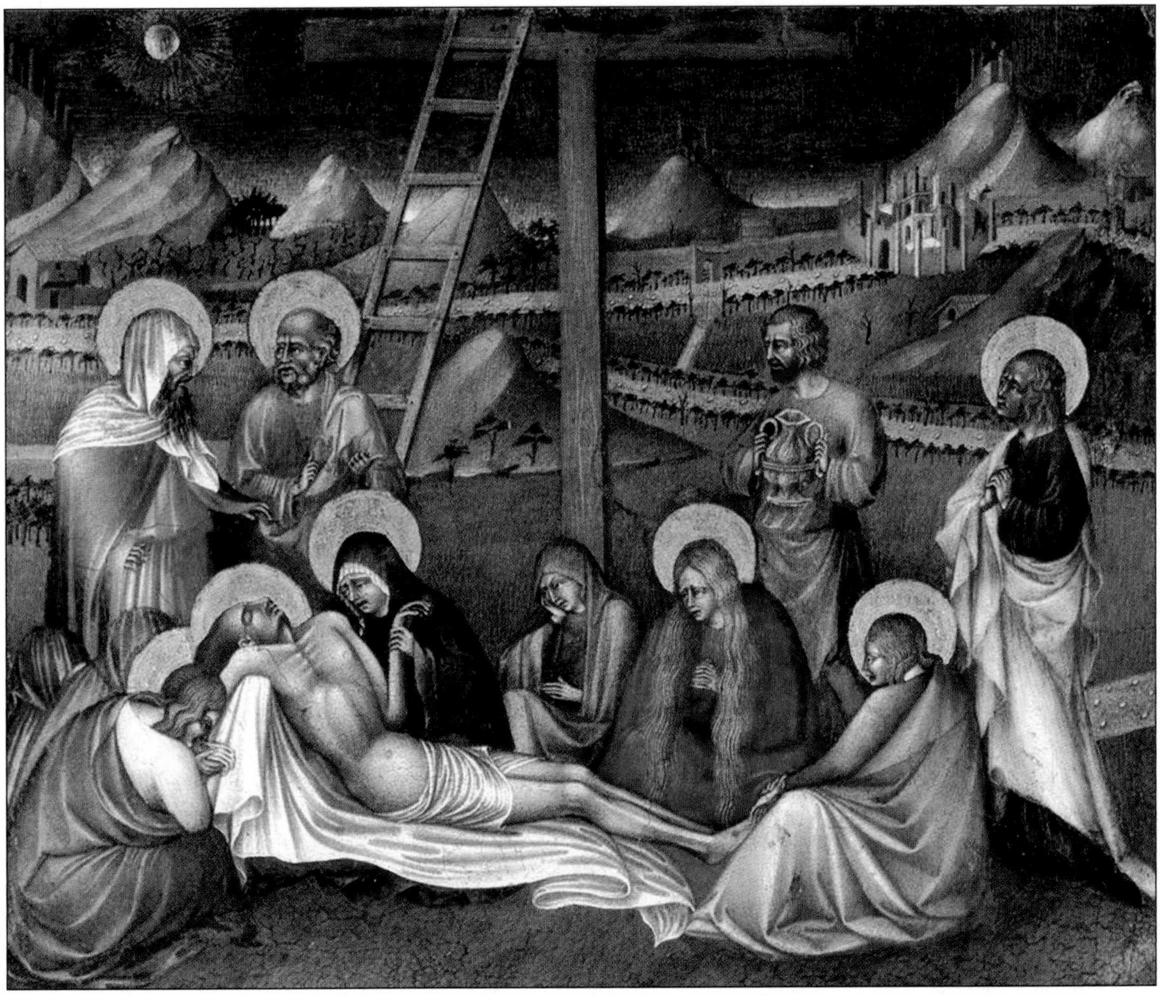

Lamentation over the Dead Christ by Giovanni di Paolo.
Every action of Christ on earth is redemptive; in the same way, his *kenosis* permeates his entire life of obedience and service.

THE *KENOSIS*

Have this in mind among yourselves, which was in Christ Jesus, who, though he was in the form of God, did not count equality with God a thing to be grasped, but emptied himself, taking the form of a servant, being born in the likeness of men. And being found in human form he humbled himself and became obedient unto death, even death on a cross. Therefore God has highly exalted him and bestowed on him the name which is above every name, that at the name of Jesus every knee should bow, in heaven and on earth and under the earth, and every tongue confess that Jesus Christ is Lord to the glory of God the Father. (Phil 2: 5-11)

St. Paul's celebrated description of Christ's life and sentiments is known as his *kenosis*, a Greek word meaning *self-emptying*. These words encapsulate Christ's life of sacrificial love and serve as the essence of his entire existence.

Jesus Christ is God the Son who took on a human nature; through his human nature he was able to become the Suffering Servant. His human nature is the vehicle of salvation and the Revelation of God's love.

The ascent to God occurs precisely in the descent of humble service, in the descent of love, for love is God's essence, and is thus the power that truly purifies man and enables him to perceive God and to see him. In Jesus Christ, God has revealed himself in his descending: "Though he was in the form of God," he "did not count equality with God a thing to be grasped, but emptied himself, taking the form of a servant, being born in the likeness of men.... He humbled himself and became

> obedient unto death, even death on a cross. Therefore God has highly exalted him" (Phil 2: 6-9). These words mark a decisive turning point in the history of mysticism. They indicate what is new in the Revelation of Jesus Christ. God descends to the point of death on the Cross. And precisely by doing so, he reveals himself in his true divinity. We ascend to God by accompanying him on this descending path. (Pope Benedict XVI, *Jesus of Nazareth*, p. 95)

The phrase, "taking the form of a servant, being born in the likeness of men,"[38] is especially reflected by his Birth in the stable and his Death on the Cross. As attested by his entire life and, in particular, by his Passion, Christ did not overwhelmingly manifest his divine power. His divine power was not used for personal benefit but instead to heal and cure in a compassionate response to the sick and the dying. For the most part, Christ's divine nature was hidden behind his humanity.

Every action of Christ on earth is redemptive; in the same way, his *kenosis* permeates his entire life of obedience and service. His *kenosis* was completed between his Agony in the Garden and his last dying breath on the Cross; it reached its climax when one of the soldiers pierced his side, from which flowed blood and water.[39] Christ offered his Body and poured out his Blood for every human being. There is absolutely no person for whom Christ did not lay down his life.

> By his obedience unto death, Jesus accomplished the substitution of the suffering Servant, who "makes himself an *offering for sin*," when "he bore the sin of many," and who "shall make many to be accounted righteous," for "he shall bear their iniquities."[40] Jesus atoned for our faults and made satisfaction for our sins to the Father.[41] (CCC 615)

By virtue of the Incarnation, Christ deserves a glory far surpassing that of all of creation combined. His life, however, was animated by loving service and ended in his Passion and Death on the Cross. The fulfillment of his Father's will to redeem man gives him a name above every other name. The immediate glory resulting from Christ's Passion and Death is his Resurrection from the dead. The Resurrection validates the victory of Christ's agonizing suffering to win forgiveness of sin and everlasting life.

The Entombment of Christ by Badalocchio.
The fulfillment of his Father's will to redeem man gives him a name above every other name.

Descent of Christ to Limbo by Andrea da Firenze.
Access to everlasting life in Heaven was barred, even for the righteous, until it was opened through our Lord's redemptive Death on the Cross and Resurrection from the dead.

HE DESCENDED TO THE DEAD

The death of a human being is the separation of the soul from the body. Once the body is no longer animated by the soul, it undergoes corruption. However, the soul is immortal and, therefore, continues in existence without the body. Like every human person, Jesus' Death—because he took on human nature—meant the separation of his Soul from his Body.

> **In his plan of salvation, God ordained that his Son should not only "die for our sins"[42] but should also "taste death," experience the condition of death, the separation of his soul from his body, between the time he expired on the cross and the time he was raised from the dead. The state of the dead Christ is the mystery of the tomb and the descent into hell.** (CCC 624)

Following his Death, Christ descended to the dead, i.e., the state of all who had died before the redemption. Access to everlasting life in Heaven was barred, even for the righteous, until it was opened through our Lord's redemptive Death on the Cross and Resurrection from the dead.

> **Scripture calls the abode of the dead, to which the dead Christ went down, "hell"—*Sheol* in Hebrew or *Hades* in Greek—because those who are there are deprived of the vision of God.[43] Such is the case for all the dead, whether evil or righteous, while they await the Redeemer.** (CCC 633)

These souls awaited eagerly the redemption, which opened the gates of Heaven. Scripture calls the state of the souls of the just the "bosom of Abraham."[44] Included among these just souls were the innumerable holy men and women of both the Chosen People and the Gentiles.

Though the details of this period between Jesus' Death and his Resurrection are not known, it is certain St. Joseph was among the first to enter into Paradise. Other illustrious figures awaiting the redemption were the souls of Adam, Eve, Abraham, Moses, David, and the prophets.

> "It is precisely these holy souls, who awaited their Savior in Abraham's bosom, whom Christ the Lord delivered when he descended into hell."[45] (CCC 633)

St. Matthew's Gospel notes, immediately after Christ's Death and Resurrection, the dead rising from their graves.

> **The tombs also were opened, and many bodies of the saints who had fallen asleep were raised, and coming out of the tombs after his resurrection they went into the holy city and appeared to many. (Mt 27:52-53)**

Many of the just in *Sheol* (a Hebrew term for the place of the dead) had not striven during their lives to be conformed totally to God's will and consequently needed purification before entering Heaven. Part of Christ's descent to the dead was to confirm to these souls their entrance into Heaven would occur after the necessary purification.

Another group of souls is the souls of the damned. Because they chose to reject any relationship with God and had refused to follow his will during their lives, they lamentably brought eternal punishment upon themselves. *Hell* applies to those individuals who have died in a state of unrepentant mortal sin. These individuals chose to be separated from God's love and friendship during their lives and are eternally separated from him in Hell.

In these days after the redemption, the souls of those who die are judged immediately by God, who determines their eternal destiny: Heaven or Hell. Those who die in the grace and friendship of God but are not perfectly pure are purified in Purgatory before entering Heaven.

> The descent into hell brings the Gospel message of salvation to complete fulfillment. This the last phase of Jesus' messianic mission, a phase which is condensed in time but vast in its real significance: the spread of Christ's redemptive work to all men of all times and all places, for all who are saved have been made sharers in the redemption. (CCC 634)

The Dead Appear in the Temple by Tissot. Part of Christ's descent to the dead was to confirm to these souls their entrance into Heaven would occur after the necessary purification.

ST. JOAN OF ARC

St. Joan of Arc was born in France in 1412. At the age of thirteen, she began to see visions in which Sts. Michael the Archangel, Margaret, and Catherine of Alexandria appeared to her. They revealed God had called her to liberate France and, in particular, the city of Orleans from the English. Moreover, they instructed her to go to the *dauphin* (the future King Charles VII) and tell him she would make his coronation possible.

It was clear St. Joan was to lead an army against the English. However, despite the certainty of God's will for her life, her mission was not easy. The first obstacle to her mission was the *dauphin* himself. Securing an audience with the French prince was difficult enough, let alone persuading him to let a poor, peasant girl lead a French army into battle.

When St. Joan finally had her chance to speak with Charles, she was aided, ironically, by the prince's own trickery. Seeking to test her, the *dauphin* had one of his aides put on the royal vestments. Upon entering the court, however, St. Joan saluted the real king, who had disguised himself as an attendant. She then revealed to the *dauphin* a secret sign the Lord had disclosed before her arrival. After these revelations, Charles was convinced and proceeded to help St. Joan carry out her mission.

In May 1429, St. Joan led a small army against the English garrison at Orleans. Under her leadership, French soldiers overwhelmed the English fortifications and drove them from the city, liberating the regions of Loire, Troyes, and Chalons.

During the battle, St. Joan was wounded by an arrow but desired to move on to Rheims, where the French kings were traditionally crowned. Rheims was finally captured in July 1429, and the *dauphin* was crowned King Charles VII.

After his coronation, Charles and his advisors grew increasingly apathetic to St. Joan's mission to liberate France. The following May, St. Joan led a small army of five hundred against a far stronger English force, during which she was captured. King Charles did not attempt to bargain for her life; with no support from the French, St. Joan was put on trial for heresy and witchcraft.

Before leading her first strike with the French forces, Charles had requested St. Joan be examined by a number of doctors and bishops. They found her sane and discovered nothing heretical in her message, but neither those officials nor their documents proving her innocence were allowed for her defense. The court was determined to find her guilty. She was convicted and burned at the stake on May 30, 1431.

Twenty-five years later, in 1456, the sentence was lifted after a re-examination by Pope Callistus III. St. Joan was beatified in 1909 and canonized in 1920. Her feast day is May 30.

Illustration: *Capture of Joan of Arc* (detail) by Dillens.

The Resurrection by Bloch. The entire Christian Faith hangs on this wonderful truth: Christ is risen from the dead, and he is alive in the fullest sense of the word.

THE RESURRECTION

The greatest sign of Christ's victory is his Resurrection from the dead. The resurrected Christ took on a new mode of existence that goes beyond simple restoration to natural life. His glorified Body is not subject to suffering or the strictures of space and time. When examining the Resurrection, it is important to bear in mind the entire Christian Faith hangs on this wonderful truth: Christ is risen from the dead, and he is alive in the fullest sense of the word.

In the Gospel accounts, Christ rose from the dead in his own Body three days after his Crucifixion. Over the years, however, there have arisen several false interpretations of the Resurrection that argue either explicitly or implicitly it should not be taken as a literal, historical event. Some opine the Resurrection is a myth that evolved from the great admiration the early Christians had for Jesus Christ. They speculate that Christ's followers, with the passage of years, gradually claimed Christ rose from the dead and imagined him having divine attributes. Others claim the Resurrection was the result of mass hysteria by which the followers of Christ convinced themselves Christ had risen. However, upon examination of the Gospel accounts, the Resurrection is a historical event. Christ truly, bodily rose from the dead.

In the Gospel accounts of the Resurrection, the Apostles' first reaction to Christ's empty tomb was one of incredulity and fear. In fact, there is absolutely no hint any of the Apostles expected Christ to rise again. St. John frankly relates his own hesitant reaction to Christ's empty tomb:

> **Peter then came out with the other disciple [John], and they went toward the tomb. They both ran, but the other disciple outran Peter and reached the tomb first; and stooping to look in, he saw the linen cloths lying there, but he did not go in. Then Simon Peter came, following him, and went into the tomb; he saw the linen cloths lying, and the napkin, which had been on his head, not lying with the linen cloths but rolled up in a place by itself. Then the other disciple, who reached the tomb first, also went in, and he saw and believed; for as yet they did not know the scripture, that he must rise from the dead (Jn 20: 3-9)**

The Gospels relate the doubts and disbelief of the Resurrection by the Apostles. While St. Thomas' disbelief is singled out, his skepticism was shared by the rest. Only through an encounter with the resurrected Christ were the Apostles able to believe he is truly risen.

> **The shock provoked by the Passion was so great that at least some of the disciples did not at once believe in the news of the Resurrection. Far from showing us a community seized by a mystical exaltation, the Gospels present us with disciples demoralized ("looking sad"[46]) and frightened. For they had not believed the holy women returning from the tomb and had regarded their words as an "idle tale."[47] (CCC 643)**

Christ first appeared to St. Mary Magdalene and other holy women. In her grief and never expecting to see him again, St. Mary Magdalene did not initially recognize Christ.

> **Supposing him to be the gardener, she said to him, "Sir, if you have carried him away, tell me where you have laid him." (Jn 20: 15)**

Christ and Mary Magdalene by Edelfelt.
In his glorified Body, Christ must not have appeared exactly in the same manner as before his Death because his followers did not always recognize him at first.

Full of joy and enthusiasm upon recognizing Christ, the women immediately announced his Resurrection to the Apostles. However, instead of accepting and believing the Good News, the Apostles' response was one of disbelief along with a degree of ridicule. Later, Christ appeared to the Apostles to demonstrate he had indeed risen from the dead; only then did they come to believe.

In his glorified Body, Christ must not have appeared exactly in the same manner as before his Death because his followers did not always recognize him at first. However, after Christ opened their eyes, they recognized him immediately. This was especially true when Christ spoke with two of his disciples on their way to Emmaus; only in the "breaking of the bread," a term the early Christians used to describe the Eucharist, did they recognize the risen Christ.

> **Their eyes were opened and they recognized him; and he vanished out of their sight. (Lk 24: 31)**

Supper at Emmaus by Bloch.
In the modern era, faith in the Resurrection is based on the account of those apostolic witnesses who saw the resurrected Christ.

These events after the Lord's Resurrection signified much more than simply being restored to life; rather, they involved the glorification of his once mortal Body. Christ's Resurrection was inherently different from the experience of those such as Lazarus, whom Christ had brought back to life during his public ministry. Those people later died like everyone else.

The Resurrection is the sign Christ's Passion and Death has overcome the power of Satan, sin, and death.

> **In his risen body he passes from the state of death to another life beyond time and space. At Jesus' Resurrection his body is filled with the power of the Holy Spirit: he shares the divine life in his glorious state, so that St. Paul can say that Christ is "the man of heaven."**[48] (CCC 646)

In the modern era, faith in the Resurrection is based on the account of those apostolic witnesses who saw the resurrected Christ. He appeared so this glorious event would be the foundation of the Christian Faith. At least as much as any reliable historical record should be taken seriously, the Gospels and the rest of the New Testament together with the early writings of the Fathers of Church should be given full credence.

The Resurrection of Christ is not only a matter of faith but also an objective, historical fact.

> **The faith of the first community of believers is based on the witness of concrete men known to the Christians and for the most part still living among them. Peter and the Twelve are the primary "witnesses to his Resurrection," but they are not the only ones—Paul speaks clearly of more than five hundred persons to whom Jesus appeared on a single occasion and also of James and of all the apostles.**[49] (CCC 642)

The Resurrection is the culminating event of Christ's Redemption. The heartbreak of his Passion was transformed into the surpassing joy of his Resurrection. This event gives meaning to every aspect of the Good News and the Church's teaching. This event shows Christ's absolute victory over sin and death, which has opened the gates of Heaven.

THE RESURRECTION AS A TRANSCENDENTAL EVENT

The Resurrection is a manifestation of the salvific power of God; it allows people of every age to have faith in Jesus Christ and his message. It corroborates the fact Jesus Christ is truly the Son of God. The Resurrection demonstrates the old man, Adam, can be overcome by the new man, Jesus Christ, and indicates all of Adam's descendants can be reconciled with God and enter into communion with him. The Resurrection teaches the way to Heaven is by way of the Cross. It gives meaning to life and gives hope for each person's resurrection on the Last Day.

According to St. Paul, about five hundred people saw Christ after his Resurrection.[50] Nevertheless, no one was an eyewitness to the moment when the Christ's Body came back to life. As a supernatural occurrence, it seems the Resurrection can never be empirically described.

The Doubting Thomas by Signorelli.
In his appearance to St. Thomas, Christ presented himself with the wounds he bore from his Passion, but these wounds reflected his glory and did not cause him any suffering.

No one was an eyewitness to Christ's Resurrection and no evangelist describes it. No one can say how it came about physically. Still less was its innermost essence, his passing over to another life, perceptible to the senses. (CCC 647)

It is clear, from the accounts following the Resurrection, Christ's relationship with his Apostles and disciples dramatically changed. No longer did Christ live among them as before, address large crowds, or heal infirmities. According to the Gospels, he appeared and disappeared.

He vanished out of their sight. (Lk 24: 31)

With his glorious, resurrected Body, Christ was able to pass through walls and locked doors. These Gospel accounts imply his Body was completely immune from suffering and death. In his appearance to St. Thomas, Christ presented himself with the wounds he bore from his Passion, but these wounds reflected his glory and did not cause him any suffering.[51] The *Catechism* describes Christ's risen state:

[T]his authentic, real body possesses the new properties of a glorious body: not limited by space and time but able to present how and when he wills; for Christ's humanity can no longer be confined to earth and belongs henceforth only to the Father's divine realm.[52] For this reason too the risen Jesus enjoys the sovereign freedom of appearing as he wishes: in the guise of a gardener or in other forms familiar to his disciples, precisely to awaken their faith.[53] (CCC 645)

Until having met the Lord in Heaven, every person must correspond with him through a life of prayer animated by faith. Given this new mode of existence, Christ wants his followers to believe without seeing, as indicated by his declaration to the doubting St. Thomas and the rest of his Apostles:

"Blessed are those who have not seen and yet believe." (Jn 20: 29)

Though Christ personally appeared to a good number of his followers, he wanted his Resurrection to be more a matter of faith than simple knowledge of a new fact. The *Catechism* explains:

Although the Resurrection was an historical event that could be verified by the sign of the empty tomb and by the reality of the apostles' encounters with the risen Christ, still it remains at the very heart of the mystery of faith as something that transcends and surpasses history. This is

why the risen Christ does not reveal himself to the world, but to his disciples, "to those who came up with him from Galilee to Jerusalem, who are now his witnesses to the people."[54] (CCC 647)

The Resurrection is a compelling invitation for every Christian to believe Jesus Christ lives. Now that he transcends space and time, everyone can have an intimate, personal relationship with him. The transcendence of Christ's glorified Body makes him present everywhere: in the Church, in the sacraments, and in the lives of his followers. In Heaven, the faithful will contemplate the risen Christ directly and eternally, but, during their sojourn on earth, they encounter him on the level of faith and love.

THE SIGNIFICANCE OF THE RESURRECTION

The word *gospel* means "good news." The Good News of the Gospel is God became man, died for the sins of all, and then rose from the dead to give forgiveness of sins and everlasting life. The ultimate Good News is not Christ's exalted moral teachings or even the perfect New Law of Love. The Good News is Christ is alive!

What if Christ had not risen from the dead? St. Paul meditated on this question long ago:

If Christ has not been raised, then our preaching is in vain and your faith is in vain. We are even found to be misrepresenting God, because we testified of God that he raised Christ, whom he did not raise if it is true that the dead are not raised. For if the dead are not raised, then Christ has not been raised. If Christ has not been raised, your faith is futile and you are still in your sins. Then those also who have fallen asleep in Christ have perished. If for this life only we have hoped in Christ, we are of all men most to be pitied. (1 Cor 15: 14-19)

Christ Appearing to His Mother by Weyden.
According to St. Paul, about five hundred people saw Christ after his Resurrection.

If there had been no Resurrection, faith in Christ is futile. People still would be prisoners to sin. Man would not have been redeemed, forgiven, or adopted children of God. Those who have died following Christ would be lost. Christians would be the most pitiful of all.

On the contrary, Christ has been raised from the dead! Therefore, Christians' faith is efficacious; it accomplishes salvation. Sins are forgiven, and God dwells in the souls of his adopted children. Those dead in Christ are alive with him. Because of hope in Christ in this life, the faithful are among the most envied. Those conformed to Christ through the sacraments of the Church can hope to attain Heaven in the next life.

Only God has power over death. If Christ rose from the dead, he really is who he claimed to be: the Son of God. If Christ is the Son of God, everyone can believe all he taught with confidence. His words about himself and about the Father and the Holy Spirit are trustworthy. People can believe what he taught about how to live their lives. The Church he established teaches the truth, and the sacraments are fountains of grace.

The Resurrection above all constitutes the confirmation of all Christ's works and teachings. All truths, even the most inaccessible to human reason, find their justification if Christ by his Resurrection has given the definitive proof of his divine authority, which he had promised. (CCC 651)

The Resurrection imprints a kind of seal of victory on every human effort performed in the name of Christ. Because our Savior conquered sin and death by rising from the dead, everything done or suffered to promote his kingdom will prove successful in the end. In light of Christ's victory, St. Paul aptly stated:

> **We know that in everything God works for good with those who love him, who are called according to his purpose. (Rom 8: 28)**

Perhaps the greatest confirmation of the victory of the Resurrection is the lives of the saints. Their days were marked by suffering and hardship; at the same time, they reflected Christ in their lives and attracted many others to him. The joy, peace, and love manifested in the lives of conscientious Christians attest to the power of the Resurrection working through the supernatural grace obtained by the redemption.

In short, the Resurrection gives great confidence to "go out to all the world and tell the good news."[55]

FORGIVENESS IS A FRUIT OF THE RESURRECTION

The Appearance of Christ at the Cenacle by Tissot.
"Receive the Holy Spirit. If you forgive the sins of any, they are forgiven; if you retain the sins of any, they are retained."

The Resurrection of Christ is a divine message: sin has been conquered, and the bondage of the human race to Satan has been shattered. Every sin, no matter how serious or heinous, can be forgiven if the sinner has faith in Christ and offers the proper dispositions of sorrow and purpose of amendment.

It is important to remember the purpose of God's plan of redemption—from the Incarnation to the Crucifixion—is to restore all people to their full dignity as children of God. Furthermore, no amount of sacrifice or personal sorrow would have been sufficient or effective to remove sin. Only God-made-man was capable of making the full reparation for sin and winning the grace to be reconciled with God.

It stands to reason, then, the forgiveness of sins appeared as the first revealed fruit of the Resurrection. On the evening of the Resurrection, the Lord appeared to his Apostles, and said:

> **"Peace be with you. As the Father has sent me, even so I send you." And when he had said this, he breathed on them, and said to them, "Receive the Holy Spirit. If you forgive the sins of any, they are forgiven; if you retain the sins of any, they are retained." (Jn 20: 21-23)**

Christ granted his authority to forgive sins to his Apostles so all who want their sins forgiven, no matter how grievous, can be forgiven. This ministry of Christ continues in the Church today, primarily through the Sacraments of Baptism and Reconciliation.

Christ at the Sea of Galilee by Tintoretto.
Christ forgave St. Peter; in addition, he reaffirmed St. Peter was the chief shepherd over his newly founded Church.

ST. PETER'S FORGIVENESS

St. Peter was one of the first beneficiaries of the forgiveness of sins after the Resurrection. At the Last Supper, St. Peter had fallen into pride; he thought he would be more faithful than the other Apostles. However, in the Garden of Gethsemane, when Christ had urged him to pray so he would not fall into temptation, St. Peter could not even stay awake. After Christ's arrest, three times St. Peter denied he knew Christ.

After the Resurrection, Christ sought out St. Peter especially to receive his love and forgiveness. St. John's Gospel relates, while the Apostles were fishing in their boats, they spotted Christ on the beach, who urged them to cast their nets to the right side of the boat. They subsequently caught a great quantity of fish.[56] After they had hauled in their catch, Christ invited them to have some breakfast, which he himself had prepared beside a charcoal fire, reminiscent of the charcoal fire before which St. Peter had denied him three times. Having eaten, Christ turned to the sorrowful, guilt-ridden St. Peter, who was his chosen leader of the Apostles.

In a moving dialogue, Christ gently led St. Peter to repentance by asking him three times to affirm his love and fidelity.[57]

> **When they had finished breakfast, Jesus said to Simon Peter, "Simon, son of John, do you love me more than these?" He said to him, "Yes, Lord; you know that I love you." He said to him, "Feed my lambs." A second time he said to him, "Simon, son of John, do you love me?" He said to him, "Yes, Lord; you know that I love you." He said to him, "Tend my sheep." He said to him the third time, "Simon, son of John, do you love me?" Peter was grieved because he said to him the third time, "Do you love me?" And he said to him, "Lord, you know everything; you know that I love you." Jesus said to him, "Feed my sheep."** (Jn 21:15-17)

Christ forgave St. Peter; in addition, he reaffirmed St. Peter was the chief shepherd over his newly founded Church. Christ also foretold St. Peter's future suffering and martyrdom. Though he had failed in his encounter with the Cross of Christ, St. Peter rose to the occasion when presented with his own crucifixion. According to tradition, St. Peter requested to be crucified upside down, not feeling worthy to die in the same manner as Christ.

Scenes from the Life of Christ: Ascension by Giotto.
With his Apostles gathered around him, Christ ascended Body and Soul into Heaven in a clear manifestation of his divinity.

THE ASCENSION

The Resurrection signified Christ's victory over sin and death and initiated his glorification. Christ's glorified Body gave him a new mode of existence that transcends time and space in such a way that he was not always immediately recognizable to his followers. However, this glorification would not be fully accomplished until his Ascension into Heaven.

> During the forty days when he eats and drinks familiarly with his disciples and teaches them about the kingdom, his glory remains veiled under the appearance of ordinary humanity.[58] Jesus' final apparition ends with the irreversible entry of his humanity into divine glory, symbolized by the cloud and by heaven, where he is seated from that time forward at God's right hand.[59] (CCC 659)

> **He opened their minds to understand the scriptures, and said to them, "Thus it is written, that the Christ should suffer and on the third day rise from the dead, and that repentance and forgiveness of sins should be preached in his name to all nations, beginning from Jerusalem. You are witnesses of these things." (Lk 24: 45-48)**

Christ spent the final days before his Ascension instructing his Apostles and confirming their faith in his Resurrection. Moreover, Christ prepared them to receive the Holy Spirit, the Third Person of the Blessed Trinity. This same Holy Spirit transformed the Apostles, enabling them to be witnesses of the Gospel, even to the point of martyrdom.

Christ's mission was fulfilled and his glorification completed with his Ascension into Heaven. With his Apostles gathered around him, Christ ascended Body and Soul into Heaven in a clear manifestation of his divinity.

> **As they were looking on, he was lifted up, and a cloud took him out of their sight. And while they were gazing into heaven as he went, behold, two men stood by them in white robes, and said, "Men of Galilee, why do you stand looking into heaven? This Jesus, who was taken up from you into heaven, will come in the same way as you saw him go into heaven." (Acts 1: 9-11)**

Christ's victory over sin and death culminated in his triumphant and glorious return to Heaven, Body and Soul. His rightful place in Heaven is at the right hand of the Father. The victorious Ascension of Christ into Heaven also indicates his kingdom will have no end.

By ascending into Heaven, Christ opened the gates to Heaven for the rest of his Church. Christ's entrance into Heaven gives his followers hope: one day the faithful will join him in his glory. At the same time, Christ constantly intercedes before the Father.

> **There Christ permanently exercises his priesthood, for he "always lives to make intercession" for "those who draw near to God through him."[60] (CCC 662)**

Christ's final instructions before his Ascension defined the mission of the Apostles and the Church until the end of time. Immediately before ascending into Heaven, Christ instructed the Apostles to evangelize all nations. This mission will not be achieved until everybody has been introduced to Christ.

> **"Go into all the world and preach the gospel to the whole creation." (Mk 16: 15)**

Fulfillment of this staggering task is impossible on a purely human level. Divine intervention was necessary for the Apostles to have accomplished their mission. For this reason, Christ assured the Apostles they would receive special powers to accomplish his work.

> **"You shall receive power when the Holy Spirit has come upon you." (Acts 1: 8)**

Ascension of Christ (detail) by Garofalo.
By ascending into Heaven, Christ opened the gates to Heaven for the rest of his Church.

Christ emphasized it was necessary for him to leave and return to his Father.

> **"I tell you the truth: it is to your advantage that I go away, for if I do not go away the Counselor will not come to you." (Jn 16: 7)**

After he will have ascended into Heaven, Christ and his Father would send the Holy Spirit, who would give the Apostles the graces needed to evangelize the world. By virtue of the graces merited by the Paschal Mystery, the Holy Spirit would transform each of Christ's followers so he or she would become the light of the world and the salt of the earth. Therefore, the Ascension of Christ into Heaven was the preliminary condition for the Holy Spirit to descend upon the Apostles and Our Lady on the day of Pentecost.

The Ascension of our Lord also initiated another kind of relationship between himself and his Church—a relationship founded on a life of faith, hope, and love. Primarily through prayer and the sacraments, his followers can be close to him. The Ascension of Christ, therefore, is an invitation to be united to him spiritually. He left these comforting words:

> **"Lo, I am with you always, to the close of the age."** (Mt 28: 20)

In a sense, the Ascension of Christ into Heaven and the subsequent descent of the Holy Spirit made Christ more accessible than he was during his public life.

Pentecost by Restout. The Ascension of Christ into Heaven was the preliminary condition for the Holy Spirit to descend upon the Apostles and Our Lady on the day of Pentecost.

THE DESCENT OF THE HOLY SPIRIT

Our Lord having confirmed his disciples in their faith, they were ready to receive the Holy Spirit. Accompanied by the Blessed Virgin Mary and other disciples, the Apostles spent the ten days from the Ascension to Pentecost to intensify the Apostles' love for Jesus Christ, increase their desire to imitate him, and prepare them for their mission.

During the Last Supper, Christ promised his Apostles he would send them a divine Advocate who would enable them and all Christians to live up to the demands of the New Covenant. While following him would mean contradiction and persecution, the Holy Spirit would give them the courage, strength, and love to carry their crosses and even suffer martyrdom. The Holy Spirit would transform them so they would reflect the life of Christ in the exercise of compassion, humility, peace, and joy. The Holy Spirit would teach them what they needed to know and what they should say. As Jesus told his disciples,

> **"The Counselor, the Holy Spirit, whom the Father will send in my name, he will teach you all things, and bring to your remembrance all that I have said to you."** (Jn 14: 26)

During the Last Supper, Christ had revealed a dramatic new teaching: the indwelling of the Blessed Trinity. The Holy Spirit would dwell in the souls of those who had accepted the fruits of the redemption to fill them with light, counsel, and charity.

> **"I will pray the Father, and he will give you another Counselor, to be with you for ever, even the Spirit of truth whom the world cannot receive, because it neither sees him nor knows him; you know him, for he dwells with you, and will be in you."** (Jn 14: 16-17)

Once the redemption was accomplished by the Word Incarnate, the Third Person of the Blessed Trinity, God the Holy Spirit, brought the effects of the redemption to the hearts of men and women in a myriad of ways.

The Apostles had heard in detail the requirements of being a follower of Christ, but they could not manage to live up to these teachings by their own efforts alone. Our Lord showed the Apostles he recognized their limitations and assured them the Holy Spirit would give them the courage and wisdom to continue his work.

> **"When the Spirit of truth comes, he will guide you into all the truth." (Jn 16: 13)**

When a person has the proper dispositions, cultivated by prayer, he or she will be receptive to the grace of the Holy Spirit. The gifts of the Holy Spirit enlighten the intellect and strengthen the will, but their effectiveness depends on openness and the desire to live by Christ's teachings. The *Catechism* reiterates the need to have proper dispositions to cooperate with the work of the Holy Spirit:

> **By this power of the Spirit, God's children can bear much fruit. He who has grafted us onto the true vine will make us bear "the fruit of the Spirit:...love, joy, peace, patience, kindness, goodness, faithfulness, gentleness, self-control."[61] "We live by the Spirit"; the more we renounce ourselves, the more we "walk by the Spirit."[62] (CCC 736)**

> **When the day of Pentecost had come, they were all together in one place. And suddenly a sound came from heaven like the rush of a mighty wind, and it filled all the house where they were sitting. And there appeared to them tongues as of fire, distributed and resting on each one of them. And they were all filled with the Holy Spirit and began to speak in other tongues, as the Spirit gave them utterance. (Acts 2: 1-4)**

St. Peter Preaching in the Presence of St. Mark (detail) by Fra Angelico. "When the Spirit of truth comes, he will guide you into all the truth." (Jn 16: 13)

This transformation was dramatic and noticeable; St. Peter's first sermon led to the conversion of 3000 people. Amazingly, people of different nationalities understood the Apostles in their own language. This divine intervention of the Holy Spirit caused the Apostles to be exceedingly joyful about Christ and his redemption. (Given the newfound enthusiasm of the Apostles, they were falsely accused of being drunk.[63]) They were now fortified with the necessary graces and gifts of the Holy Spirit to carry out the mission Christ had given them.

St. Paul, in his Letter to the Romans, spoke about this grace received from the Holy Spirit:

> **God's love has been poured into our hearts through the Holy Spirit who has been given to us. (Rom 5: 5)**

This new, divine love was facilitated by the seven gifts of the Holy Spirit: wisdom, understanding, counsel, fortitude, knowledge, piety, and fear of the Lord. These permanent dispositions sanctify the recipient by making him or her attentive to the voice of God and rendering him or her more obedient and docile to the inspirations of the Holy Spirit.

A central part of this new love infused by the Holy Spirit consists in loving as Christ loved.

> **This love (the "charity" of *1 Cor* 13) is the source of new life in Christ, made possible because we have received "power" from the Holy Spirit.[64] (CCC 735)**

The Holy Spirit gives the grace to sacrifice oneself for the needs of others. The new heart formed by the Holy Spirit sees Christ in everyone, especially in the suffering and poor. The charity of Christ knows no bounds. This loving strength enables a follower of Christ to struggle against temptations and to stay faithful to the Gospel under the most adverse circumstances.

Evangelization proved an arduous work. It soon became a capital offense to profess the Christian Faith, let alone introduce others to it. Nevertheless, the power of the Holy Spirit in the lives of the early Christians overcame all obstacles and won over a significant portion of the population of the Roman Empire. They were able to accomplish the humanly impossible not on account of dazzling talents or spellbinding eloquence but through the charity infused by the Holy Spirit. The secret to their effectiveness was the ability to reflect the life of the Master by the work of the Holy Spirit.

CONCLUSION

Resurrection by Bouts.
The Resurrection was Christ's greatest miracle because it proved he is truly the Son of God.

Christ's Passion, Death, and Resurrection is man's redemption. Christ offered himself to his heavenly Father to save all people from sin and sanctify them. Christ's act of loving obedience by dying on the Cross was more pleasing to the Father than sins were displeasing to him. Christ reversed Adam's fault: "As by one man's disobedience many were made sinners, so by one man's obedience many will be made righteous."[65] Christ Jesus was the Suffering Servant foretold by the prophets; he "[made] himself an offering for sin" when "he bore the sin of many," and he "[makes] many to be accounted righteous" for "he [bears] their iniquities."[66] Christ atoned for the faults of all people and made satisfaction for those sins to the Father.[67]

From Christ's Paschal Mystery, people have learned to appreciate the great evil of sin and the even greater love of God. The harm sin causes to souls cannot be seen directly, but meditating on the crucifix helps realize the enormous evil of sin that resulted in the Passion and Death of Jesus Christ, our Lord.

Christ said he would rise from the dead on the third day. The Resurrection was Christ's greatest miracle because it proved he is truly the Son of God. The Resurrection confirms Christ's works and teachings.

Forty days after his Resurrection, in the presence of his Apostles, Christ ascended, Body and Soul, into Heaven. In Heaven, Christ intercedes as our Eternal High Priest and Mediator. On Pentecost, the Father and the Son gave the gift of the Holy Spirit to the Church. The Father, the Son, and the Holy Spirit dwell in the souls of Christians, helping them on their journeys and assisting in the mission he has given to the Church, which is the means of salvation for all people.

FROM THE CATECHISM

535 Jesus' public life begins with his baptism by John in the Jordan.[68] John preaches "a baptism of repentance for the forgiveness of sins."[69] A crowd of sinners[70]—tax collectors and soldiers, Pharisees and Sadducees, and prostitutes—come to be baptized by him. "Then Jesus appears." The Baptist hesitates, but Jesus insists and receives baptism. Then the Holy Spirit, in the form of a dove, comes upon Jesus and a voice from heaven proclaims, "This is my beloved Son."[71] This is the manifestation ("Epiphany") of Jesus as Messiah of Israel and Son of God.

561 "The whole of Christ's life was a continual teaching: his silences, his miracles, his gestures, his prayer, his love for people, his special affection for the little and the poor, his acceptance of the total sacrifice on the Cross for the redemption of the world, and his Resurrection are the actualization of his word and the fulfillment of Revelation" (John Paul II, *CT* 9).

599 Jesus' violent death was not the result of chance in an unfortunate coincidence of circumstances, but is part of the mystery of God's plan, as St. Peter explains to the Jews of Jerusalem in his first sermon on Pentecost: "This Jesus [was] delivered up according to the definite plan and foreknowledge of God."[72] This Biblical language does not mean that those who handed him over were merely passive players in a scenario written in advance by God.[73]

600 To God, all moments of time are present in their immediacy. When therefore he establishes his eternal plan of "predestination," he includes in it each person's free response to his grace: "In this city, in fact, both Herod and Pontius Pilate, with the Gentiles and the peoples of Israel, gathered together against your holy servant Jesus, whom you anointed, to do whatever your hand and your plan had predestined to take place."[74] For the sake of accomplishing his plan of salvation, God permitted the acts that flowed from their blindness.[75]

607 The desire to embrace his Father's plan of redeeming love inspired Jesus' whole life,[76] for his redemptive passion was the very reason for his Incarnation. And so he asked, "And what shall I say? 'Father, save me from this hour'? No, for this purpose I have come to this hour."[77] And again, "Shall I not drink the cup which the Father has given me?"[78] From the cross, just before "It is finished," he said, "I thirst."[79]

614 This sacrifice of Christ is unique; it completes and surpasses all other sacrifices.[80] First, it is a gift from God the Father himself, for the Father handed his Son over to sinners in order to reconcile us with himself. At the same time it is the offering of the Son of God made man, who in freedom and love offered his life to his Father through the Holy Spirit in reparation for our disobedience.[81]

639 The mystery of Christ's resurrection is a real event, with manifestations that were historically verified, as the New Testament bears witness. In about A.D. 56 St. Paul could already write to the Corinthians: "I delivered to you as of first importance what I also received, that Christ died for our sins in accordance with the scriptures, and that he was buried, that he was raised on the third day in accordance with the scriptures, and that he appeared to Cephas, then to the Twelve..."[82] The Apostle speaks here of the living tradition of the Resurrection which he had learned after his conversion at the gates of Damascus.[83]

641 Mary Magdalene and the holy women who came to finish anointing the body of Jesus, which had been buried in haste because the Sabbath began on the evening of Good Friday, were the first to encounter the Risen One.[84] Thus the women were the first messengers of Christ's Resurrection for the apostles themselves.[85] They were the next to whom Jesus appears: first Peter, then the Twelve. Peter had been called to strengthen the faith of his brothers,[86] and so sees the Risen One before them; it is on the basis of his testimony that the community exclaims: "The Lord has risen indeed, and has appeared to Simon!"[87]

FROM THE CATECHISM Continued

642 Everything that happened during those Paschal days involves each of the apostles—and Peter in particular—in the building of the new era begun on Easter morning. As witnesses of the Risen One, they remain the foundation stones of his Church. The faith of the first community of believers is based on the witness of concrete men known to the Christians and for the most part still living among them. Peter and the Twelve are the primary "witnesses to his Resurrection," but they are not the only ones—Paul speaks clearly of more than five hundred persons to whom Jesus appeared on a single occasion and also of James and of all the apostles.[88]

Man of Sorrows (detail) by Geertgen.

ENDNOTES - CHAPTER FOUR

1. Jn 1:14.
2. Cf. Jn 1:29.
3. Mt 3:15.
4. Jn 1:29; cf. Is 53:12.
5. Cf. Mk 10:38; Lk 12:50.
6. Mt 3:15; cf. 26:39.
7. Mt 3:17.
8. Jn 2:3.
9. Jn 2:5.
10. Thomas A Kempis, *Imitation of Christ*, XI. Book II: Admonitions Concerning the Inner Life.
11. Cf. Ps 95:10; Mk 3:27.
12. Cf. Jn 8:44.
13. Cf. Jn 18:15-27.
14. Cf. Mt 16:22-23; Mt 17:23; Lk 9:45.
15. Cf. Mt 17:1-8 and parallels; 2 Pt 1:16-18.
16. Lk 24:26.
17. Cf. Lk 24:27.
18. Cf. Is 42:1.
19. St. Thomas Aquinas, *STh* III, 45, 4, ad 2.
20. Phil 3:21.
21. Acts 14:22.
22. Jn 15:5.
23. *SC* 47.
24. *LG* 3; St. Ignatius of Antioch, *Ad Eph.* 20, 2: SCh 10, 76.
25. 1 Pt 2:24; cf. Mt 26:42.
26. Mt 27:46.
27. Cf. Mt 16:21-23.
28. Heb 4:15.
29. Is 53:3.
30. Jn 10:18.
31. Cf. Jn 18:4-6; Mt 26:53.
32. Mk 27:21.
33. Mt 27:24.
34. Jn 19:30.
35. Jn 13:1.
36. Cf. Gal 2:20; Eph 5:2, 25.
37. 2 Cor 5:14.
38. Phil 2:7.
39. Cf. Jn 19:34.
40. Is 53:10-12.
41. Cf. Council of Trent (1547): DS 1529.
42. 1 Cor 15:3.
43. Cf. Phil 2:10; Acts 2:24; Rev 1:18; Eph 4:9; Ps 6:6; 88:11-13.
44. Lk 16:22; Ps 89:48.
45. *Roman Catechism* I, 6, 3.
46. Lk 24:17; cf. Jn 20:19.
47. Lk 24:11; cf. Mk 16:11, 13.
48. Cf. 1 Cor 15:35-50.
49. 1 Cor 15:4-8; cf. Acts 1:22.
50. Cf. 1 Cor 15:4-8; Act 1:22.
51. Cf. Jn 20:27.
52. Cf. Mt 28:9, 16-17; Lk 24:15, 36; Jn 20:14, 17, 19, 26; 21:4.
53. Cf. Mk 16:12; Jn 20:14-16; 21:4, 7.
54. Acts 13:31; cf. Jn 14:22.
55. Responsorial Psalm, Twenty-First Sunday of the Year.
56. Cf. Jn 21:6.
57. Cf. Jn 21:15-18.
58. Cf. Acts 1:3; 10:41; Mk 16:12; Lk 24:15; Jn 20:14-15; 21:4.
59. Cf. Acts 1:9; 2:33; 7:56; Lk 9:34-35; 24:51; Ex 13:22; Mk 16:19; Ps 110:1.
60. Heb 7:25.
61. Gal 5:22-23.
62. Gal 5:25; cf. Mt 16:24-26.
63. Cf. Acts 2:13.
64. Acts 1:8; cf. 1 Cor 13.
65. Rom 5:19.
66. Is 53:10-12.
67. Cf. Council of Trent (1547): DS 1529; cf. CCC 615.
68. Cf. Lk 3:23; Acts 1:22.
69. Lk 3:3.
70. Cf. Lk 3:10-14; Mt 3:7; 21:32.
71. Mt 3:13-17.
72. Acts 2:23.
73. Cf. Acts 3:13.
74. Acts 4:27-28; cf. Ps 2:1-2.
75. Cf. Mt 26:54; Jn 18:36; 19:11; Acts 3:17-18.
76. Cf. Lk 12:50; 22:15; Mt 16:21-23.
77. Jn 12:27.
78. Jn 18:11.
79. Jn 19:30; 19:28.
80. Cf. Heb 10:10.
81. Cf. Jn 10:17-18; 15:13; Heb 9:14; 1 Jn 4:10.
82. 1 Cor 15:3-4.
83. Cf. Acts 9:3-18.
84. Mk 16:1; Lk 24:1; Jn 19:31, 42.
85. Cf. Lk 24:9-10; Mt 28:9-10; Jn 20:11-18.
86. Cf. 1 Cor 15:5; Lk 22:31-32.
87. Lk 24:34, 36.
88. 1 Cor 15:4-8; cf. Acts 1:22.

The Mystery of Redemption

CHAPTER 5

Christ Redeems Through His Church

Through her teaching and sacraments, the Church has continued and will continue Christ's work of redemption until he comes again.

The Mystery of Redemption

CHAPTER 5

Christ Redeems Through His Church

Why did God create human beings? The eternal Father, in his wisdom and goodness, created the whole world in order to raise men and women to share in his love and happiness and to participate in his divine life. God wanted to create a people who could knowingly and freely unite themselves with him. God created human beings though he foreknew each man and woman would, to some degree, reject his offer. This rejection began with the Fall of Adam and Eve and continues with the personal sins of every human person except the Blessed Virgin Mary. (Jesus Christ, as a divine Person, likewise never sinned.)

The Good News is God did not leave man to his own devices. Instead, he ceaselessly offered help to man in view of Christ the Redeemer, who "is the image of the invisible God."[1]

Before time began, the Father "foreknew and predestined" the elect—those who would cooperate in God's plan—"to be conformed to the image of his Son, in order that he might be the first-born among many brethren."[2] The Father planned to assemble in his holy Church all who believe in Christ. Thus, already from the beginning of the world, the Church was foreshadowed.

In the fullness of time, God sent his Son into the world. Fulfilling the will of his Father, Christ announced the Kingdom of Heaven on earth, and, by his obedience unto death, he brought about redemption. Christ founded his Church, and, in unison with the Father, he sent the Holy Spirit, who gave birth to the Church and continues to provide for her growth.

At the end of time the Church will achieve her glorious completion, when all the just—from Adam to "Abel, the just one, to the last of the elect"[3]—will be gathered together with the Father in the universal Church. God's plan in creating the universe will then be revealed, and everyone will be judged with perfect justice.

Pope Benedict XVI Celebrates Mass.
Throughout the centuries, the bishops in union with the pope have faithfully governed the Church, transmitted the Gospel to each generation, and celebrated the sacraments instituted by Christ.

Christ Giving the Keys to St. Peter by Bentele.
The Gospels reveal Christ founded one Church, which he entrusted to the Twelve Apostles. He chose St. Peter to lead the Twelve and appointed him to be his representative on earth. For this reason, the pope, who is the successor of St. Peter, is the Vicar of Christ.

THIS CHAPTER WILL ADDRESS SEVERAL QUESTIONS:

- Why was redemption necessary?
- How is the fruit of Christ's redemption received?
- What is the Kingdom of God?
- How is the Church the Mystical Body of Christ?
- Why is the Church necessary for salvation?
- What are the marks of the Church?
- What is the role of a bishop in the Church?
- What is the Magisterium?
- What are sacraments, and what is their importance in the Christian life?
- What are the Last Things?
- What is the Final Judgment?

INTRODUCTION

The Lord Jesus set [the Church] on its course by preaching the Good News, that is, the coming of the Kingdom of God, which, for centuries, had been promised in the scriptures. (*Lumen Gentium*, 5)

Christ's mission was to accomplish the Father's plan of salvation in the fullness of time. To accomplish his Father's will, Christ ushered in the Kingdom of Heaven. On earth, this Kingdom of Heaven subsists in the Catholic Church, whose members form part of Christ's Mystical Body. This new People of God will continue his salvific mission until he comes again. The Second Vatican Council described the Church as "the Kingdom of heaven on earth and revealed to us the mystery."[4]

Moses and Aaron Speak to the People by Tissot.
The Church is a people chosen and set apart by God; this idea has its origin in the Old Testament. The assembly of the Israelites, God's Chosen People, is called *qahal.*

Christ's entire mission—from the moment of his Incarnation until his Ascension into Heaven—was directed toward the redemption of man. Christ's sacrifice of the Cross made this redemption possible (objective redemption), yet it needs to be applied to the life of each human person (subjective redemption).

For this reason, Christ established the Church to be his instrument to bring the Good News and the grace of his redemption to all people. Through her teaching and sacraments, the Church has continued and will continue Christ's work of redemption until he comes again.

The Church is a people chosen and set apart by God; this idea has its origin in the Old Testament. The assembly of the Israelites, God's Chosen People, is called *qahal* (in Greek, *ekklesia*), which is translated *church*. The Greek *ekklesia* is derived from *ekkalein*, "to call out." The word *church* indicates the Church is the successor of God's Chosen People of the Old Testament.

Membership in the Church is thus a calling. The Church is an assembly of people called together by God. More than merely a human organization, it is a divine institution designed by God and established by Christ.

The Church, then, is the People of God. United in Christ, the members of the Church serve God in holiness. Those who comprise the Church

- are designated by God to be a chosen race, a royal priesthood, a holy nation;
- are given new life by rebirth in water and the Spirit;
- have the status of children of God formed in the image of Christ;
- are called to love God and neighbor with the heart of Christ;
- have a mission to be salt of the earth and light of the world;
- are given the means to be saved; and
- are destined to be brought to perfection by God at the end of time.

The New Testament attests to how St. Peter and the Apostles, guided by the Holy Spirit, fulfilled their mission to lead the early Church. However, the mission Christ had entrusted to the Apostles was not to die with them but endure until he comes again. This continuation of the apostolic ministry was first seen in the election of St. Matthias to fulfill the office left vacant by Judas. Later, St. Paul was called to be an Apostle by Christ himself, and others, such as Sts. Timothy and Titus, also had a share in the teaching ministry of the Apostles.

In time, the Apostles ordained other bishops to assist them in their ministry to the local churches and to succeed them in the leadership of the Church. The early Fathers of the Church, such as Pope St. Clement I (d. ca. AD 99), testify these bishops succeeded the Apostles in the apostolic ministry of the Church:

> **Our Apostles knew through our Lord Jesus Christ that there would be strife over the name of the bishop's office. For this cause therefore, having received complete foreknowledge, they appointed the aforesaid persons, and afterwards they provided a continuance, that if these should fall asleep, other approved men should succeed to their ministration.** (I Clement, 44: 1-3)

Throughout the centuries, the bishops in union with the pope have faithfully governed the Church, transmitted the Gospel to each generation, and celebrated the sacraments instituted by Christ.

GUARDIAN OF CHRIST'S MESSAGE

> **"Go therefore and make disciples of all nations...teaching them to observe all that I have commanded you." (Mt 28: 19-20)**

Christ commanded the Church to teach the Good News. The *Magisterium* is the universal teaching authority of the Catholic Church, which she received from her founder. To ensure the Church would always teach the truth, Christ promised the Apostles the special assistance of the Holy Spirit: "The Counselor, the Holy Spirit, whom the Father will send in my name, he will teach you all things, and bring to your remembrance all that I have said to you."[45] The Holy Spirit guarantees that the teachings of the Church in matters of Faith and morals are *infallible* (incapable of error).

Communion of the Apostles (detail) by Signorelli. Christ established the Church with a visible structure and hierarchy.

> **"The Roman Pontiff, head of the college of bishops, enjoys this infallibility in virtue of his office, when, as supreme pastor and teacher of all the faithful—who confirms his brethren in the faith—he proclaims by a definitive act a doctrine pertaining to Faith or morals....The infallibility promised to the Church is also present in the body of bishops when, together with Peter's successor, they exercise the supreme Magisterium," above all in an Ecumenical Council.[46] When the Church through its supreme Magisterium proposes a doctrine "for belief as being divinely revealed,"[47] and as the teaching of Christ, the definitions "must be adhered to with the obedience of faith."[48] This infallibility extends as far as the deposit of divine Revelation itself.[49] (CCC 891)**

The Church teaches infallibly when she defines a doctrine of Faith or morals to be held by all the faithful. This can be done by the pope alone, as the supreme pastor of all the faithful, or through the pope and the bishops in communion with him.

The doctrine of papal infallibility was solemnly defined at the First Vatican Council in 1870:

> **When the Roman Pontiff speaks *ex cathedra*, that is, when, in the exercise of his office as shepherd and teacher of all Christians, in virtue of his supreme apostolic authority, he defines a**

> **doctrine concerning Faith or morals to be held by the whole Church, he possesses, by the divine assistance promised to him in blessed Peter, that infallibility which the divine Redeemer willed his Church to enjoy in defining doctrine concerning Faith or morals.** (DS 3074)

When the pope teaches infallibly, he is said to speak *ex cathedra* ("from the chair" of St. Peter) as supreme pastor and teacher of all the faithful. The doctrine he defines must be accepted by all Catholics.

THE GRACE OF REDEMPTION THROUGH THE SACRAMENTS

Christ instituted the Church to be the means by which his salvation would be brought to all people until he comes again. This is achieved primarily through preaching the Word of God and the celebration of the sacraments. The sacraments were instituted by Christ as the primary means to impart the grace of his redemption, which enables a person to share in his divine life and assists to reach his or her heavenly home.

> **The sacraments are efficacious signs of grace, instituted by Christ and entrusted to the Church, by which divine life is dispensed to us. The visible rites by which the sacraments are celebrated signify and make present the graces proper to each sacrament. They bear fruit in those who receive them with the required dispositions.** (CCC 1131)

All grace comes from God, and he alone has the authority to confer it. Jesus Christ, who is both God and man, is the principal author of the sacraments. Before his Ascension, Christ told his Apostles, "All authority in heaven and on earth has been given to me."[50] Christ had shown this authority before his Resurrection many times by performing miracles and forgiving sins. The risen Christ granted authority to the Apostles, giving them the mission and power to "make disciples of all nations, baptizing...[and] teaching them."[51]

The Apostles and their successors, through teaching and the celebration of the sacraments, share directly in the mission of Christ. The Seven Sacraments are Baptism, Confirmation, the Eucharist, Reconciliation, the Anointing of the Sick, Holy Orders, and Matrimony. The signs are *efficacious*, or effective, because Christ works through them. Though the visible actions of the minister and the sacramental signs are seen, Christ himself accomplishes the sacramental action by his grace.

The rite of each sacrament signifies and makes present the particular graces conferred by that sacrament. Each sacrament bears spiritual fruit through the cooperation and good dispositions of those who receive it. Each sacrament has a particular function to help reach a full life in Christ while supplying the grace to help the individual accomplish his or her plan of salvation and the salvation of others.

Last Supper (detail) by Caliari.
Each sacrament bears spiritual fruit through the cooperation and good dispositions of those who receive it.

THE SEVEN SACRAMENTS

SACRAMENT	EVIDENCE IN SCRIPTURE	SOURCE
Baptism	"Go therefore and make disciples of all nations, baptizing them in the name of the Father and of the Son and of the Holy Spirit."	Mt 28: 19-20
Confirmation	"When Paul had laid his hands upon them, the Holy Spirit came on them."	Acts 19: 6 Cf. Lk 24: 49 Acts 2: 1-4
Eucharist	"Take, eat; this is my body...Drink of it, all of you; for this is my blood of the covenant, which is poured out for many for the forgiveness of sins."	Mt 26: 26-28 Cf. Mk 14: 22-25 Lk 22: 19-20 Jn 6: 22-23
Reconciliation	"If you forgive the sins of any, they are forgiven."	Jn 20: 22-23 Cf. Mt 16: 19; 18: 18
Anointing of the Sick	"Let them pray over him, anointing him with oil in the name of the Lord."	Jas 5: 14-15 Cf. Mk 6: 13
Holy Orders	"Do this in remembrance of me."	Lk 22: 19 Cf. Acts 6: 6
Matrimony	"What therefore God has joined together, let not man put asunder."	Mk 10: 7-9 Cf. Jn 2: 1-11

THE LAST THINGS

The Soul of the Good Thief by Tissot.
A soul separated from its body, being pure spirit, does not occupy a place.

The Church can be described as the divinely authorized institution that seeks the eternal life of all souls. For the faithful, the end of their pilgrim journey culminates with entrance into Heaven and the resurrection of the body at the end of time. By keeping his or her eyes fixed on the goal and cooperating with God's grace, each person can attain holiness and obtain perfect happiness in Heaven.

Through his Passion, Death, and Resurrection, Jesus Christ opened the gates of Heaven, which is an essential part of redemption. However, to attain everlasting happiness, each individual must choose to accept Christ and follow all his teachings. Each person can, however, also opt to reject or ignore his gift of salvation. The decision to embrace Christ can only be made in this life because, at the moment of death, the time God has given to respond to his call ends.

At the moment of death, the soul is judged by God (the Particular Judgment) and rewarded with eternal communion with God in Heaven—either immediately or following purification in Purgatory—or condemned to eternal separation from God in Hell.

In all you do, remember the end of your life, and then you will never sin. (Sir 7:36)

Heaven, Purgatory, and Hell do not indicate *places* but *states*. A soul separated from its body, being pure spirit, does not occupy a place.

Heaven

This perfect life with the Most Holy Trinity—this communion of life and love with the Trinity, with the Virgin Mary, the angels and all the blessed—is called "heaven." Heaven is the ultimate end and fulfillment of the deepest human longings, the state of supreme, definitive happiness. (CCC 1024)

Heaven is the state of eternal communion with God. In Heaven, a person enjoys the immediate vision of God as he or she becomes like him in glory. This contemplation of the glory of God face-to-face is called the *Beatific Vision*. The souls that enter into this communion with the Blessed Trinity and with all of the angels and saints in Heaven have been perfectly purified of their sins either on earth or in Purgatory.

Purgatory

All who die in God's grace and friendship, but still imperfectly purified, are indeed assured of their eternal salvation; but after death they undergo purification, so as to achieve the holiness necessary to enter the joy of heaven. (CCC 1030)

Following the Particular Judgment, those who are in a state of grace are assured of eternal life with God in Heaven. However, before entering into God's presence, a soul must be free of every trace of attachment to sin. By purifying a soul of these imperfections before it enters his presence, God shows not only his justice but also his great love and mercy.

Every sin, even venial, entails an unhealthy attachment to creatures, which must be purified either here on earth, or after death in the state called Purgatory. This purification frees one from what is called the "temporal punishment" of sin. (CCC 1472)

The souls in Purgatory share in God's love and are no farther from him than when on earth. Furthermore, they are completely assured of their place in Heaven. Their punishment, however, is the delay to see God, whom they desire above all things.

Hell

To die in mortal sin without repenting and accepting God's merciful love means remaining separated from him for ever by our own free choice. This state of definitive self-exclusion from communion with God and the blessed is called "hell." (CCC 1033)

Hell is the state of eternal self-exclusion from communion with God and the blessed in Heaven. A person who dies in mortal sin without having repented or sought refuge in the compassionate love of God will remain separated from God forever because of his or her free choice.

The souls in Hell suffer the loss of eternal communion with God and also punishments according to the sins committed on earth. From this state of separation from God there can be no salvation. As the blessed enjoy eternal love and joy, the damned suffer eternal hatred and unhappiness. In the company of Satan, his demons, and the other lost souls, those in Hell will only be able to express bitterness and despair for having turned away from God.

The teaching of the Church affirms the existence of hell and its eternity. Immediately after death the souls of those who die in a state of mortal sin descend into hell, where they suffer the punishments of hell, "eternal fire."[52] The chief punishment of hell is eternal separation from God, in whom alone man can possess the life and happiness for which he was created and for which he longs. (CCC 1035)

The Hell (detail) Mosaic by Coppo, ca. 1301.
In the company of Satan, his demons, and the other lost souls, those in Hell will only be able to express bitterness and despair for having turned away from God.

THE FULLNESS OF THE KINGDOM OF GOD

The Last Judgment and the Mass of St. Gregory by Master of the Artés Family. Keeping the eternal destination in mind helps people choose the correct course on earth.

The return of Christ at the end of time is known as the *Parousia*, a Greek word meaning *apparition* or *presence*. At the *Parousia*, Christ will appear in power and majesty as judge and establish his kingdom in all its fullness.

In salvation history, the *Parousia* marks the definitive triumph of Christ over sin and death. This triumph was manifested in Christ's Resurrection and Ascension and can be shared through sanctifying grace, but it will be fully demonstrated only at the end of the world. The *Parousia* is the culmination of the history of salvation. The plan of God will reach complete fulfillment in a renewed universe inhabited by glorified bodies.

In the Apostles' and Nicene Creeds, Christians profess "[Christ] will come again in glory to judge the living and the dead." This judgment at the end of time is known as the *General*, or *Last, Judgment*. When Christ will return, every human soul will rise in its own body. Everyone's moral decisions, including the circumstances and motivations surrounding them, will be revealed. Each person will be rewarded or punished for what he or she did in this life, "according to his [or her] acceptance or refusal of grace."[53]

At the *Parousia*, God's majesty, wisdom, justice, and mercy will be made evident, and Christ's victory on earth will be manifested. Every person will know why God allowed the good to suffer and the wicked to prosper. All the good and bad effects of every human action will be understood.

At the end of time, the Kingdom of God will come in its fullness. After the universal judgment, the righteous will reign for ever with Christ, glorified in body and soul. The universe itself will be renewed:

> **The Church...will receive her perfection only in the glory of heaven, when will come the time of the renewal of all things. At that time, together with the human race, the universe itself, which is so closely related to man and which attains its destiny through him, will be perfectly re-established in Christ.[54] (CCC 1042)**

God's plan of redemption to establish the *Kingdom of God* on earth will come to its fullness at the end of time.[55] The Church will be perfected and the universe transformed into a heavenly city, a New Jerusalem, and God will live among his people.[56]

Keeping the eternal destination in mind helps people choose the correct course on earth. Christ has shown the way, but each person must respond to his gift of salvation and follow him:

> **"Enter by the narrow gate; for the gate is wide and the way is easy, that leads to destruction, and those who enter by it are many. For the gate is narrow and the way is hard, that leads to life, and those who find it are few." (Mt 7:13-14)**

CHRIST THE KING

The Ghent Altarpiece: God Almighty by Van Eyck.
Christ wants to reign in every person's life, and his followers want Christ to reign both in them and in the world.

Christ wants to reign in every person's life, and his followers want Christ to reign both in them and in the world. Thus, the Our Father includes the phrases, "Thy kingdom come; thy will be done."[57] The reign of Christ first becomes a reality in a person's heart and then grows to inspire his or her entire existence. The Gospels describe the nature of the kingdom Christ came to establish: it is neither burdensome nor tyrannical but a kingdom of peace, joy, and love. As Christ said, "My yoke is easy and my burden is light."[58]

As recounted in the Gospels, Christ established a spiritual kingdom. This teaching disappointed many of the Jews at the time of Christ, who wrongly assumed the promised messiah would be a military leader who would restore David's temporal kingdom. Christ, however, explicitly rejected this idea, telling Pilate, "My kingship is not of this world; if my kingship were of this world, my servants would fight, that I might not be handed over."[59] Instead, his is a spiritual kingdom, the entrance to which is opened to any person through Baptism and a living faith. This is why Christ said, "The kingdom of God is in the midst of you."[60]

Christ refused any kingly authority on earth; nevertheless, it would be incorrect to think the Kingdom of God has no place in this world. By instructing his Apostles to go to all nations, teaching and baptizing, Christ intended his kingdom to embrace everyone. Christ taught his followers were to be like leaven; as yeast transforms the entire loaf, Christians are called to renew the entire world according to Christ's New Commandment of Love. By preaching the Good News, the Church hands on the means to guide the faithful in this transformation. The laity has a paramount responsibility to bring the light of Christ into the heart of the world.

He did not come to rule over peoples and territories but to set people free from the slavery of sin and to reconcile them with God.[61]

Oh, what happiness would be ours if all men, individuals, families, and nations, would but let themselves be governed by Christ![62]

When once men recognize, both in private and in public life, that Christ is King, society will at last receive the great blessings of real liberty, well-ordered discipline, peace and harmony.[63]

Christ taught—by word and example—his kingdom is one of self-sacrifice, offered for love of God and neighbor. The Cross is the throne from which Christ reigns; from there he defeated Satan and ushered in his kingdom. Christ's kingship was inadvertently recognized by Pontius Pilate, who ordered an inscription be placed on the Cross: "Jesus of Nazareth, the King of the Jews."[64] This kingdom, established by Christ on the Cross, will be fully unveiled at the end of time; Satan will then suffer his final defeat, and Christ will reign over the new creation.

> Though already present in his Church, Christ's reign is nevertheless yet to be fulfilled "with power and great glory" by the King's return to earth. This reign is still under attack by the evil powers, even though they have been defeated definitively by Christ's Passover.[65] Until everything is subject to him, "until there be realized new heavens and a new earth in which justice dwells, the pilgrim Church, in her sacraments and institutions, which belong to this present age, carries the mark of this world which will pass, and she herself takes her place among the creatures which groan and travail yet and await the revelation of the sons of God."[66] That is why Christians pray, above all in the Eucharist, to hasten Christ's return by saying to him:[67] *Marana tha!* "Our Lord, come!"[68] (CCC 671)

CONCLUSION

The Mystical Body of Christ, the People of God, in St. Peter's Square, Vatican City.

"The Church is on earth the seed and beginning of the kingdom of God" (cf. *LG* 5), the earthly reign of the glorified Christ in the hearts of his people. She is the Mystical Body of Christ wherein each member—in Heaven, in Purgatory, and on earth—is united both to Christ the head and to each other. This *qahal*, or assembly, of the People of God is necessary for salvation because all the graces of the redemption flow through this instrument. Thus, anyone who knowingly rejects the Church cannot be saved. Still, Christ offers his grace—in a way known only to him—to allow those ignorant of him to find a way to salvation.

The Church is one under her head, Christ. She is holy because of the holiness of Christ. She is catholic, that is, for all men and women, in all places, at all times. She is apostolic because she was founded on the Apostles, preserves the doctrines Christ entrusted to the Apostles, and is governed by their successors. The pope and bishops, who have inherited the offices of St. Peter and the Apostles, are the authentic teachers of the Faith. The Church's Magisterium exercises the charism of infallibility when the pope solemnly defines a doctrine of Faith or morals *ex cathedra*—or the bishops do the same united to the pope—especially in an Ecumenical Council.

The Church transmits the graces of Christ's redemption primarily through the Seven Sacraments, which were established by Christ.

At death, each person receives the Particular Judgment, followed by Hell, Purgatory, or Heaven. At the end of time, Christ will return in glory for the Final Judgment; all will rise in glorified bodies, and those faithful to God's grace will enjoy the renewed creation forever with Christ their King.

The Church's One Foundation

Samuel John Stone (1839-1900)

Christ is the foundation and cornerstone of his Church. By his Incarnation, God's love was made manifest. By his death on the Cross, the ultimate act of love, Christ established a New Covenant between God and man, founding his Church.

"In Jesus Christ the divine presence in the world and in man has been made manifest in a new way and in visible form. In him 'the grace of God has appeared' indeed" (cf. Ti 2: 11).

"The love of God the Father, as a gift, infinite grace, source of life, has been made visible in Christ, and in his humanity that love has become 'part' of the universe, the human family and history." (*DV* 54)

The Church's one foundation
Is Jesus Christ her Lord;
She is his new creation
By water and the word;
From heaven he came and sought her
To be his holy bride;
With his own blood he bought her,
And for her life he died.

Elect from every nation,
Yet one o'er all the earth;
Her charter of salvation,
One Lord, one faith, one birth;
One holy name she blesses,
Partakes one holy food,
And to one hope she presses,
With ev'ry grace endued.

SUPPLEMENTARY READING

1. *The Eschatological Character of the Pilgrim Church*

The Church, to which we are all called in Christ Jesus, and in which we acquire sanctity through the grace of God, will attain its full perfection only in the glory of heaven, when there will come the time of the restoration of all things. At that time the human race as well as the entire world, which is intimately related to man and attains to its end through him, will be perfectly reestablished in Christ.

Christ, having been lifted up from the earth has drawn all to Himself. Rising from the dead He sent His life-giving Spirit upon His disciples and through Him has established His Body which is the Church as the universal sacrament of salvation. Sitting at the right hand of the Father, He is continually active in the world that He might lead men to the Church and through it join them to Himself and that He might make them partakers of His glorious life by nourishing them with His own Body and Blood. Therefore the promised restoration which we are awaiting has already begun in Christ, is carried forward in the mission of the Holy Spirit and through Him continues in the Church in which we learn the meaning of our terrestrial life through our faith, while we perform with hope in the future the work committed to us in this world by the Father, and thus work out our salvation.

Already the final age of the world has come upon us and the renovation of the world is irrevocably decreed and is already anticipated in some kind of a real way; for the Church already on this earth is signed with a sanctity which is real although imperfect. However, until there shall be new heavens and a new earth in which justice dwells, the pilgrim Church in her sacraments and institutions, which pertain to this present time, has the appearance of this world which is passing and she herself dwells among creatures who groan and travail in pain until now and await the revelation of the sons of God

— Second Vatican Council, *Lumen Gentium*, 48-50

2. *Without Real Effort, No One Wins the Crown*

The Roman Church remains the head of all the churches and the source of Catholic teaching. Of this there can be no doubt. Everyone knows that the keys of the kingdom of Heaven were given to Peter. Upon his faith and teaching the whole fabric of the Church will continue to be built until we all reach full maturity in Christ and attain to unity in faith and knowledge of the Son of God.

Of course many are needed to plant and many to water now that the faith has spread so far and the population become so great. Even in ancient times when the people of God had only one altar, many teachers were needed; how much more now for an assembly of nations which Lebanon itself could not provide with fuel for sacrifice, and which neither Lebanon nor the whole of Judea could supply with beasts for burnt offerings! Nevertheless, no matter who plants or waters, God gives no harvest unless what he plants is the faith of Peter, and unless he himself assents to Peter's teaching. All important questions that arise among God's people are referred to the judgment of Peter in the person of the Roman Pontiff. Under him the ministers of Mother Church exercise the powers committed to them, each in his own sphere of responsibility.

Remember then how our fathers worked out their salvation; remember the sufferings through which the Church has grown, and the storms the ship of Peter has weathered because it has Christ on board. Remember how the crown was attained by those whose sufferings gave new radiance to their faith. The whole company of saints bears witness to the unfailing truth that without real effort no one wins the crown.

— St. Thomas Becket

SUPPLEMENTARY READING Continued

3. *Christ Is Present to His Church*

Christ is always present in His Church, especially in her liturgical celebrations. He is present in the sacrifice of the Mass, not only in the person of His minister, "the same now offering, through the ministry of priests, who formerly offered himself on the cross," but especially under the Eucharistic species. By His power He is present in the sacraments, so that when a man baptizes it is really Christ Himself who baptizes. He is present in His word, since it is He Himself who speaks when the holy scriptures are read in the Church. He is present, lastly, when the Church prays and sings, for He promised: "Where two or three are gathered together in my name, there am I in the midst of them" (Mt 18: 20).

Christ indeed always associates the Church with Himself in this great work wherein God is perfectly glorified and men are sanctified. The Church is His beloved Bride who calls to her Lord, and through Him offers worship to the Eternal Father.

Rightly, then, the liturgy is considered as an exercise of the priestly office of Jesus Christ. In the liturgy the sanctification of the man is signified by signs perceptible to the senses, and is effected in a way which corresponds with each of these signs; in the liturgy the whole public worship is performed by the Mystical Body of Jesus Christ, that is, by the Head and His members.

From this it follows that every liturgical celebration, because it is an action of Christ the priest and of His Body which is the Church, is a sacred action surpassing all others; no other action of the Church can equal its efficacy by the same title and to the same degree.

In the earthly liturgy we take part in a foretaste of that heavenly liturgy which is celebrated in the holy city of Jerusalem toward which we journey as pilgrims, where Christ is sitting at the right hand of God, a minister of the holies and of the true tabernacle; we sing a hymn to the Lord's glory with all the warriors of the heavenly army; venerating the memory of the saints, we hope for some part and fellowship with them; we eagerly await the Saviour, Our Lord Jesus Christ, until He, our life, shall appear and we too will appear with Him in glory....

By a tradition handed down from the apostles which took its origin from the very day of Christ's resurrection, the Church celebrates the paschal mystery every eighth day; with good reason this, then, bears the name of the Lord's day or Sunday. For on this day Christ's faithful are bound to come together into one place so that; by hearing the word of God and taking part in the eucharist, they may call to mind the passion, the resurrection and the glorification of the Lord Jesus, and may thank God who "has begotten them again, through the resurrection of Jesus Christ from the dead, unto a living hope" (1 Pt 1: 3). Hence the Lord's day is the original feast day, and it should be proposed to the piety of the faithful and taught to them so that it may become in fact a day of joy and of freedom from work. Other celebrations, unless they be truly of greatest importance, shall not have precedence over the Sunday which is the foundation and kernel of the whole liturgical year.

— Second Vatican Council, *Sacrosanctum Concilium*, 7-8, 106

Pentecost (detail) by Duccio.
"And there appeared to them tongues as of fire, distributed and resting on each one of them. And they were all filled with the Holy Spirit and began to speak in other tongues, as the Spirit gave them utterance." (Acts 2: 3-4)

SUPPLEMENTARY READING Continued

4. *The Church in Her Unity Speaks in the Language of Every Nation*

The disciples spoke in the language of every nation. At Pentecost God chose this means to indicate the presence of the Holy Spirit: whoever had received the Spirit spoke in every kind of tongue. We must realize, dear brothers, that this is the same Holy Spirit by whom love is poured out in our hearts. It was love that was to bring the Church of God together all over the world. And as individual men who received the Holy Spirit in those days could speak in all kinds of tongues, so today the Church, united by the Holy Spirit, speaks in the language of every people.

Therefore if somebody should say to one of us, "You have received the Holy Spirit, why do you not speak in tongues?" his reply should be, "I do indeed speak in the tongues of all men, because I belong to the body of Christ, that is, the Church, and she speaks all languages. What else did the presence of the Holy Spirit indicate at Pentecost, except that God's Church was to speak in the language of every people?"

This was the way in which the Lord's promise was fulfilled: "No one puts new wine into old wineskins. New wine is put into fresh skins, and so both are preserved." So when the disciples were heard speaking in all kinds of languages, some people were not far wrong in saying: "They have been drinking too much new wine." The truth is that the disciples had now become fresh wineskins, renewed and made holy by grace. The new wine of the Holy Spirit filled them, so that their fervor brimmed over and they spoke in manifold tongues. By this spectacular miracle they became a sign of the Catholic Church, which embraces the language of every nation.

Keep this feast, then, as members of the one body of Christ. It will be no empty festival for you if you really become what you are celebrating. For you are the members of that Church which the Lord acknowledges as his own, being himself acknowledged by her, that same Church which he fills with the Holy Spirit as she spreads throughout the world. He is like a bridegroom who never loses sight of his own bride; no one could ever deceive him by substituting some other woman.

To you men of all nations, then, who make up the Church of Christ, you the members of Christ, you, the body of Christ, you, the bride of Christ—to all of you the Apostle addresses these words: "*Bear with one another in love; do all you can to preserve the unity of the Spirit in the bond of peace.*" Notice that when Paul urges us to bear with one another, he bases his argument on love, and when he speaks of our hope of unity, he emphasizes the bond of peace. This Church is the house of God. It is his delight to dwell here. Take care, then, that he never has the sorrow of seeing it undermined by schism and collapsing in ruins.

— St. Gregory of Agrigentum

The Last Supper (detail) by Fra Angelico.
"I tell you I shall not drink again of this fruit of the vine until that day when I drink it new with you in my Father's kingdom." (Mt 26: 29)

VOCABULARY

APOSTOLIC SUCCESSION
The bishops of the Church, through their ordination, form an uninterrupted, unbroken chain of succession, historically traceable to the Twelve Apostles.

BRIDE OF CHRIST
Christ described himself as the bridegroom and the Church as his bride. This symbolism represents the intimate union between Christ and the members of his Mystical Body, the Church.

CHURCH
The assembly of people God has called together from the ends of the earth. This word has three meanings: the people God gathers together, the local church (diocese), and the liturgical assembly. It is also the name given to a building used for public Christian worship.

ELECT
Those chosen by God from the beginning to participate in his plan of salvation and to enjoy his eternal friendship in Heaven.

EX CATHEDRA
Latin for *from the chair* (of St. Peter). It indicates a solemn and infallible definition by a pope of a doctrine concerning matters of Faith or morals to be held by the faithful.

EXTRA ECCLESIAM NULLA SALUS
Latin for *outside the Church there is no salvation.* This doctrine teaches all salvation comes from Jesus Christ through his Church.

FINAL JUDGMENT
Also called the Last, or General, Judgment. This judgment of everyone at the end of time will follow the Second Coming of Christ and the resurrection of the dead.

HEAVEN
The dwelling of God. In Heaven, the elect enjoy eternal friendship and communion with God and with the angels and saints. Those in Heaven enjoy perfect happiness and see God face-to-face, i.e., the Beatific Vision.

HELL
The dwelling of Satan and the other fallen angels. By their own choice, those in hell suffer eternal separation from God and the company of the blessed.

INDEFECTIBILITY
The quality or characteristic of the Church by which she will exist until the end of time.

INFALLIBILITY
Immunity from error and any possibility of error. The pope enjoys this charism by virtue of his office when, "as supreme pastor and teacher of the faithful...he proclaims by a definitive act a doctrine pertaining to faith or morals" (CCC 891). The college of bishops is also infallible when, in union with the pope and above all in an Ecumenical Council, it definitively proclaims a doctrine pertaining to Faith and morals to be held by the universal Church.

INVINCIBLE IGNORANCE
Ignorance that cannot be overcome by ordinary diligence. The guilt of a sin committed under invincible ignorance is not imputed to the sinner. This ignorance can be caused by a lack of knowledge, either of fact or of law, by a scarcity of evidence, by insufficient time or talent in the person, or by some other factor.

KINGDOM OF GOD
The Kingdom of God is based on union with Jesus Christ by the work of the Holy Spirit. This kingdom, which is spiritual, begins here on earth and is perfected at the end of time. It is a kingdom of peace, love, and justice.

MAGISTERIUM
The teaching authority of the Church, which is entrusted to the pope and the bishops in communion with him.

MARKS OF THE CHURCH
Four characteristics identified in the early Church by which one can distinguish whether an ecclesial body is part of the Church established by Christ. The marks are listed in the Nicene Creed: "one, holy, catholic and apostolic."

VOCABULARY Continued

MYSTICAL BODY OF CHRIST
Taught in St. Paul's First Letter to the Corinthians, believers are united to Christ in the way the individual parts of the body, each with its own function, are united to the head.

PARABLE
A usually fictitious narrative or allegory (usually of something that might naturally occur) used to illustrate and explain moral or spiritual principles.

PARTICULAR JUDGMENT
The eternal recompense received by each soul at the moment of death in accordance with that person's faith and works.

PAROUSIA
Greek for *presence* or *arrival*; the Second Coming of Christ at the end of time.

PILGRIM CHURCH
Term for the Church on earth, whose members are on a journey, the destination of which has not yet been reached. Although people face difficulties and temptations, they are already united—albeit imperfectly—with Christ in Heaven.

PURGATORY
A state of final purification after death but before entrance into Heaven for those who have died in God's friendship but are only imperfectly purified.

SACRAMENT
An efficacious sign of grace instituted by Christ and entrusted to the Church by which divine life is dispensed through the work of the Holy Spirit. There are seven.

STUDY QUESTIONS

1. How does God make it possible for human beings to participate in the divine life?
2. What is the core message of the Gospel according to Mark 1:15?
3. How is the Kingdom of God like a mustard seed?
4. What is the Kingdom of God according to Pope Benedict XVI?
5. What did the Evangelists mean when they wrote Christ came in the *fullness of time*?
6. What is the Mystical Body of Christ?
7. What is the vertical dimension of the Mystical Body of Christ?
8. What is the horizontal dimension of the Mystical Body of Christ?
9. What does it mean to say the Church is necessary for salvation?
10. What is the importance of the four marks of the Church?
11. What does it mean to say the Church is one?
12. How can the Church claim to be holy if it is made up of sinful members?
13. What is the meaning of *catholic* as it pertains to the Catholic Church?
14. In what three ways is the Church apostolic?
15. What is Apostolic Succession?
16. What did the Fathers of the Second Vatican Council mean when they taught the Church *subsists* in the Catholic Church?
17. What is the indefectibility of the Church?
18. According to the *Catechism*, no. 797, what effect does the Holy Spirit have on the Church?

STUDY QUESTIONS Continued

19. What was the immediate effect of the descent of the Holy Spirit on the nascent Church?
20. What gifts does the Holy Spirit give the members of the Church?
21. How are St. Peter and his successors Vicars of Christ?
22. How is the Church hierarchy a *college* according to the *Catechism*, no. 880?
23. What evidence exists to claim the mission entrusted to the Apostles did not die with them?
24. From where did the first bishops come?
25. Where did the Church receive her authority to teach?
26. What is the Magisterium?
27. What is the role of the Holy Spirit in the Magisterium?
28. What is papal infallibility?
29. What is the basic work of the Church?
30. Who instituted the sacraments, and when?
31. What is a sacrament according to the *Catechism*, no. 1131?
32. What is the Particular Judgment?
33. What is the Beatific Vision?
34. What is the purpose of Purgatory?
35. What is Hell?
36. Which souls go to Hell?
37. What does a soul experience in Hell?
38. Why is there no happiness in Hell?
39. What is the *Parousia*?
40. What will happen at the General Judgment?
41. How difficult is it to live under the reign of Christ on earth according to Matthew 11: 30?
42. What would be the effect on the world if each person were to embrace the Kingdom of God within him- or herself?
43. What is the attitude of Christians toward the end of the world?

PRACTICAL EXERCISES

1. Outside the Church there is no salvation. At first glance, this might seem an inhuman doctrine, condemning all non-Catholics, even those who have never heard of Christ, to Hell. Explain why this is not a correct interpretation of "*extra Ecclesiam nulla salus*."

2. Research an early Christian heretical group and explain how it fails to conform to one or more of the four marks of the Church.

3. During the summer of 1999, Pope John Paul II gave a series of Wednesday audiences to address Heaven, Hell, and Purgatory. They can be found at the following Web site:

www.ewtn.com/library/PAPALDOC/JP2HEAVN.HTM

Have each student choose one of the three audiences, read it, and then write and answer three Focus Questions about what the pope taught about Heaven, Hell, or Purgatory.

FROM THE CATECHISM

765 The Lord Jesus endowed his community with a structure that will remain until the Kingdom is fully achieved. Before all else there is the choice of the Twelve with Peter as their head.[69] Representing the twelve tribes of Israel, they are the foundation stones of the new Jerusalem.[70] The Twelve and the other disciples share in Christ's mission and his power, but also in his lot.[71] By all his actions, Christ prepares and builds his Church.

766 The Church is born primarily of Christ's total self-giving for our salvation, anticipated in the institution of the Eucharist and fulfilled on the cross. "The origin and growth of the Church are symbolized by the blood and water which flowed from the open side of the crucified Jesus."[72] "For it was from the side of Christ as he slept the sleep of death upon the cross that there came forth the 'wondrous sacrament of the whole Church.'"[73] As Eve was formed from the sleeping Adam's side, so the Church was born from the pierced heart of Christ hanging dead on the cross.[74]

767 "When the work which the Father gave the Son to do on earth was accomplished, the Holy Spirit was sent on the day of Pentecost in order that he might continually sanctify the Church."[75] Then "the Church was openly displayed to the crowds and the spread of the Gospel among the nations, through preaching, was begun."[76] As the "convocation" of all men for salvation, the Church in her very nature is missionary, sent by Christ to all the nations to make disciples of them.[77]

768 So that she can fulfill her mission, the Holy Spirit "bestows upon [the Church] varied hierarchic and charismatic gifts, and in this way directs her."[78] "Henceforward the Church, endowed with the gifts of her founder and faithfully observing his precepts of charity, humility and self-denial, receives the mission of proclaiming and establishing among all peoples the Kingdom of Christ and of God, and she is on earth the seed and the beginning of that kingdom."[79]

769 "The Church...will receive its perfection only in the glory of heaven,"[80] at the time of Christ's glorious return. Until that day, "the Church progresses on her pilgrimage amidst this world's persecutions and God's consolations."[81] Here below she knows that she is in exile far from the Lord, and longs for the full coming of the Kingdom, when she will "be united in glory with her king."[82] The Church, and through her the world, will not be perfected in glory without great trials. Only then will "all the just from the time of Adam, 'from Abel, the just one, to the last of the elect,'... be gathered together in the universal Church in the Father's presence."[83]

772 It is in the Church that Christ fulfills and reveals his own mystery as the purpose of God's plan: "to unite all things in him."[84] St. Paul calls the nuptial union of Christ and the Church "a great mystery." Because she is united to Christ as to her bridegroom, she becomes a mystery in her turn.[85] Contemplating this mystery in her, Paul exclaims: "Christ in you, the hope of glory."[86]

773 In the Church this communion of men with God, in the "love [that] never ends," is the purpose which governs everything in her that is a sacramental means, tied to this passing world.[87] "[The Church's] structure is totally ordered to the holiness of Christ's members. And holiness is measured according to the 'great mystery' in which the Bride responds with the gift of love to the gift of the Bridegroom."[88] Mary goes before us all in the holiness that is the Church's mystery as "the bride without spot or wrinkle."[89] This is why the "Marian" dimension of the Church precedes the "Petrine."[90]

775 "The Church, in Christ, is like a sacrament—a sign and instrument, that is, of communion with God and of unity among all men."[91] The Church's first purpose is to be the sacrament of the *inner union of men with God*. Because men's communion with one another is rooted in that union with God, the Church is also the sacrament of the *unity of the human race*. In her, this unity is already begun, since she gathers men "from every nation, from all tribes and peoples and tongues";[92] at the same time, the Church is the "sign and instrument" of the full realization of the unity yet to come.

FROM THE CATECHISM Continued

811 "This is the sole Church of Christ, which in the Creed we profess to be one, holy, catholic and apostolic."[93] These four characteristics, inseparably linked with each other,[94] indicate essential features of the Church and her mission. The Church does not possess them of herself; it is Christ who, through the Holy Spirit, makes his Church one, holy, catholic, and apostolic, and it is he who calls her to realize each of these qualities.

812 Only faith can recognize that the Church possesses these properties from her divine source. But their historical manifestations are signs that also speak clearly to human reason. As the First Vatican Council noted, the "Church herself, with her marvelous propagation, eminent holiness, and inexhaustible fruitfulness in everything good, her catholic unity and invincible stability, is a great and perpetual motive of credibility and an irrefutable witness of her divine mission."[95]

865 The Church is ultimately *one, holy, catholic, and apostolic* in her deepest and ultimate identity, because it is in her that "the Kingdom of heaven," the "Reign of God,"[96] already exists and will be fulfilled at the end of time. The kingdom has come in the person of Christ and grows mysteriously in the hearts of those incorporated into him, until its full eschatological manifestation. Then all those he has redeemed and made "holy and blameless before him in love,"[97] will be gathered together as the one People of God, the "Bride of the Lamb,"[98] "the holy city Jerusalem coming down out of heaven from God, having the glory of God."[99] For "the wall of the city had twelve foundations, and on them the twelve names of the *twelve apostles of the Lamb*."[100]

Suffer the Little Children to Come Unto Me by Tissot.
"And they were bringing children to him, that he might touch them; and the disciples rebuked them. But when Jesus saw it he was indignant, and said to them, 'Let the children come to me, do not hinder them; for to such belongs the kingdom of God. Truly, I say to you, whoever does not receive the kingdom of God like a child shall not enter it.' And he took them in his arms and blessed them, laying his hands upon them." (Mk 10:13-16)

Sermon of St. Mark in Alexandria by Bellini. "Go therefore and make disciples of all nations, baptizing them in the name of the Father and of the Son and of the Holy Spirit, teaching them to observe all that I have commanded you; and lo, I am with you always, to the close of the age." (Mt 28: 19-20)

ENDNOTES - CHAPTER FIVE

1. Col 1: 15.
2. Rom 8: 29.
3. Cf. St. Gregory the Great, *Hom in Evang.* 19, 1: PL 76, 1154 B. St. Augustine, *Serm.* 341, 9, 11: PL 39, 1499 s. St. John Damascene, *Adv. Iconocl.* 11: PG 96, 1357.
4. *LG* 3.
5. Lk 12: 32; cf. Mt 10: 16; 26: 31; Jn 10: 1-21.
6. Cf. Mt 12: 49.
7. Cf. Mt 5-6.
8. *Roman Catechism* I, 10, 20.
9. Cf. 1 Cor 12: 27.
10. Cf. 1 Cor 12: 12.
11. Cf. 1 Cor 12: 1-11.
12. Cf. 1 Cor 12: 26.
13. Cf. 1 Cor 12.
14. 2 Cor 11: 2.
15. Jn 3: 29.
16. Mk 2: 19.
17. Cf. Mt 22: 1-14; 25: 1-13; 1 Cor 6: 15-17; 2 Cor 11: 2.
18. Cf. Rev 22: 17; Eph 1: 4; 5: 27.
19. Eph 5: 25-26.
20. Cf. Eph 5: 29.
21. *LG* 9 § 2, 48 § 2; *GS* 45 § 1.
22. Paul VI, June 22, 1973; *AG* 7 § 2; cf. *LG* 17.
23. Cf. Mk 16: 16; Jn 3: 5.
24. *LG* 16; cf. DS 3866-3872.
25. *DH* 1.
26. *AG* 7; cf. Heb 11: 6; 1 Cor 9: 16.
27. Cf. 1 Cor 8: 6; Eph 4: 1-4.
28. *MR*, 2008.
29. Cf. Eph 4: 4-5.
30. Cf. *UR* 2; *LG* 14; CIC, can. 205.
31. *SC* 10.
32. *UR* 3 § 5.
33. *LG* 48.
34. Eph 2: 20; Rev 21: 14.
35. Cf. Mt 28: 16-20; Acts 1: 8; 1 Cor 9: 1; 15: 7-8; Gal 1: 1; etc.
36. Cf. Acts 2: 42.
37. Cf. 2 Tm 1: 13-14.
38. *AG* 5.
39. *LG* 8 § 2.
40. St. Augustine, *Sermo* 267, 4: PL 38, 1231D.
41. Pius XII, encyclical, *Mystici Corporis*: DS 3808.
42. 2 Cor 6: 16; cf. 1 Cor 3: 16-17; Eph 2: 21.
43. *LG* 19; cf. Lk 6: 13; Jn 21: 15-17.
44. *LG* 22; cf. CIC, can. 330.
45. Jn 14: 26.
46. *LG* 25; cf. Vatican Council I: DS 3074.
47. *DV* 10 § 2.
48. *LG* 25 § 2.
49. Cf. *LG* 25.
50. Mt 28: 18.
51. Mt 28: 19-20.
52. Cf. DS 76; 409; 411; 801; 858; 1002; 1351; 1575; Paul VI, *CPG* § 12.
53. CCC 682.
54. *LG* 48; cf. Acts 3: 21; Eph 1: 10; Col 1: 20; 2 Pt 3: 10-13.
55. Cf. CCC 1042.
56. Cf. CCC 1043-1044.
57. Mt 6: 10.
58. Mt 11: 30.
59. Jn 18: 36.
60. Lk 17: 21.
61. Pope Benedict XVI, Angelus, November 26, 2006.
62. *Quas Primas*, 20.
63. *Quas Primas*, 19.
64. Jn 19: 19.
65. Lk 21: 27; cf. Mt 25: 31; 2 Thes 2: 7.
66. *LG* 48 § 3; cf. 2 Pt 3: 13; Rom 8: 19-22; 1 Cor 15: 28.
67. Cf. 1 Cor 11: 26; 2 Pt 3: 11-12.
68. 1 Cor 16: 22; Rev 22: 17, 20.
69. Cf. Mk 3: 14-15.
70. Cf. Mt 19: 28; Lk 22: 30; Rev 21: 12-14.
71. Cf. Mk 6: 7; Lk 10: 1-2; Mt 10: 25; Jn 15: 20.
72. *LG* 3; cf. Jn 19: 34.
73. *SC* 5.
74. Cf. St. Ambrose, *In Luc.* 2, 85-89: PL 15, 1666-1668.
75. *LG* 4; cf. Jn 17: 4.
76. *AG* 4.
77. Cf. Mt 28: 19-20; *AG* 2; 5-6.
78. *LG* 4.
79. *LG* 5.
80. *LG* 48.
81. St. Augustine, *De civ. Dei*, 18, 51: PL 41, 614; cf. *LG* 8.
82. *LG* 5; cf. 6; 2 Cor 5: 6.
83. *LG* 2.
84. Eph 1: 10.
85. Eph 5: 32; 3: 9-11; 5: 25-27.
86. Col 1: 27.
87. 1 Cor 13: 8; cf. *LG* 48.
88. John Paul II, *MD* 27.
89. Eph 5: 27.
90. Cf. John Paul II, *MD* 27.
91. *LG* 1.
92. Rev 7: 9.
93. *LG* 8.
94. Cf. DS 2888.
95. Vatican Council I, *De Filius* 3: DS 3013.
96. Rev 19: 6.
97. Eph 1: 4.
98. Rev 21: 9.
99. Rev 21: 10-11.
100. Rev 21: 14.

The Mystery of Redemption

CHAPTER 6

Called to Be Another Christ

In addition to the grace of God merited by Christ's redemption, his followers must spare no effort to imitate the example he presented and implement his teachings in their own lives.

The Mystery of Redemption

CHAPTER 6

Called to Be Another Christ

The Lord Jesus, the divine Teacher and Model of all perfection, preached holiness of life to each and every one of His disciples of every condition. He himself stands as the author and consummator of this holiness of life: "Be you therefore perfect, even as your heavenly Father is perfect."[1] Indeed he sent the Holy Spirit upon all men that he might move them inwardly to love God with their whole heart and their whole soul, with all their mind and all their strength[2] and that they might love each other as Christ loves them.[3]

The followers of Christ are called by God, not because of their works, but according to his own purpose and grace. They are justified in the Lord Jesus, because in the baptism of faith they truly become sons of God and sharers in the divine nature. In this way they are really made holy. Then too, by God's gift, they must hold on to and complete in their lives this holiness they have received. They are warned by the Apostle to live "as becomes saints,"[4] and to put on "as God's chosen ones, holy and beloved a heart of mercy, kindness, humility, meekness, patience,"[5] and to possess the fruit of the Spirit in holiness.[6] Since truly we all offend in many things[7] we all need God's mercies continually and we all must daily pray: "Forgive us our debts."[8]

Thus it is evident to everyone, that all the faithful of Christ of whatever rank or status, are called to the fullness of the Christian life and to the perfection of charity; by this holiness as such a more human manner of living is promoted in this earthly society. In order that the faithful may reach this perfection, they must use their strength accordingly as they have received it, as a gift from Christ. They must follow in His footsteps and conform themselves to his image seeking the will of the Father in all things. They must devote themselves with all their being to the glory of God and the service of their neighbor. In this way, the holiness of the People of God will grow into an abundant harvest of good, as is admirably shown by the life of so many saints in Church history. (*Lumen Gentium*, 40)

Third Station of the Cross.
Jesus falls the first time.

INTRODUCTION

The Christian vocation is to be another Christ. This lifelong duty encompasses every thought, word, and deed. The decision to pursue good and avoid evil in life is the first step to follow Christ.

Every human being is made in the image and likeness of God and, therefore, has the natural law written in his or her heart by God himself. The manner in which a person lives this natural law, which is required by human nature, determines the degree of happiness in this life and the next.

Agony in the Garden (detail) by Botticelli. The decision to pursue good and avoid evil in life is the first step to follow Christ.

In the Old Testament, God chose a people, the Israelites, to whom he revealed the Decalogue, or Ten Commandments—a privileged and explicit expression of the natural law. The teachings of the Mosaic Law were later elevated and perfected by Jesus Christ. There is a clear connection between the natural law, the Ten Commandments, and Christ's Law of Love.

Having received the graces merited by Christ's Death and Resurrection in Baptism, every Christian is empowered to be *another Christ* and to put his teachings into practice. In fact, every follower of Christ is expected to lead an exemplary life. Primarily through prayer and the reception of the sacraments, the faithful receive the graces needed to help reflect the holiness of Christ through the increase and practice of the theological virtues. The sacraments increase the gifts of the Holy Spirit, which enhance the capacity to embrace God's will in life. These gifts of the Holy Spirit are manifested in the fruits of the Holy Spirit—good actions that show forth love of Christ and reflect the love Christ taught in the Beatitudes.

In addition to the grace of God merited by Christ's redemption, his followers must spare no effort to imitate the example he presented and implement his teachings in their own lives. This effort to grow in holiness achieved enormous good for everyone in society. By striving to conform their lives to the life of the Master, the baptized transform society by attracting family, friends, and colleagues to Christ.

Thus, the call to be another Christ entails the imitation of Christ with the help of all the means he has made available through his Redemption. It involves exercising the common priesthood of all the faithful and pursuing the universal call to holiness.

THIS CHAPTER WILL ADDRESS SEVERAL QUESTIONS:

- What is the universal call to holiness?
- What is grace, and how is it given?
- What is the common priesthood of all the faithful and the vocation of the laity?
- How is Christian morality an imitation of Christ?
- What is conversion of heart?
- What is the relationship between the natural law, the Decalogue, and the New Law?
- What are the Beatitudes?
- What are the Precepts of the Church?
- What are the theological virtues and sins against them?
- What are the gifts and fruits of the Holy Spirit?

LAY PERSONS ARE CALLED TO HOLINESS

Catholic Youth Service Project in Mexico.
The special task of lay persons is the sanctification of the world in which they live and work.

Though called to imitate Christ, not all are called to live the same state in life. God chooses some men to minister to the rest through the Sacrament of Holy Orders; this is their particular path to holiness. Others are called to the religious life. However, the vast majority of Christians are called to a life of holiness in the *laity*.

The laity can be defined as all the faithful who have not received Holy Orders or been consecrated in the religious life. Living amid the world, those in the lay state are characterized by their *secular* nature, which involves a particular *vocation* or calling from God.

Christians in the lay state are called to engage in everyday, secular activities amid the world, evangelizing and sanctifying the world "from within." In this way, as Pope Pius XII stated, these Christians are in the "front lines" of the Church's evangelical mission.[13] According to the Second Vatican Council:

> The laity, by their very vocation, seek the Kingdom of God by engaging in temporal affairs and by ordering them according to the plan of God. They live in the world, that is, in each and in all of the secular professions and occupations. They live in the ordinary circumstances of family and social life, from which the very web of their existence is woven. They are called there by God that by exercising their proper function and led by the spirit of the Gospel they may work for the sanctification of the world from within as a leaven. In this way they may make Christ known to others, especially by the testimony of a life resplendent in faith, hope and charity. Therefore, since they are tightly bound up in all types of temporal affairs it is their special task to order and to throw light upon these affairs in such a way that they may come into being and then continually increase according to Christ to the praise of the Creator and the Redeemer. (*Lumen Gentium*, 31)

Thus, the special task of lay persons is the sanctification of the world in which they live and work. This is something only those in the lay state can do. Many today only experience Christ through the lay faithful who live and work side-by-side with them.

GRACE TO RESPOND TO GOD'S CALL

Through the graces merited by the sacrifice of Jesus Christ on the Cross, God gives the grace of forgiveness and calls people to lives of holiness. Though God depends on freedom to redeem each person, it is impossible to answer God's call to holiness and conform one's life to Christ by human effort alone. God, therefore, provides all the graces necessary to answer his call.

> **Grace is the help God gives us to respond to our vocation of becoming his adopted sons. It introduces us into the intimacy of the Trinitarian life.** (CCC 2021)

> **The divine initiative in the work of grace precedes, prepares, and elicits the free response of man. Grace responds to the deepest yearnings of human freedom, calls freedom to cooperate with it, and perfects freedom.** (CCC 2022)

Grace brings the baptized into the very life of Christ and helps reproduce his life in their own lives. Grace does not force itself upon anyone but assists each person to exercise true freedom, desire what ought to be desired, and achieve what ought to be achieved. For example, the decision to commit oneself to pray or to grow in kindness toward another person is the work of personal freedom assisted by grace.

There are two kinds of grace: sanctifying and actual. Through sanctifying grace, one shares in the life and love of the Blessed Trinity—Father, Son, and Holy Spirit.

There are two kinds of grace: sanctifying and actual. Through sanctifying grace, one shares in the life and love of the Blessed Trinity—Father, Son, and Holy Spirit. This grace is first received in the Sacrament of Baptism. It is meant to grow in each Christian, intensifying his or her union with God. This grace remains always, unless it is lost through mortal sin. Mortal sins can be forgiven in the Sacrament of Reconciliation, which restores the life of sanctifying grace in the soul.

Actual grace refers to all the particular, temporary help or aid God gives to perform a holy action that unites the recipient to his will. As the *Catechism of the Catholic Church* teaches, actual grace may precede a good act and help a person carry it out.[14]

Grace is a supernatural gift that elevates and transforms the soul. According to Christ, the Kingdom of God is within. The work of grace, together with the gifts of the Holy Spirit, instills an eagerness for holiness. Part of this strong desire to follow Christ involves a greater sensitivity of conscience, which empowers a person to choose actions that reflect the teachings of Christ and be sorrowful when an action falls short of these teachings.

> **It is important for every person to be sufficiently present to himself in order to hear and follow the voice of his conscience. This requirement of interiority is all the more necessary as life often distracts us from any reflection, self-examination or introspection:**
>
> > **Return to your conscience, question it....Turn inward, brethren, and in everything you do, see God as your witness.**[15] (CCC 1779)

Grace brings a person deeper into the life of the Blessed Trinity through the life of Jesus Christ. The presence of Christ grows in the soul and transforms it as sanctifying grace increases. A saint is simply an individual who has allowed the presence of Christ to transform the soul to the point he or she approaches the goal of loving God and others with the heart of Christ.

Pope Benedict XVI prays at the site of the Crucifixion in the Basilica of the Holy Sepulchre in Jerusalem.
The main altar belongs to the Greek Orthodox Church. The Rock of Calvary can be seen under glass on both sides of the altar. Beneath the main altar is the hole said to be the place where the Cross was placed. A Roman Catholic altar is on the right.

As a person grows closer to Christ and becomes more like him, he or she prompts others to conversion or at least to consider the Good News. As more individuals aspire to holiness, the world is brought nearer to Christ.

A living witness to Christ's presence will lead others to respond in like manner. This change is enhanced by growth in holiness through the exercise of the theological virtues of faith, hope, and charity received in Baptism, which have brought the recipient into contact with Christ and his graces.

An increase in sanctifying grace signifies a greater union with Jesus Christ. This growing friendship with Our Lord involves becoming like him in the order of love, peace, joy, and wisdom. The witness and example of kindness and charity make the Gospel both credible and attractive to others. In ordinary experiences, a Christian can have a great impact on others. The love that comes from a profound relationship with Christ wins others over to him effectively.

The Martyrdom of St. Sebastian by Memling.

The power of God's grace allows people to love beyond their natural, human capacities. History attests to the great number of Christians who had such an extraordinary love for Christ they willingly laid down their lives for the Faith. Others, amid the ordinary circumstances of life, led lives of incredible humility, chastity, kindness, and service in stark contrast to the sensuality and materialism of their cultures. The words of Christ are especially poignant: "He who abides in me, and I in him, he it is that bears much fruit."[16]

THE MORAL LIFE

The source of all holiness is the grace Christ has merited. Through the work of the Holy Spirit, this grace gradually transforms people into the image and likeness of Christ. Nevertheless, holiness involves cooperation with God's grace by living the natural law as revealed in the Decalogue and the perfection of Christ's New Commandment of Love, especially as taught in the Sermon on the Mount and the Last Supper.

Christ's call to holiness is also powerfully illustrated in his dialogue with the rich young man. First, Christ makes it clear God is the ultimate good; only he can truly fulfill anyone and make him or her happy. Secondly, the Lord insists people follow the Commandments. Finally, he told the rich young man to sell everything and follow him.[17]

These are the elements of Christian discipleship:

- *Call, or vocation*: The Christian life stems from a call from God. Hence, the Christian life is a vocation, or calling, to a particular type of life. Christ told the rich young man, "Follow me."
- *Response*: The Christian must respond in the affirmative to God's call. This response is essential because faith, which begins with God's call, cannot flourish without it. The rich young man went away sad, unwilling to say *yes* because of his many possessions.
- *Discipleship*: The call of Christ is ordered toward being his disciple since he is the Teacher. The word disciple indicates adopting another person's way of life, taking on his or her particular discipline. As with various human disciplines in which a student follows a teacher by imitation, every Christian has to imitate the life of Christ. Christian morality and discipleship is an imitation of Christ.

The call to discipleship involves putting one's whole life at the service of Christ. "If you would be perfect, go, sell what you possess and give to the poor, and you will have treasure in heaven; and come, follow me" (Mt 19:21). Christ also addresses these words to every person in every age, and this call begs a response expressed in a willingness to give one's mind and heart to Jesus Christ and to imitate him in every action.

THE TEN COMMANDMENTS

Every human being—regardless of religious belief—is obliged to obey the natural law. This interior code of conduct is written, as it were, on the human heart by God. The natural law can be known through reason; although, because of Original Sin, people often distort it to accommodate sinful behavior. Nevertheless, everyone knows, at least on some level, he or she has an obligation to live according to the natural law.

Through Moses, God revealed the Decalogue, or Ten Commandments, to his Chosen People. This explicit articulation of the natural law gave them certainty about what is morally right and wrong. Fidelity to the Decalogue carried with it God's promise of divine blessings, and it was the Israelites' duty to transmit these Commandments to future generations.

As detailed in the Gospels, every Christian vocation to holiness begins with an invitation to embrace the Ten Commandments. Thus, when responding to the call to follow Christ, it is vital to live the Ten Commandments, which map out the revealed natural law and correspond to the human requirements of dignity and friendship with God.

The moral life in Christ is not a set of arbitrary rules determined by social agreement. It is based on objective moral principles discoverable by reason, revealed by God, and taught and perfected by Jesus Christ.

> **The Ten Commandments belong to God's revelation. At the same time they teach us the true humanity of man. They bring to light the essential duties, and therefore, indirectly, the fundamental rights inherent in the nature of the human person. The Decalogue contains a privileged expression of the natural law. (CCC 2070)**

THE TEN COMMANDMENTS

Moses with the Ten Commandments by Champaigne.

1. **I am the Lord your God: you shall not have strange gods before me.**
2. **You shall not take the name of the Lord your God in vain.**
3. **Remember to keep holy the Lord's Day.**
4. **Honor your father and your mother.**
5. **You shall not kill.**
6. **You shall not commit adultery.**
7. **You shall not steal.**
8. **You shall not bear false witness against your neighbor.**
9. **You shall not covet your neighbor's wife.**
10. **You shall not covet your neighbor's goods. (cf. Ex 20)**

The Sermon on the Mount by Fra Angelico.
The Ten Commandments were not abolished by the moral teaching of Jesus Christ; rather, he elevated them to a new and higher level.

PERFECTION OF THE MOSAIC LAW

The Ten Commandments reflect the natural law and so are valid in all times and all places. The Ten Commandments were not abolished by the moral teaching of Jesus Christ; rather, he elevated them to a new and higher level. As Christ said, "Think not that I have come to abolish the law and the prophets; I have come not to abolish them but to fulfill them."[18]

> **Since they express man's fundamental duties towards God and towards his neighbor, the Ten Commandments reveal, in their primordial content, *grave* obligations. They are fundamentally immutable, and they oblige always and everywhere. No one can dispense from them. The Ten Commandments are engraved by God in the human heart.** (CCC 2072)

Christians are called to obey the New Law of Christ, which is the restored and perfected expression of the Decalogue. The following are a few examples of how Christ perfected the Commandments of the Decalogue.

- The First Commandment requires people to place God above all things. In the Law of Christ, the acceptance and worship of the one God is enhanced by the revelation of God as not an impersonal force but *our Father* who loves his children infinitely. Moreover, each person is called to have a personal relation with the Three Persons of the Blessed Trinity: Father, Son, and Holy Spirit.
- The Fifth Commandment requires people to defend the dignity of human life. The Law of Christ goes further, admonishing his disciples not to harbor resentment toward any person and instructing them to love neighbors and even enemies in word and deed.
- The Sixth Commandment requires people to make the correct use of sexuality, while the Law of Christ demands internal chastity even in thought and desire.[19]

In the history of Divine Revelation, the clear development of the moral life is seen from the natural law to the Ten Commandments and finally to Christ's New Law of Love. Love for the whole human race.

Sermon on the Mount by Rosselli.
The disciple who truly lives the Beatitudes experiences a plenitude of grace based on intimate union with Christ.

THE BEATITUDES

In St. Matthew's Gospel, Christ began his Sermon on the Mount with the Beatitudes, which describe the moral life at its highest level—a level only possible through the grace of the Holy Spirit. Precisely by conforming one's heart to the teachings of the Beatitudes can he or she enjoy the greatest happiness in this life and perfect happiness in the next.

Christian tradition calls these teachings of Christ the *Beatitudes* because each begins with the Latin word *beati*, meaning *blessed* or *happy*.

- Blessed are the poor in spirit, for theirs is the kingdom of heaven.
- Blessed are those who mourn, for they shall be comforted.
- Blessed are the meek, for they shall inherit the earth.
- Blessed are those who hunger and thirst for righteousness, for they shall be satisfied.
- Blessed are the merciful, for they shall obtain mercy.
- Blessed are the pure in heart, for they shall see God.
- Blessed are the peacemakers, for they shall be called sons of God.
- Blessed are those who are persecuted for righteousness' sake, for theirs is the kingdom of heaven.
- Blessed are you when men revile you and persecute you and utter all kinds of evil against you falsely on my account. Rejoice and be glad, for your reward is great in heaven. (Mt 5:3-12)

Popular culture often stresses indulgence, material gain, and riches are indispensable for happiness and fulfillment. Christ declares exactly the opposite. Self-denial and detachment from material things are necessary conditions for true human perfection and lasting happiness. Only a heart formed in a spirit of meekness and humility can be filled with the life of Christ. Suffering on account of Christ and the Gospel, though counterintuitive, leads to real joy in this life and rich rewards in the next.

According to the *Catechism*, the Beatitudes "confront us with decisive choices concerning earthly goods; they purify our hearts in order to teach us to love God above all things."[20] Following Jesus Christ means accepting a life of sacrifice for the salvation of others, as he did. In this way, the Beatitudes go beyond the Ten Commandments and lead to perfection. The *Catechism* offers these further insights into the Beatitudes:

> The Beatitudes depict the countenance of Jesus Christ and portray his charity. They express the vocation of the faithful associated with the glory of his Passion and Resurrection; they shed light on the actions and attitudes characteristic of the Christian life; they are the paradoxical promises that sustain hope in the midst of tribulations; they proclaim the blessings and rewards already secured, however dimly, for Christ's disciples; they have begun in the lives of the Virgin Mary and all the saints. (CCC 1717)

The Beatitudes express the meaning of Christian discipleship.

> First, the Beatitudes express the meaning of discipleship. They become more concrete and real the more completely the disciple dedicates himself to service in the way that is illustrated for us in the life of Saint Paul. What the Beatitudes mean cannot be expressed in purely theoretical terms; it is proclaimed in the life and suffering, and in the mysterious joy, of the disciple who gives himself over completely to following the Lord. This leads to the second point: the Christological character of the Beatitudes. The disciple is bound to the mystery of Christ. His life is immersed in communion with Christ: "It is no longer I who live, but Christ who lives in me" (Gal 2:20). The Beatitudes are the transposition of Cross and Resurrection into discipleship. But they apply to the disciple because they were first paradigmatically lived by Christ himself. (Pope Benedict XVI, *Jesus of Nazareth*, 73-74)

The disciple who truly lives the Beatitudes experiences a plenitude of grace based on intimate union with Christ.

THE PRECEPTS OF THE CHURCH

The Church specifies certain duties to help live in accordance with the Ten Commandments and the morality taught by Christ. Among those expected of Catholics are the following:

1. You shall attend Mass on Sundays and on Holy Days of Obligation and rest from servile labor.	This precept requires the faithful to participate in the Eucharistic celebration when the Christian community gathers together on the day commemorating the Resurrection of the Lord and other important feast days.
2. You shall confess your sins at least once a year.	This precept ensures preparation for the Eucharist by reception of the Sacrament of Reconciliation, which continues Baptism's work of conversion and forgiveness.
3. You shall receive the sacrament of the Eucharist at least during the Easter season.	This precept guarantees as a minimum the reception of the Lord's Body and Blood in connection with the Paschal feasts, the origin and center of the Christian liturgy.
4. You shall observe the days of fasting and abstinence established by the Church.	This precept requires periods of asceticism and penance, which prepare for the liturgical feasts. It also helps acquire freedom of heart and mastery over the passions.
5. You shall help provide for the needs of the Church.	This precept requires the faithful to contribute to the Church according to their ability.

The Precepts of the Church oblige Catholics under penalty of sin, but they are not by their nature immutable. The Church can change them from time to time as she prudentially decides.

Christ in the House of Mary and Martha by Overbeck.
"'Lord, do you not care that my sister has left me to serve alone? Tell her then to help me.' But the Lord answered her, 'Martha, Martha, you are anxious and troubled about many things; one thing is needful. Mary has chosen the good portion, which shall not be taken away from her.'" (Lk 10:40-42)

THE THEOLOGICAL VIRTUES AND GROWTH IN HOLINESS

A virtue is an habitual and firm disposition to do the good. It allows the person not only to perform good acts, but to give the best of himself. The virtuous person tends toward the good with all his sensory and spiritual powers; he pursues the good and chooses it in concrete actions.

The goal of a virtuous life is to become like God.[21] (CCC 1803)

Virtues can be natural or supernatural. *Natural virtues* are good habits: a fruit of the repetition of good moral actions. For example, if someone wants to acquire the virtue of temperance with regard to food, he or she will need to expend effort to eat less over a period of time. After a while, consumption becomes easier to control, habitual, and happy. Through the performance of virtuous actions, one acquires the corresponding natural virtue.

Supernatural virtues, accompanied by sanctifying grace, are gratuitously imparted to the soul at Baptism. "They are infused by God into the souls of the faithful to make them capable of acting as his children and of meriting eternal life."[22] These virtues are called *supernatural* because they make it possible to perform supernatural acts.

The most notable infused virtues are the theological virtues: faith, hope, and charity. They are called theological because their object is union with God. Growth in the theological virtues comes through prayer, reception of the sacraments, and practice of the virtues; these practices assist growth in holiness through becoming more imbued with the life of Christ.

- **Faith** elevates the natural intellect and moves the will so a person can assent to the truths supernaturally revealed by God and put those truths into practice.
- **Hope** gives the mind and will the power to trust God will give all the means necessary to achieve everlasting life.
- **Charity** enables a person to love God above all things and his neighbor as him- or herself with the love of Christ.

Of the three theological virtues, the most important is charity. Without it, faith and hope, if present at all, are formless or dead and are ineffective to attain holiness and eternal life.

Faith, hope, love abide, these three; but the greatest of these is love. (1 Cor 13: 13)

FAITH

Faith is the theological virtue by which we believe in God and believe all that he has said and revealed to us, and that the Holy Church proposes for our belief, because he is truth itself. (CCC 1814)

God infuses the virtue of faith into the soul at Baptism to assist in accepting the truths he has revealed through his Church. Faith signifies a person's belief in God and the adherence of his or her heart and soul to God's Revelation.

To have faith means to accept truths guaranteed by the authority of God. Because it is based on God's revealed truth, faith cannot contradict human reason; rather, it enables a person to believe and understand truths beyond the scope of human reason. Some examples include the doctrines of God as a Trinity of Persons; Jesus Christ as one divine Person with two natures, human and divine; and Christ as truly present in the Holy Eucharist under the appearance of bread and wine. Once these truths are accepted, human reason attempts to understand and defend them. This is the proper role of theological studies, which may be understood as *faith seeking understanding*.

Nevertheless, the practice of the virtue of faith should never be reduced to a mere intellectual or academic acceptance of Catholic doctrine. Faith is meant to be lived in a manner that inspires every facet of life. For instance, faith in the Real Presence of Christ in the Eucharist is only exercised fully when there is an eagerness to receive Communion often and spend time in prayer before the Blessed Sacrament.

Faith, a great gift from God, is given to all who ask for it; nonetheless, it can be lost if it is neglected. In order to safeguard and increase faith, one must live the Faith. Studying the truths God has revealed to the Church through Jesus Christ and praying for greater understanding is necessary, but a person cannot expect God's assistance if he or she is not also striving to live according to the moral teachings of Jesus Christ. Loss of faith often has less to do with intellectual doubts than a reluctance to embrace God's moral law. For example, someone who ignores Christ's teaching to avoid being angry with people will be more likely to ignore the related Commandment against murder.

Doubting Thomas by Strozzi.
Loss of faith often has less to do with intellectual doubts than a reluctance to embrace God's moral law.

Christ and the Centurion (detail) by Veronese.
The virtue of faith requires the baptized not only to believe in Christ but also to spread the Faith to others.

Since faith is necessary for salvation, each person has the serious obligation to protect his or her faith and avoid anything that might harm it. Faith can be damaged or even lost by exposure to false teachings, which plant doubts concerning the truth of God's Revelation.

For example, books that criticize, distort, or ridicule the Faith should be avoided. The most profound convictions can be obscured when attacked by incorrect ideologies, which are often presented in clever and appealing ways. Exercising prudence also requires the same discretion to choose what to watch or listen to, whom to befriend, and even how to assess what teachers say. Unfortunately, many educational authorities advocate anti-Christian ideologies.

It is wise to have someone who can give advice concerning questions about books, movies, or activities that might harm faith. Such an advisor might be a parent, godparent, teacher, or priest. The obligation to use prudence in exposure to contrary ideas does not mean the Church is afraid of certain ideas or cannot refute them; the problem lies in individuals, who sometimes lack sufficient formation and can be overwhelmed by false ideas.

The virtue of faith requires the baptized not only to believe in Christ but also to spread the Faith to others. This call to evangelize (also called the apostolate) is part of the Christian vocation. However, before a Christian can share the Faith with others, he or she must know it and live it. Once a life bears witness to interior faith, there will be many opportunities to share it with others.

Faith requires more from us than simply caring for it within oneself.

> **The disciple of Christ must not only keep the faith and live on it, but also profess it, confidently bear witness to it, and spread it.** (CCC 1816)

Sins Against Faith

The five primary sins against faith are *voluntary doubt*, *schism*, *heresy*, *apostasy*, and *atheism*.

Voluntary doubt intentionally calls into question or ignores some aspect of Divine Revelation. This indicates a lack of humility and a lack of openness to embrace the Faith fully. Voluntary doubt is different from questioning, which seeks greater understanding of the mysteries of Faith.

Schism is a refusal to submit oneself to the authority of the pope or to the bishops in communion with him even though no formal rejection of a truth of Faith is necessarily made. Schism opposes the unity of the Church and the authority established by Christ himself.

Heresy is the decisive denial by a baptized person of one or more tenets of the Faith. A person who obstinately denies the truth of the Immaculate Conception or the Real Presence of Christ in the Eucharist, for example, falls into heresy.

Apostasy is an implicit or explicit total repudiation of the Christian Faith.

Atheism denies the very existence of God. With God's existence rejected, any personal relationship with him and any sense of objective morality are impossible. Several atheistic political regimes of the twentieth century are a painful testimony to the evil that can occur when the rejection of God is mandated by law.

HOPE

Hope is the theological virtue by which we desire the kingdom of heaven and eternal life as our happiness, placing our trust in Christ's promises and relying not on our own strength, but on the help of the grace of the Holy Spirit....The virtue of hope responds to the aspiration to happiness which God has placed in the heart of every man; it takes up the hopes that inspire men's activities and purifies them so as to order them to the Kingdom of heaven; it keeps man from discouragement; it sustains him during times of abandonment; it opens up his heart in expectation of eternal beatitude. Buoyed up by hope, he is preserved from selfishness and led to the happiness that flows from charity. (CCC 1817-1818)

The virtue of hope is the confident expectation God will give the capacity to respond to his love so as to achieve a life of sanctity. Hope enables a person to rely on God's grace and trust in his promises of salvation and everlasting life in Heaven.

God calls every person to a life of holiness. The response, however, cannot rest solely on human strength; God's help is necessary. The virtue of hope signifies a joyful expectation: God—not by reason of any human merit but out of his supreme goodness—will give the necessary graces to return his love and follow his will in this life, thereby attaining eternal life. Through hope, one can expect God will supply all of the graces necessary for salvation.

To this end we toil and strive, because we have our hope set on the living God, who is the Savior of all men, especially of those who believe. (1 Tm 4: 10)

Hope, like the other theological virtues, must be nurtured. The virtue of hope can be fostered in life through prayer. It can also be cultivated in others by reminding them of God's love and mercy and by praying God will give them hope in difficult situations.

Sins Against Hope

The sins against hope are *despair* and *presumption*.

Despair is the loss of trust in God because of doubt in his fidelity or his interest in each person.

By *despair*, man ceases to hope for his personal salvation from God, for help in attaining it or for the forgiveness of his sins. Despair is contrary to God's goodness, to his justice—for the Lord is faithful to his promises—and to his mercy. (CCC 2091)

An example of despair was Judas' suicide. Judas falsely thought he could never have been forgiven for betraying Christ.

Presumption is either expecting salvation without personal effort or trusting solely in human effort without the aid of the Holy Spirit.

There are two kinds of *presumption*. Either man presumes upon his own capacities (hoping to be able to save himself without help from on high), or he presumes upon God's almighty power or his mercy (hoping to obtain his forgiveness without conversion and glory without merit). (CCC 2092)

Christ in the Wilderness by Kramskoy.
Presumption is either expecting salvation without personal effort or trusting solely in human effort without the aid of the Holy Spirit.

Satan's temptation for Christ to hurl himself from the pinnacle of the Temple was the sin of presumption. In effect, Satan said God would automatically save Christ though he would have been wrongly putting his life at risk. Christ's answer: "You shall not tempt the Lord your God."[23]

Legend of St. Francis: St. Francis Giving his Mantle to a Poor Man (detail) by Giotto.
The greatest fruit of the redemption is the capacity to love as Christ loved through the infusion of the theological virtue of charity.

CHARITY

Charity is the theological virtue by which we love God above all things for his own sake, and our neighbor as ourselves for the love of God. (CCC 1822)

Charity enables a person to love God above all things. God loves his creatures freely and unconditionally, without limits or requirements. It is just and right, then, his love should be returned. Every person ought to love God because he is Creator, Father, and Savior. Love for God should reflect his love. People should love God "because he first loved us."[24]

The greatest fruit of the redemption is the capacity to love as Christ loved through the infusion of the theological virtue of charity. In fact, every virtue is at the service of the fullness of charity. The saints show a tremendous love for God and neighbor in imitation of Christ. As charity is practiced, it grows until he or she actually becomes Christlike in the ability to love God and neighbor.

As a consequence of Original Sin, the call to love God is sometimes difficult. People often do evil or fail to do what should be done. These sins cause separation from God. On his or her own, every person falls short in love of God. Only with God's help, through the virtue of charity, will he or she receive the graces needed to respond to his love and to love neighbor as self.

To foster the virtue of charity, it is helpful to recall God's goodness. He calls people into existence and sustains their lives; he freely loves people and calls them to love in return. Man was created, in fact, to love and to be loved by God. Every person needs to reflect often on the greatness of God's love as expressed in the Passion and Death of his Son, Jesus Christ.

See what love the Father has given us, that we should be called children of God; and so we are. (1 Jn 3:1)

ST. FRANCIS DE SALES

St. Francis de Sales was born in 1567, the oldest of twelve children. His father belonged to an aristocratic family, and he wanted St. Francis to become a magistrate. St. Francis, on the other hand, dreamed of being a soldier. When St. Francis was twelve, his father sent him to Paris, where he studied rhetoric and humanities in a college run by the Jesuits. While there, St. Francis suffered a particularly intense religious crisis which left him physically ill. Upon visiting the Church of St. Stephen, St. Francis recovered and made a vow of chastity, consecrating himself to the Blessed Virgin Mary.

St. Francis, however, did not tell his family he intended to become a priest. He continued in school, eventually becoming a lawyer and being appointed a senator. It was not until his father arranged a marriage for him that St. Francis declared his intention to enter the priesthood. This created a deep conflict with his father, who opposed the idea. Eventually, the Bishop of Geneva resolved the issue by giving St. Francis a position under the patronage of the pope. In 1593, Francis received the Sacrament of Holy Orders.

St. Francis worked tirelessly to preach the Gospel, hear confessions, and give spiritual direction to the lay faithful. The next year, full of apostolic zeal, he volunteered to evangelize an area of Switzerland where the Reformed Protestant religion had taken root. He left on this mission full of hope but with no money and only his cousin to assist him.

Though St. Francis worked tirelessly and suffered immense hardships, he found no one would listen to him. At the end of three years, he had made no converts, and even his cousin left him. St. Francis was patient, however, and did not give up. He tried a new tactic. If people would not listen to him, then maybe they would read what he had to say. He prepared pamphlets of his sermons explaining and defending the Catholic Faith and began to distribute them to people in the area. When doors were slammed in his face, he would slide the pamphlets under the door. Gradually, more and more people began to read the pamphlets. Before he left the area, more than 40,000 people had converted to the Catholic Faith.

In 1602, St. Francis was consecrated bishop of Geneva. As a bishop, St. Francis lived a very simple and ascetic life. He always had a great love for the laity, and he began his role as bishop by providing for the catechetical instruction of the faithful in his diocese. Emphasizing that God calls all people to a life of holiness, he guided his priests to offer good formation and spiritual direction to those entrusted to their care. In fact, his best known book, *Introduction to the Devout Life*, was directed toward helping the laity grow in the life of piety.

St. Francis died in 1622 and was canonized in 1665, being proclaimed a Doctor of the Church in 1877. His feast day is January 24 (January 29 in the extraordinary form of the Latin Rite).

Illustration: *The Blessed Virgin Appearing to St. Francis de Sales* (detail) by Maratta.

The Mercy of Fra Martin de Vizcaya (detail) by Zurbaran.
The Lord makes it abundantly clear, especially in a culture that may be indifferent or even hostile to the Faith, Christian charity is the only response.

Charity also moves Christians to love their neighbors out of love for God with the heart of Christ. In other words, it empowers them to love others as Christ loves because they are children of God bought with the Blood of Christ's redemption. Holiness, then, can be summed up as the *fullness of charity*.

The call to be faithful to Christ's New Commandment of Love is not based on mere emotional sentiment but on a generous spirit of sacrifice. Aided by grace and a generous response, the exercise of charity is expressed in a selfless service that tries to bring about happiness in others.

In imitation of Christ's life of service and redemptive sacrifice, Christians must strive to lay down their lives for others. The Lord makes it abundantly clear, especially in a culture that may be indifferent or even hostile to the Faith, Christian charity is the only response.

Sins Against Charity

Sins against God's love take various forms:

Indifference is the refusal to reflect on the prior goodness and power of divine charity. It results in a lack of commitment to exercise the Faith.

Ingratitude is the refusal to acknowledge divine charity or try to respond to God's love. It is a failure to recognize and acknowledge God's blessings.

Lukewarmness is failure or hesitation to respond to divine love; it can imply refusal to obey the prompting of charity. It consists in a lackluster, lazy, or perfunctory fulfillment of the Faith.

Acedia, or sloth, is the refusal of the joy God gives, and it causes a person to be repelled by divine goodness. It is a form of depression that leads to discouragement or even despair.

Hatred of God opposes the love of God, denies his goodness, and curses him as the one who forbids sin and inflicts punishment. It is a result of pride.

THE GIFTS OF THE HOLY SPIRIT

The gifts of the Holy Spirit are supernatural habits that are infused into the soul together with sanctifying grace at Baptism. Sacred Scripture lists seven gifts of the Holy Spirit.[25] Of these, four act on the intellect (wisdom, understanding, counsel, and knowledge), while three act on the will (fortitude, piety, and fear of the Lord).

WISDOM (Enjoying the Presence of God):

The fruit of perfect charity, wisdom strengthens the loving knowledge of God and all that leads to and comes from him. Wisdom allows contemplation of God and enjoyment of his divine life, savoring the things of God.

> **Wisdom is a fountain of life to him who has it.** (Prv 16: 22)

UNDERSTANDING (Discerning Divine Truths):

The gift of understanding enhances the perception of the mysteries of the Faith, enabling deeper penetration of the divine truths revealed by God. This gift enables appreciation of the fullness of the Catholic Faith and comprehension of Divine Revelation hidden from the human intellect.

> **Happy is the man who finds wisdom, and the man who gets understanding.** (Prv 3: 13)

COUNSEL (Making Wise Decisions):

Counsel helps to judge promptly, correctly, and according to the will of God. It enables one to choose wisely actions intended for the glory of God, for salvation, and to help others. Flowing from the gifts of wisdom and understanding, counsel perfects the virtue of prudence and helps to know what should or should not be done in situations requiring a moral decision.

> **Thy testimonies are my delight, they are my counselors.** (Ps 119: 24)

St. John Baptizing by Unknown Master.
Sacred Scripture lists seven gifts of the Holy Spirit. Of these, four act on the intellect (wisdom, understanding, counsel, and knowledge), while three act on the will (fortitude, piety, and fear of the Lord).

Crucifixion of St. Peter by Giordano.
Fortitude gives the strength and courage to profess and defend the truths of the Faith.

FORTITUDE (Having Strength of Character):

Fortitude causes steadfastness in the Faith, constancy in struggle, and faithfulness in perseverance, communicating vigor and encouragement to the soul beyond human capability. It gives the strength and courage to profess and defend the truths of the Faith, to endure long and trying difficulties, to avoid dangers and temptations, and to complete the tasks God has planned.

The LORD is the strength of his people, he is the saving refuge of his anointed. (Ps 28: 8)

KNOWLEDGE (Using Created Things Wisely):

Knowledge enables discovery of the real purpose of God's creation and the path to Heaven. It permits a life of detachment, using created things as God intended. It helps to understand created things and their relationship with God.

Take my instruction instead of silver, and knowledge rather than choice gold. (Prv 8: 10)

PIETY (Knowing God as "Abba"):

The gift of piety teaches the meaning of divine filiation; comprehends the joyful, supernatural awareness of being children of God; and recognizes brothers and sisters in all mankind. Piety leads to a true love for God as a merciful Father and for all human beings as his children; it allows people to give him the honor and glory that are due him.

All who are led by the Spirit of God are sons of God. (Rom 8: 14)

FEAR OF THE LORD (Serving God Faithfully):

Fear of the Lord deepens a sense of sovereign respect in the presence of the all-powerful and loving God. This gift leads to an appreciation and detestation of the evil of sin and also impresses upon the heart a spirit of adoration for God and a profound and sincere humility.

The fear of the LORD is the beginning of wisdom. (Ps 111: 10)

THE FRUITS OF THE HOLY SPIRIT

The fruits of the Holy Spirit are those supernatural acts, performed with peace and joy, that flow from the gifts of the Holy Spirit. In a certain sense, they can be seen as twelve aspects of the virtue of charity. Their designation as *fruits* signifies they are performed with pleasure and ease—all difficulties disappearing in light of the satisfaction that results from the good accomplished. Scripture lists the fruits of the Holy Spirit: charity, joy, peace, patience, kindness, goodness, generosity, gentleness, faithfulness, modesty, self-control, and chastity. While traditionally designated as twelve in number, the fruits of the Holy Spirit may be extended to include all acts of a similar nature.

> **"Justified in the name of the Lord Jesus Christ and in the Spirit of our God,"[26] "sanctified... [and] called to be saints,"[27] Christians have become the temple of the *Holy Spirit*.[28] This "Spirit of the Son" teaches them to pray to the Father[29] and, having become their life, prompts them to act so as to bear "the fruit of the Spirit"[30] by charity in action. Healing the wounds of sin, the Holy Spirit renews us interiorly through a spiritual transformation.[31] He enlightens and strengthens us to live as "children of light" through "all that is good and right and true."[32] (CCC 1695)**

CONCLUSION

The redemption has made it possible for God to call everyone to be another Christ and to live a life of holiness. This vocation invites each person to use both human and supernatural means to pursue sanctity in his or her everyday activities, offering the circumstances and events of life as spiritual sacrifices. While living a moral life in Christ is impossible by human effort alone, God gives abundant graces to make it possible.

The Martyrdom of St. Stephen (detail) by Stella.
The Holy Spirit gave St. Stephen wisdom, counsel, and fortitude.
There are as many ways to become saints as there are people.

The moral law within Christianity is grounded in the natural law God gave to all people and in the Ten Commandments he gave to Moses. Christ perfected the moral law in his Law of Love, which calls for conversion of heart. Christians imitate Christ by loving their neighbors the way God loves. The Beatitudes show how the human heart must be conditioned and transformed to reflect the heart of Christ.

To help achieve holiness, God gives the infused theological virtues of faith, hope, and charity. The gifts of the Holy Spirit facilitate the practice of these virtues.

Among the many opportunities for success in this life, any vocation offers the possibility of becoming a true saint. As St. Paul noted, every person has been called by God to play a special role in his Mystical Body, the Church.

There are as many ways to become saints as there are people. There will be disappointments and human failings along the way, but, as long as a person is doing his or her best to serve God, success is guaranteed. All this is made possible by participation in those graced actions of Christ called sacraments, initiated by Baptism and intensified by Reconciliation and the Eucharist. God expects each person to choose these means he has provided through the Church to help every person reach the goal of eternal life.

SUPPLEMENTARY READING

1. *Keep Watch: He Is to Come Again*

To prevent his disciples from asking the time of his coming, Christ said: "About that hour no one knows, neither the angels nor the Son. It is not for you to know times or moments." He has kept those things hidden so that we may keep watch, each of us thinking that he will come in our own day. If he had revealed the time of his coming, his coming would have lost its savor: it would no longer be an object of yearning for the nations and the age in which it will be revealed. He promised that he would come but did not say when he would come, and so all generations and ages await him eagerly.

Though the Lord has established the signs of his coming, the time of their fulfillment has not been plainly revealed. These signs have come and gone with a multiplicity of change; more than that, they are still present. His final coming is like his first. As holy men and prophets waited for him, thinking that he would reveal himself in their own day, so today each of the faithful longs to welcome him in his own day, because Christ has not made plain the day of his coming.

— St. Ephrem, *Commentary on the Diatessaron*

2. *The Cross Exemplifies Every Virtue*

Why did the Son of God have to suffer for us? There was a great need, and it can be considered in a twofold way: in the first place, as a remedy for sin, and secondly, as an example of how to act.

It is a remedy, for, in the face of all the evils which we incur on account of our sins, we have found relief through the passion of Christ. Yet, it is no less an example, for the passion of Christ completely suffices to fashion our lives. Whoever wishes to live perfectly should do nothing but disdain what Christ disdained on the cross and desire what he desired, for the cross exemplifies every virtue.

If you seek the example of love: Greater love than this no man has, than to lay down his life for his friends. Such a man was Christ on the cross. And if he gave his life for us, then it should not be difficult to bear whatever hardships arise for his sake.

If you seek patience, you will find no better example than the cross. Great patience occurs in two ways: either when one patiently suffers much, or when one suffers things which one is able to avoid and yet does not avoid. Christ endured much on the cross, and did so patiently, because when he suffered he did not threaten; he was led like a sheep to the slaughter and he did not open his mouth. Therefore Christ's patience on the cross was great. In patience let us run for the prize set before us, looking upon Jesus, the author and perfecter of our faith who, for the joy set before him, bore his cross and despised the shame.

If you seek an example of humility, look upon the crucified one, for God wished to be judged by Pontius Pilate and to die.

If you seek an example of obedience, follow him who became obedient to the Father even unto death. For just as by the disobedience of one man, namely, Adam, many were made sinners, so by the obedience of one man, many were made righteous.

If you seek an example of despising earthly things, follow him who is the King of kings and the Lord of lords, in whom are hidden all the treasures of wisdom and knowledge. Upon the cross he was stripped, mocked, spat upon, struck, crowned with thorns, and given only vinegar and gall to drink.

— St. Thomas Aquinas, *Colatio 6 super Credo in Deum*

SUPPLEMENTARY READING Continued

3. *Without Love Everything Is in Vain*

Charity is a right attitude of mind which prefers nothing to the knowledge of God. If a man possesses any strong attachment to the things of this earth, he cannot possess true charity. For anyone who really loves God prefers to know and experience God rather than his creatures. The whole set and longing of his mind is ever directed toward him.

For God is far superior to all his creation, since everything which exists has been made by God and for him. And so, in deserting God, who is beyond compare, for the inferior works of creation, a man shows that he values God, the author of creation, less than creation itself.

The Lord himself reminds us: "Whoever loves me will keep my commandments. And this is my commandment: that you love one another." So the man who does not love his neighbor does not obey God's command. But one who does not obey his command cannot love God. A man is blessed if he can love all men equally. Moreover, if he truly loves God, he must love his neighbor absolutely. Such a man cannot hoard his wealth. Rather, like God himself, he generously gives from his own resources to each man according to his needs.

Since he imitates God's generosity, the only distinction he draws is the person's need. He does not distinguish between a good man and a bad one, a just man and one who is unjust. Yet his own goodness of will makes him prefer the man who strives after virtue to the one who is depraved.

A charitable mind is not displayed simply in giving money; it is manifested still more by personal service as well as by the communication of God's word to others: In fact, if a man's service toward his brothers is genuine and if he really renounces worldly concerns, he is freed from selfish desires. For he now shares in God's own knowledge and love. Since he does possess God's love, he does not experience weariness as he follows the Lord his God. Rather, following the prophet Jeremiah, he withstands every type of reproach and hardship without even harboring an evil thought toward any man.

For Jeremiah warns us: 'Do not say: "We are the Lord's temple." Neither should you say: "Faith alone in our Lord Jesus Christ can save me."' By itself faith accomplishes nothing. "For even the devils believe and shudder."

No, faith must be joined to an active love of God which is expressed in good works. The charitable man is distinguished by sincere and long-suffering service to his fellow man: it also means using things aright.

—St. Maximus the Confessor, *A Treatise on Charity*

Bl. Teresa of Calcutta, (1910-1997), born Agnesë Gonxhe Bojaxhiu, was an Albanian Catholic nun with Indian citizenship who founded the Missionaries of Charity in Calcutta, India in 1950. For over 45 years, she ministered to the poor, sick, orphaned, and dying, while guiding the Missionaries of Charity's expansion, first throughout India and then in other countries.

At the time of her death, Bl. Teresa's Missionaries of Charity operated 610 missions in 123 countries, including hospices and homes for people with AIDS, leprosy, and tuberculosis; soup kitchens; family counseling programs; orphanages; and schools.

She was beatified by Pope John Paul II on October 19, 2003.

VOCABULARY

ACTUAL GRACE
This supernatural, free, and undeserved help from God is given in specific circumstances to help choose the good and avoid evil.

BEATITUDES
The teachings of Christ in the Sermon on the Mount about the meaning and way to true happiness (cf. Mt 5: 3-12). They are at the heart of Christ's preaching and fulfill the promises of God starting with Abraham.

CHRISTIAN DISCIPLESHIP
Being a follower of Christ. This involves a conversion of heart and a life centered on Jesus Christ as well as following his teachings and being a witness to others.

COMMON PRIESTHOOD OF THE FAITHFUL
The participation in the priesthood of Christ shared by all the faithful through Baptism.

CONSCIENCE
The inner voice of a human being, in whose heart is inscribed the Law of God. Moral conscience is a judgment of practical reason about the moral quality of a human action that a person may do, is in the process of doing, or has already done.

GIFTS OF THE HOLY SPIRIT
The seven gifts of the Holy Spirit are wisdom, understanding, counsel, fortitude, knowledge, piety, and fear of the Lord. They belong in their fullness to Christ as Son of David. They complete and perfect the virtues of those who receive them. They make the faithful docile in readily accepting divine inspirations (cf. CCC 1831). These gifts are given to Christians to assist in following Christ and are conferred in a special way in the Sacrament of Confirmation.

GRACE
The free and undeserved gift of God to respond to one's vocation to become his adopted son or daughter.

HOLINESS
Principally an attribute of God describing his complete separation from the sphere of the profane. Individual human beings may become holy by dedicating themselves completely to God. Holiness is the perfection of charity.

LAITY
The faithful who, having been incorporated into Christ through Baptism, are made part of the People of God, the Church. They are not in Holy Orders or the consecrated life.

LAW OF LOVE
Christ taught his followers to love God above all else and love their neighbors as themselves. This teaching elevated and perfected the Old Law.

MINISTERIAL PRIESTHOOD
Distinct from the common priesthood of the faithful, the ministerial priesthood consists of those men who have received the Sacrament of Holy Orders in order to minister to the needs of the faithful.

NATURAL LAW
The objective order established by God that determines the requirements for people to thrive and reach fulfillment. The participation of man in the plan of God in relation to human life and action insofar as the mind can understand it. Natural law "enables man to discern by reason the good and the evil, the truth and the lie" (CCC 1954).

PRECEPTS OF THE CHURCH
Duties required by the Catholic Church of her members in order to ensure a certain minimum in their spiritual and moral lives.

SAINT
A person on earth, in Purgatory, or in Heaven notable for holiness and heroic virtue. The saints share in God's life, glory, and happiness. The Church may officially declare someone a saint through the process of beatification and canonization.

VOCABULARY Continued

SANCTIFICATION
The process of being made holy. This begins with Baptism, continues throughout the life of the Christian, and is completed when a person enters Heaven and becomes totally and irrevocably united with God in the Beatific Vision.

THEOLOGICAL VIRTUES
Faith, hope, and charity. Infused in the soul at Baptism, these enable a Christian to partake of the divine nature; they are called *theological* because they have God as their object.

UNIVERSAL CALL TO HOLINESS
Every baptized person is called to seek holiness regardless of his or her state in life. This call was reaffirmed by the Second Vatican Council.

STUDY QUESTIONS

1. Of what does holiness consist according to *Lumen Gentium*?
2. Who is called to holiness according to *Lumen Gentium*?
3. What is morality?
4. What is a moral life in Christ?
5. What does it mean to be created in the image of God?
6. What supernatural gifts did Adam and Eve possess?
7. What does it mean to say man is born in a *fallen* state?
8. What is objective redemption?
9. What is subjective redemption?
10. What is the relationship between freedom and sanctity?
11. Which aspects of life can be oriented toward God?
12. Why does God give grace?
13. What is sanctifying grace?
14. What is actual grace?
15. What is conscience?
16. What kind of friendship does grace help establish?
17. Do Christians have to obey the Ten Commandments? Why or why not?
18. What did Christ mean when he said he did not come to abolish the Law but to fulfill it?
19. What is an example of Christ perfecting the Mosaic Law?
20. What is paradoxical about the Beatitudes?
21. What is the double meaning of *blessed* in the Beatitudes?
22. What is a virtue?
23. What is the difference between a natural and a supernatural virtue?
24. What are faith, hope, and charity?

STUDY QUESTIONS Continued

25. How does faith relate to reason?
26. Why must Catholics be prudent when exposing themselves to books, films, music, and the Internet?
27. Identify and briefly define some sins against faith.
28. What is desired by the virtue of hope?
29. Identify and briefly define the sins against hope.
30. Why should a person love God?
31. Why should a person love his or her neighbor?
32. What is the essence of charity toward a neighbor?
33. Identify and briefly define some sins against charity.
34. What are the gifts of the Holy Spirit?
35. What are the fruits of the Holy Spirit?
36. In what three offices of Christ do the faithful also share?

Sermon on the Mount (detail) by Carbonero.
Only a heart formed in a spirit of meekness and humility can be filled with the life of Christ.

PRACTICAL EXERCISES

1. Because Christ's followers share in everything of Christ, they have the vocation to live as kings, priests, and prophets. How can you live this amazing vocation now? Provide one concrete way you can live as a king, a priest, and a prophet in imitation of Christ.

2. What aspect of the faith do you find the most challenging with respect to conversion of heart? Is there any aspect or teaching of the Church you find difficult to understand? How might you overcome this difficulty?

3. Read the Sermon on the Mount in its entirety (Matthew 5-7). Choosing one of the following topics, explain how Christ fulfilled the Mosaic Law:

- killing
- adultery
- marriage
- swearing of oaths
- justice toward enemies
- public piety

4. Choose one of the Beatitudes and show how it relates to the Ten Commandments. Then show how it goes beyond the Commandments, leading to Christian perfection.

5. Some 500 years before Christ, the Greek philosopher Aristotle explained most natural virtues represent a golden mean between two contradictory vices: one a deficiency of the virtue and one an excess of it. Choose one of the virtues below and (1) define the virtue, its vice of deficiency, and its vice of excess; (2) explain how the vices could harm and the virtue could help your natural life; and (3) do the same for your spiritual life.

Natural Virtue	*Vice of Deficiency*	*Vice of Excess*
Courage	cowardice	foolhardiness
Generosity	miserliness	prodigality
Perseverance	fickleness	bullheadedness
Obedience	disobedience	slavishness
Industriousness	laziness	workaholism
Chastity	impurity	prudery

6. Find a spiritual director, someone who can help you to pray every day, to choose appropriate spiritual reading, and to make important decisions about your future. To get started you may want to try a priest, sister, devout family member, teacher, or other adviser.

The Prodigal Son by Rosa.
The parable of the Prodigal Son (Lk 15:11-32) is a story about Vices of Deficiency, Vices of Excess, and, finally, a story of Obedience and Redemption.

FROM THE CATECHISM

1717 The Beatitudes depict the countenance of Jesus Christ and portray his charity. They express the vocation of the faithful associated with the glory of his Passion and Resurrection; they shed light on the actions and attitudes characteristic of the Christian life; they are the paradoxical promises that sustain hope in the midst of tribulations; they proclaim the blessings and rewards already secured, however dimly, for Christ's disciples; they have begun in the lives of the Virgin Mary and all the saints.

1719 The Beatitudes reveal the goal of human existence, the ultimate end of human acts: God calls us to his own beatitude. This vocation is addressed to each individual personally, but also to the Church as a whole, the new people made up of those who have accepted the promise and live from it in faith.

1721 God put us in the world to know, to love, and to serve him, and so to come to paradise. Beatitude makes us "partakers of the divine nature" and of eternal life.[33] With beatitude, man enters into the glory of Christ[34] and into the joy of the Trinitarian life.

1804 *Human virtues* are firm attitudes, stable dispositions, habitual perfections of intellect and will that govern our actions, order our passions, and guide our conduct according to reason and faith. They make possible ease, self-mastery, and joy in leading a morally good life. The virtuous man is he who freely practices the good.

The moral virtues are acquired by human effort. They are the fruit and seed of morally good acts; they dispose all the powers of the human being for communion with divine love.

1805 Four virtues play a pivotal role and accordingly are called "cardinal"; all the others are grouped around them. They are: prudence, justice, fortitude, and temperance. "If anyone loves righteousness, [Wisdom's] labors are virtues; for she teaches temperance and prudence, justice, and courage."[35] These virtues are praised under other names in many passages of Scripture.

1806 *Prudence* is the virtue that disposes practical reason to discern our true good in every circumstance and to choose the right means of achieving it; "the prudent man looks where he is going."[36] "Keep sane and sober for your prayers."[37] Prudence is "right reason in action," writes St. Thomas Aquinas, following Aristotle.[38] It is not to be confused with timidity or fear, nor with duplicity or dissimulation. It is called *auriga virtutum* (the charioteer of the virtues); it guides the other virtues by setting rule and measure. It is prudence that immediately guides the judgment of conscience. The prudent man determines and directs his conduct in accordance with this judgment. With the help of this virtue we apply moral principles to particular cases without error and overcome doubts about the good to achieve and the evil to avoid.

1807 *Justice* is the moral virtue that consists in the constant and firm will to give their due to God and neighbor. Justice toward God is called the "virtue of religion." Justice toward men disposes one to respect the rights of each and to establish in human relationships the harmony that promotes equity with regard to persons and to the common good. The just man, often mentioned in the Sacred Scriptures, is distinguished by habitual right thinking and the uprightness of his conduct toward his neighbor. "You shall not be partial to the poor or defer to the great, but in righteousness shall you judge your neighbor."[39] "Masters, treat your slaves justly and fairly, knowing that you also have a Master in heaven."[40]

1808 *Fortitude* is the moral virtue that ensures firmness in difficulties and constancy in the pursuit of the good. It strengthens the resolve to resist temptations and to overcome obstacles in the moral life. The virtue of fortitude enables one to conquer fear, even fear of death, and to face trials and persecutions. It disposes one even to renounce and sacrifice his life in defense of a just cause. "The Lord is my strength and my song."[41] "In the world you have tribulation; but be of good cheer, I have overcome the world."[42]

FROM THE CATECHISM Continued

1809 *Temperance* is the moral virtue that moderates the attraction of pleasures and provides balance in the use of created goods. It ensures the will's mastery over instincts and keeps desires within the limits of what is honorable. The temperate person directs the sensitive appetites toward what is good and maintains a healthy discretion: "Do not follow your inclination and strength, walking according to the desires of your heart."[43] Temperance is often praised in the Old Testament: "Do not follow your base desires, but restrain your appetites."[44] In the New Testament it is called "moderation" or "sobriety." We ought "to live sober, upright, and godly lives in this world."[45]

> To live well is nothing other than to love God with all one's heart, with all one's soul and with all one's efforts; from this it comes about that love is kept whole and uncorrupted (through temperance). No misfortune can disturb it (and this is fortitude). It obeys only [God] (and this is justice), and is careful in discerning things, so as not to be surprised by deceit or trickery (and this is prudence).[46]

1812 The human virtues are rooted in the theological virtues, which adapt man's faculties for participation in the divine nature:[47] for the theological virtues relate directly to God. They dispose Christians to live in a relationship with the Holy Trinity. They have the One and Triune God for their origin, motive, and object.

1813 The theological virtues are the foundation of Christian moral activity; they animate it and give it its special character. They inform and give life to all the moral virtues. They are infused by God into the souls of the faithful to make them capable of acting as his children and of meriting eternal life. They are the pledge of the presence and action of the Holy Spirit in the faculties of the human being. There are three theological virtues: faith, hope, and charity.[48]

2014 Spiritual progress tends toward ever more intimate union with Christ. This union is called "mystical" because it participates in the mystery of Christ through the sacraments—"the holy mysteries"—and, in him, in the mystery of the Holy Trinity. God calls us all to this intimate union with him, even if the special graces or extraordinary signs of this mystical life are granted only to some for the sake of manifesting the gratuitous gift given to all.

2015 The way of perfection passes by way of the Cross. There is no holiness without renunciation and spiritual battle.[49] Spiritual progress entails the ascesis and mortification that gradually lead to living in the peace and joy of the Beatitudes:

> He who climbs never stops going from beginning to beginning, through beginnings that have no end. He never stops desiring what he already knows.[50]

2028 "All Christians . . . are called to the fullness of Christian life and to the perfection of charity" (*LG* 40 § 2). "Christian perfection has but one limit, that of having none" (St. Gregory of Nyssa, *De vita Mos.*: *PG* 44, 300D).

2029 "If any man would come after me, let him deny himself and take up his cross and follow me" (Mt 16:24).

Christ and the Pilgrims of Emmaus (detail) by Velázquez.
"God put us in the world to know, to love, and to serve him, and so to come to paradise." (CCC 1721)

The Lord's Prayer by Tissot.
"Pray then like this: Our Father who art in heaven, Hallowed be thy name. Thy kingdom come. Thy will be done, On earth as it is in heaven. Give us this day our daily bread; And forgive us our debts, As we also have forgiven our debtors; And lead us not into temptation, But deliver us from evil." (Mt 6: 9-13)

ENDNOTES - CHAPTER SIX

1. Mt 5: 48; cf. St. Gregory the Great, *Hom in Evang.* 19, 1: PL 76, 1154 B. St. Augustine, *Serm.* 341, 9, 11: PL 39, 1499 s. St. John Damascene, *Adv. Iconocl.* 11: PG 96, 1357.
2. Cf. Mk 12: 30.
3. Cf Jn 13: 34; 15: 12.
4. Eph 5: 3.
5. Col 3: 12.
6. Cf. Gal 5: 22; Rom 6: 22.
7. Cf. Jas 3: 2.
8. Mt 6: 12.
9. Cf. Mt 5: 23-24, 44-45; 6: 7, 14-15, 21, 25, 33.
10. Mt 5: 44.
11. Cf. Mt 25: 31-46.
12. Col 1: 24.
13. Pope Pius XII, Discourse, February 20, 1946: AAS 38 (1946) 149.
14. Cf. CCC 2022.
15. St. Augustine, *In ep Jo.* 8, 9: PL 35, 2041.
16. Jn 15: 5.
17. Cf. Mt 19: 16-22.
18. Mt 5: 17.
19. Cf. Mt 5: 17-48.
20. CCC 1728.
21. St. Gregory of Nyssa, *De beatitudinibus*, 1: PG 44, 1200D.
22. CCC 1813.
23. Mt 4: 7.
24. 1 Jn 4: 19.
25. Cf. Is 11: 2-3.
26. 1 Cor 6: 11.
27. 1 Cor 1: 2.
28. Cf. 1 Cor 6: 19.
29. Cf. Gal 4: 6.
30. Gal 5: 22, 25.
31. Cf. Eph 4: 23.
32. Eph 5: 8, 9.
33. 2 Pt 1: 4; cf. Jn 17: 3.
34. Cf. Rom 8: 18.
35. Wis 8: 7.
36. Prv 14: 15.
37. 1 Pt 4: 7.
38. St. Thomas Aquinas, *STh* II-II, 47, 2.
39. Lv 19: 15.
40. Col 4: 1.
41. Ps 118: 14.
42. Jn 16: 33.
43. Sir 5: 2; cf. 37: 27-31.
44. Sir 18: 30.
45. Ti 2: 12.
46. St. Augustine, *De moribus eccl.* 1, 25, 46: PL 32, 1330-1331.
47. Cf. 2 Pt 1: 4.
48. Cf. 1 Cor 13: 13.
49. Cf. 2 Tm 4.
50. St. Gregory of Nyssa, *Hom in Cant.* 8: PG 44, 941C.

The Mystery of Redemption

CHAPTER 7

The Call to Evangelization

People can grow in holiness through prayer—an intimate conversation with God—and the sacraments—seven privileged channels of grace instituted by Christ and entrusted to the Church.

The Mystery of Redemption

CHAPTER 7

The Call to Evangelization

[Jesus] was praying in a certain place, and when he ceased, one of his disciples said to him, "Lord, teach us to pray, as John taught his disciples." And he said to them, "When you pray, say:

'Father, hallowed be thy name. Thy kingdom come. Give us each day our daily bread; and forgive us our sins, for we ourselves forgive every one who is indebted to us; and lead us not into temptation.'"

He said to them, "Which of you who has a friend will go to him at midnight and say to him, 'Friend, lend me three loaves; for a friend of mine has arrived on a journey, and I have nothing to set before him'; and he will answer from within, 'Do not bother me; the door is now shut, and my children are with me in bed; I cannot get up and give you anything'? I tell you, though he will not get up and give him anything because he is his friend, yet because of his importunity he will rise and give him whatever he needs.

And I tell you, Ask, and it will be given you; seek, and you will find; knock, and it will be opened to you. For every one who asks receives, and he who seeks finds, and to him who knocks it will be opened. What father among you, if his son asks for a fish, will instead of a fish give him a serpent; or if he asks for an egg, will give him a scorpion? If you then, who are evil, know how to give good gifts to your children, how much more will the heavenly Father give the Holy Spirit to those who ask him!" (Lk 11: 1-13)

INTRODUCTION

Through his Death and Resurrection, Jesus Christ redeemed every person. Everyone who approaches Jesus Christ with the right dispositions is a beneficiary of God's merciful love. The magnanimous heart of Christ the Redeemer forgives, purifies, and sanctifies through the superabundance of grace he has merited. How should a Christian approach Jesus Christ for a share in his redeeming grace? Through prayer and participation in the sacraments he or she is immersed in the heart and life of Christ.

People can grow in holiness through prayer—an intimate conversation with God—and the sacraments—seven privileged channels of grace instituted by Christ and entrusted to the Church.

Illustration: *Christ Praying in the Garden* (detail) by Basaiti.

Resurrection (detail) by Piero.
The magnanimous heart of Christ the Redeemer forgives, purifies, and sanctifies through the superabundance of grace he has merited.

THIS CHAPTER WILL ADDRESS SEVERAL QUESTIONS:

- Why are prayer and the sacraments necessary to be like Christ?
- What is prayer?
- What is unique about the Lord's Prayer?
- Does God always answer prayers?
- What are the chief expressions and forms of prayer?
- What are some difficulties in prayer?
- What are the Seven Sacraments, and how are they the source of the Christian life?
- What does it mean to bear witness to Christ and love one's neighbor?

St. Francis of Assisi at Prayer (detail) by Murillo.
In the history of the Church, the saints bear witness to the necessity and power of prayer in the Christian life.

PART I: PRAYER IN THE CHRISTIAN LIFE

A relationship between friends rests and grows on mutual communication and dialogue. In a similar fashion, friendship and union with God rests on communication through personal prayer and the sacramental life. Prayer is an inner communion or conversation with God. Through prayer, spiritual nourishment comes from God, who becomes more and more present.

In the history of the Church, the saints bear witness to the necessity and power of prayer in the Christian life. No matter how active a saint might have been in preaching; teaching; writing; performing the corporal and spiritual works of mercy; or building and administering churches, hospitals, or schools, they were all, first and foremost, men and women of prayer. On their own they could achieve very little, but with God all things—even miracles—are possible.

LORD, TEACH US TO PRAY

If being human is essentially about relation to God, it is clear that speaking with, and listening to, God is an essential part of it. This is why the Sermon on the Mount also includes a teaching about prayer. The Lord tells us how we are to pray. (Pope Benedict XVI, *Jesus of Nazareth*, 128-129)

In St. Matthew's account of the Sermon on the Mount, Christ taught his disciples to pray using these words:

> **Our Father who art in heaven,**
> **Hallowed be thy name.**
> **Thy kingdom come.**
> **Thy will be done,**
> **On earth as it is in heaven.**
> **Give us this day our daily bread;**
> **And forgive us our debts,**
> **As we also have forgiven our debtors;**
> **And lead us not into temptation,**
> **But deliver us from evil.**
> **(Mt 6: 9-13)**

This prayer, which Christ taught his disciples, is called the *Lord's Prayer*, or the *Our Father*, and it is a model for all Christian prayer. It is sometimes called the *perfect prayer* as it sums up the entire Gospel of Jesus Christ. It teaches prayer is a communication with the Father and people should rely upon him for everything, both material and spiritual. The Lord's Prayer helps resist temptation and is an effective petition for personal forgiveness that rests on one's willingness to forgive others. It contains the most essential petitions for holiness, which pertain to everyone.

> **The Lord's Prayer "is truly the summary of the whole gospel."[1] "Since the Lord...after handing over the practice of prayer, said elsewhere, 'Ask and you will receive,' and since everyone has petitions which are peculiar to his circumstances, the regular and appropriate prayer [the Lord's Prayer] is said first, as the foundation of further desires."[2]** (CCC 2761)

Our Father

Reinhold Schneider, the great German poet, wrote with moving insight:

> **The Our Father begins with a great consolation: we are allowed to say "Father." This one word contains the whole history of redemption. We are allowed to say "Father," because the Son was our brother and has revealed the Father to us; because, thanks to what Christ has done, we have once more become children of God.[3]**

The Lord's Prayer begins with the recognition of God as our Father. In his public ministry, Christ called upon God as *Abba*, a term similar to the English word *daddy*. One of the many blessings of Christ's redemption is the capacity to call upon God as Father, and, during prayer, his children are invited to acknowledge God's paternal love.

Christ Retreats to the Mountain at Night by Tissot.
"Heaven and earth will pass away, but my words will not pass away." (Lk 21: 33)

In his own prayer, Christ addressed God the Father as *my* Father and taught his disciples to call God *our* Father. It is interesting to note the Lord did not instruct his followers to use the phrase *my* Father—a term reserved exclusively to Christ to indicate he is the Only-Begotten Son of the Father by nature. Through the merits of the redemption, human beings are incorporated into the Mystical Body of Christ and become children of God by adoption. Calling upon God as *our* Father emphasizes Christians are members of a community and live as a part of the Communion of Saints that embraces Heaven, earth, and Purgatory.

Hallowed be thy name

> **"You shall not take the name of the LORD your God in vain."** (Ex 20: 7)

The Old English word *hallowed* means *holy* or *sacred*. The Second Commandment teaches God's name is holy, and, in the Lord's Prayer, this truth is proclaimed and praise is given to his name, thereby giving glory to God.

In addition to respecting and venerating God's name, this petition asks for the ultimate goal of the redemption, i.e., sanctification. By stating a desire for the name of God to be glorified, it asks for, in essence, holiness of life.

Old Man Praying by Falat.
Those who follow the will of God help establish his kingdom on earth as it is in Heaven.

Thy kingdom come

> **"Seek first his kingdom and his righteousness, and all these things shall be yours as well."** (Mt 6: 33)

The Revelation and description of the Kingdom of God formed an essential part of Christ's teaching. His New Commandment of Love shows the way to live in this kingdom, and establishing it affects every aspect of life.

The Kingdom of God, which consists of the reign of Christ in the hearts of the faithful and an intimate communion with the Blessed Trinity through Jesus Christ, was established on earth from the moment of the Incarnation and will find its ultimate fulfillment at the end of time. Entrance into this kingdom of peace, joy, truth, and holiness was made possible by Christ's redemption.

This petition asks for the kingdom to continue to spread throughout the world, and prayer is the most effective means to bring others into this kingdom.

Thy will be done on earth as it is in heaven

> Earth becomes "heaven" when and insofar as God's will is done there. (Pope Benedict XVI, *Jesus of Nazareth*, 147)

Christians strive to follow the will of God and live the two Greatest Commandments Christ taught his disciples: love of God and love of neighbor as self. Those who follow the will of God help establish his kingdom on earth as it is in Heaven.

God has a plan for each person, but how can one know his will in life? Through Sacred Tradition and Sacred Scripture as transmitted by the Magisterium, everyone can come to a greater understanding of the teachings of Christ. When these teachings are considered in prayer, a person is led by the Holy Spirit to discern the will of God in life and is given the grace to put it into practice. By following God's will, earth becomes Heaven; in other words, the Kingdom of Heaven becomes established on earth.

Give us this day our daily bread

> Though the Lord directs our eyes to the essential, to the "one thing necessary," he also knows about and acknowledges our earthly needs. While he says to his disciples, "Do not be anxious about your life, what you shall eat,"[4] he nevertheless invites us to pray for our food and thus to turn our care over to God. (Pope Benedict XVI, *Jesus of Nazareth*, 150)

As created beings, people are entirely dependent on God, and, as Scripture relates, he is intimately concerned about every aspect of everyone's life. Nothing expresses the truth of the human condition and its relationship with God better than a petition to give what is best for everyone.

In addition to a plea for assistance in material needs, *our daily bread* recalls Christ's words, "I am the bread of life";[5] it thus forms a humble request for the Eucharist. The bread of Christians is the Holy Eucharist, which nourishes, and strengthens, and unites people together in Christ.

Forgive us our trespasses as we forgive those who trespass against us

> **"If you are offering your gift at the altar, and there remember that your brother has something against you, leave your gift there before the altar and go; first be reconciled to your brother, and then come and offer your gift."** (Mt 5: 23-24)

Christ came to redeem man, and, through his sacrifice of the Cross, people have perennial recourse to the forgiveness of sins. However, before anyone can ask for God's infinite mercy, he or she must first have mercy on others. Likewise, all people should seek forgiveness from those they have wronged. Lastly, this phrase implies a commitment to love all people with an unconditional love.

Lead us not into temptation, but deliver us from evil

> God certainly does not lead us into temptation....Temptation comes from the devil, but part of Jesus' messianic task is to withstand the great temptations that have led man away from God and continue to do so. As we have seen, Jesus must suffer through these temptations to the point of dying on the Cross, which is how he opens the way of redemption for us. (Pope Benedict XVI, *Jesus of Nazareth*, 160, 161)

While Baptism cleanses from Original Sin, a Christian is left with a fallen nature that makes it difficult to live a virtuous life. This inclination to sin is called concupiscence. However, God's grace gives the necessary strength to overcome all of the temptations in life. It is important to remember every temptation presents a moral choice and an opportunity to say yes to God and ask for his help.

The Virgin in Prayer by Sassoferrato.
The *Amen* at the end of a prayer expresses faith in God and trust that the things prayed for will come to pass.

Amen

Amen is Hebrew for *so be it*, and it expresses ratification of what has been said. Because it was used so commonly by Christ (e.g., "Amen, Amen, I say to you..."), it is one of the few Hebrew words still used in modern languages. The *Amen* at the end of a prayer expresses faith in God and trust that the things prayed for will come to pass.

Christ not only gave the Lord's Prayer to his disciples, but he showed them how to pray by example. The Gospels recount Christ often went off by himself to pray. This habitual withdrawal for prayer exemplifies the importance of spending time with God. The Lord's zeal to love and serve others found their source in his life of prayer. Undoubtedly, Christian discipleship involves a prayer life marked by habitual periods of silence and exclusive focus on Christ. This commitment to silent meditation is a common characteristic of the saints.

Through his own example of eagerness and commitment to speak with the Father, Christ revealed the importance and the power of prayer. In the Gospels, Christ prayed before the most decisive events of his ministry. Before he began his public life, he spent forty days in the desert, praying and fasting. He prayed before he called the Twelve Apostles. He prayed St. Peter's faith might not be tempted. He prayed before the raising of Lazarus. He prayed in Gethsemane the night before his Crucifixion, and he prayed while on the Cross.

If a person thinks he or she is not quite ready to pray, it is good to go to Christ—as his disciples did—and say to him, "Lord, teach me how to pray." The Holy Spirit will, little by little, assist and support all sincere prayer.

PRAYER IS A DIALOGUE WITH GOD

God addresses every individual by a name that no one else knows, as Scripture tells us.[6] God's love for each individual is totally personal and includes this mystery of a uniqueness that cannot be divulged to other human beings. (Pope Benedict XVI, *Jesus of Nazareth*, 128-129)

Pope Benedict XVI Prays at the Western Wall in Jerusalem.
A life of prayer forms the interior habit of being always in the presence of God and in communion with him.

God created man in his own image and likeness.[7] Because of this unique beginning, human beings have a special bond with God. Though they often turn away from him, there is still a sense he is calling the sinner back. This innate desire for God is placed deep within the human heart.

The graces of the redemption, bestowed upon the faithful in Baptism, raise each Christian to the status of a son or daughter of God. Through the power of grace, a person is not only made in the image and likeness of God but also becomes an adopted child of God. This filial relationship with the Father causes each person to sense his presence, and it invites everyone to share fully in his divine life.

The desire for God is written in the human heart, because man is created by God and for God; and God never ceases to draw man to himself. Only in God will he find the truth and happiness he never stops searching for:

The dignity of man rests above all on the fact that he is called to communion with God. This invitation to converse with God is addressed to man as soon as he comes into being. For if man exists, it is because God has created him through love, and through love continues to hold him in existence. He cannot live fully according to truth unless he freely acknowledges that love and entrusts himself to his creator.[8] (CCC 27)

People often assume they can satisfy this inherent need for God through material things or through relationships with other people.

Crucifixion by Mantegna.
Christ prayed before he called the Twelve Apostles. He prayed St. Peter's faith might not be tempted. He prayed before the raising of Lazarus. He prayed in Gethsemane the night before his Crucifixion, and he prayed while on the Cross.

Some people will try to deny these innate desires or will attempt to put them to rest through a spirituality whose only goal is inner peace. Christians, however, recognize this restlessness in the heart for what it truly is: a desire to be in intimate communion with God. As St. Augustine famously wrote, "You have made us for yourself, O Lord, and our heart is restless until it rests in you."

Prayer can be defined as *raising one's heart and mind* to God. Prayer, then, in whatever form, is a person's response to God's call. God knows the only way to find true happiness is to unite oneself to him and do his will. The call to prayer, then, is a call to love, to follow his will, and to experience his love. A life of prayer forms the interior habit of being always in the presence of God and in communion with him.

> **Where does prayer come from? Whether prayer is expressed in words or gestures, it is the whole man who prays. But in naming the source of prayer, Scripture speaks sometimes of the soul or the spirit, but most often of the heart (more than a thousand times). According to Scripture, it is the *heart* that prays. If our heart is far from God, the words of prayer are in vain.** (CCC 2562)

A regular life of prayer leads a person to know God's will and enables him or her to do his will more easily. Through consistent prayer, it becomes clear Christ is always there and that he will help get through every difficult situation. Through prayer, the Holy Spirit increases the life of Christ within. The effects of this transformation are manifested in a greater capacity to love as Christ loves. When a Christian is more Christlike, he or she is able to bring others to God.

> **Prayer is the life of the new heart. It ought to animate us at every moment. But we tend to forget him who is our life and our all. This is why the Fathers of the spiritual life in the Deuteronomic [the law of Moses] and prophetic traditions insist that prayer is a remembrance of God**

often awakened by the memory of the heart: "We must remember God more often than we draw breath."[9] But we cannot pray "at all times" if we do not pray at specific times, consciously willing it. These are the special times of Christian prayer, both in intensity and duration. (CCC 2697)

The Church never ceases to call the faithful to a life of prayer. First of all, on Sundays and Holy Days of Obligation, she calls everyone to participate in the highest form of prayer, the Holy Mass. Additionally, the faithful are strongly encouraged to participate in the other liturgical prayers of the Church, e.g., the Liturgy of the Hours, as well as personal prayer and other traditional devotions such as the Holy Rosary, the *Angelus*, and blessings before and after meals.

The *Christian family* is the first place of education in prayer. Based on the sacrament of marriage, the family is the "domestic church" where God's children learn to pray "as the Church" and to persevere in prayer. For young children in particular, daily family prayer is the first witness of the Church's living memory as awakened patiently by the Holy Spirit. (CCC 2685)

Life in Heaven (the Beatific Vision) consists of constant, intimate prayer—an eternal conversation with the Blessed Trinity, one God in three divine Persons. Prayer on earth is a preparation for the face-to-face conversation with God each person hopes to enjoy in Heaven. Christ will always give the necessary graces to cultivate a life of prayer, but each person must do his or her part to develop a relationship with him.

SCRIPTURE AS A SOURCE OF PRAYER

Through his Word, God speaks to man. By words, mental or vocal, our prayer takes flesh. Yet it is most important that the heart should be present to him to whom we are speaking in prayer: "Whether or not our prayer is heard depends not on the number of words, but on the fervor of our souls."[10] (CCC 2700)

Prayer is communication with God. One of the primary ways a person can hear what God is saying is by prayerfully reading his Word in Sacred Scripture.

Sacred Scripture has always been a rich source of prayer in the Church. First of all, a great majority of the prayers of the Mass and the other liturgies of the Church are based on Sacred Scripture. In the Mass, for example, the readings, the Entrance Antiphon, the Gospel Acclamation, the Sanctus, the Lamb of God, "Lord, I am not worthy..." and the Communion Antiphon are quoted from Sacred Scripture.

The Liturgy of the Hours is a liturgical prayer based primarily on readings from the Psalms. Other traditional prayers of the Church such as the *Lord's Prayer*, the *Hail Mary*, and the *Angelus* all come from the words of Sacred Scripture. For example, the *Hail Mary* repeats the words of the Archangel Gabriel in the Annunciation[11] and St. Elizabeth's greeting at the Visitation.[12]

The Church also encourages the faithful to practice *lectio divina*, the prayerful or meditative reading of Sacred Scripture. In this ascetical practice, an individual reads a verse or a few verses from Scripture and then prays about what God is saying to him or her.

St. John the Evangelist by Martini.
Life in Heaven (the Beatific Vision) consists of constant, intimate prayer—an eternal conversation with the Blessed Trinity, one God in three divine Persons.

The practice of *lectio divina* is often described as having four steps:

- *Lectio* (reading): The scriptural passage is read slowly, focusing on what the Word of God is saying.
- *Meditatio* (meditation): The person meditates or reflects on the reading, thinking about the words and events presented and how they apply to his or her life.
- *Oratio* (prayer): Prayer is the human response to the Word of God. The person prays, speaking to God about the subject of his or her meditation.
- *Contemplatio* (contemplation): Believing God always answers prayer, the person listens to what God has to say.

Sacred Scripture also gives the example of many saintly men and women who can be imitated in one's prayer life:

- Abel offered the best of his flock in a sacrifice that was found acceptable by God. (cf. Gn 4: 4)
- Noah was a righteous man who walked with God. (cf. Gn 6: 9)
- Abraham believed in God's promise—Sarah would bear a child in her old age—and was obedient when God asked him to sacrifice Isaac. Although he struggled to understand, he trusted God when he was tested. (cf. Gn 15: 5-6; Gn 22)
- Moses spoke to God face-to-face and was a mediator for his people. (cf. Ex 33: 11)
- David was a man after God's own heart. (cf. Acts 13: 22)
- Elijah was a righteous man who prayed fervently and without ceasing. (cf. Jas 5: 16-17)
- Christ is the perfect example: "Not my will, but thine, be done." (cf. Lk 22: 42)

Abraham Praying Before the Three Angels by Tiepolo.
Sacred Scripture gives the example of many saintly men and women who can be imitated in one's prayer life.

GOD ANSWERS ALL PRAYERS

God answers every prayer, though not always in the way one might wish or expect. This is because particular petitions do not always conform to his plan. When this happens, he responds by offering the grace to accept his will. Unfortunately, many people refuse this grace. The goal, therefore, is to accept his will; when a petition does not meet his will, God's plan should take precedence for the good of the soul. Given God's infinite love, it is always possible to have firm faith and trust in his plans; they are always what is best.

> **Filial trust is put to the test when we feel that our prayer is not always heard. The Gospel invites us to ask ourselves about the conformity of our prayer to the desire of the Spirit.** (CCC 2756)

Jesus Christ is the eternal Mediator, or Intercessor, in Heaven. Attested to in Scripture, Christ presents prayers to the Father, and everything asked in his name will be granted. God hears every prayer and will either grant the request or give something even greater.

Jesus also prays for us—in our place and on our behalf. All our petitions were gathered up, once for all, in his cry on the Cross and, in his Resurrection, heard by the Father. This is why he never ceases to intercede for us with the Father.[13] If our prayer is resolutely united with that of Jesus, in trust and boldness as children, we obtain all that we ask in his name, even more than any particular thing: the Holy Spirit himself, who contains all gifts. (CCC 2741)

EXPRESSIONS AND FORMS OF PRAYER

There is no other way of Christian prayer than Christ. Whether our prayer is communal or personal, vocal or interior, it has access to the Father only if we pray "in the name" of Jesus. The sacred humanity of Jesus is therefore the way by which the Holy Spirit teaches us to pray to God our Father. (CCC 2664)

The Church has identified three expressions of prayer:

- Vocal prayer: This is simple conversation with God using traditional prayers such as the *Lord's Prayer*, the *Hail Mary*, or using one's own words.
- Meditative prayer: This is prayer of understanding that involves dwelling on some element of divine wisdom found in Sacred Scripture, Sacred Tradition, or a spiritual writing in order to discern God's will and apply it to one's life.
- Contemplative prayer: This is prayer that consists in abiding and resting in God's presence.

Pope John Pope II in Vocal Prayer with the Holy Rosary.
A person can pray aloud or in the silence of his or her own heart.

VOCAL PRAYER is prayer that uses words. For example, the Liturgy of the Hours and the Holy Rosary utilize vocal prayers. This type of prayer can be said individually or with others. Established prayers or one's own words can be used.

Normally, thought precedes word; it seeks and formulates the word. But praying the Psalms and liturgical prayer in general is exactly the other way round: The word, the voice, goes ahead of us, and our mind must adapt to it. (Pope Benedict XVI, *Jesus of Nazareth*, 131)

A person can pray aloud or in the silence of his or her own heart. In vocal prayer, one simply talks to God, sharing joys and sorrows with him, praising him, and growing in love and understanding. Christ is a loving God and calls each person into a mysterious encounter with him.

Vocal prayer is an essential element of the Christian life. To his disciples, drawn by their Master's silent prayer, Jesus teaches a vocal prayer, the Our Father. He not only prayed aloud the liturgical prayers of the synagogue but, as the Gospels show, he raised his voice to express his personal prayer, from exultant blessing of the Father to the agony of Gesthemani.[14] (CCC 2701)

MEDITATIVE PRAYER is used to gain a greater understanding of the life of Christ or a particular mystery of the Faith as well as to come to a deeper understanding of how this truth could be applied to life.

Meditation is above all a quest. The mind seeks to understand the why and how of the Christian life, in order to adhere and respond to what the Lord is asking. The required attentiveness is difficult to sustain. We are usually helped by books, and Christians do not want for them:

> the Sacred Scriptures, particularly the Gospels, holy icons, liturgical texts of the day or season, writings of the spiritual fathers, works of spirituality, the great book of creation, and that of history—the page on which the "today" of God is written. (CCC 2705)

While vocal prayer may arise spontaneously, meditation usually requires choosing a particular topic and disciplined focus and concentration. In meditation, a person is generally assisted by reading Sacred Scripture, especially the Gospels, the New Testament, or some other spiritual writing or image to provide content on which to focus. Meditative prayer engages the entire person through the heart and mind.

> Meditation engages thought, imagination, emotion, and desire. This mobilization of faculties is necessary in order to deepen our convictions of faith, prompt the conversion of our heart, and strengthen our will to follow Christ. Christian prayer tries above all to meditate on the mysteries of Christ, as in *lectio divina* or the Rosary. This form of prayerful reflection is of great value, but Christian prayer should go further: to the knowledge of the love of the Lord Jesus, to union with him. (CCC 2708)

CONTEMPLATIVE PRAYER keeps a person in God's presence as he or she abides in his love. It is the prayerful habit to focus the entire heart and mind on the Lord. It has been compared to the experience of good friends or spouses who enjoy being in each other's presence even without words.

> What is contemplative prayer? St. Teresa answers: "Contemplative prayer [*oracion mental*] in my opinion is nothing else than a close sharing between friends; it means taking time frequently to be alone with him who we know loves us."[15]
>
> Contemplative prayer seeks him "whom my soul loves."[16] It is Jesus, and in him, the Father. We seek him, because to desire him is always the beginning of love, and we seek him in that pure faith which causes us to be born of him and to live in him. In this inner prayer we can still meditate, but our attention is fixed on the Lord himself. (CCC 2709)

The teachings of Christ, especially in the Lord's Prayer, show there are particular forms of prayer.

- *Blessing and Adoration.* In a prayer of blessing, a person beseeches the Father, the source of all blessing, for his gifts and protection.[17] Adoration is worship and veneration given to God because of his eternal and infinite goodness. Adoration is a devotion that recognizes God as the source of all goodness, who enjoys infinite transcendence above every creature.
- *Petition* requests favors and blessings from God. It is assured God will honor requests by either granting what is asked or giving something even more beneficial.
- *Intercession* prays on behalf of another or asks others to pray on one's behalf. Everyone should pray constantly for those closest to him or her, beginning with the family. Anyone can also pray for anyone else, anywhere, as charity so moves. In doing so, Christ is imitated, whose redemption consists in being the Mediator between God and all people. Being the Mother of Christ, our Blessed Mother is a great intercessor. Because of the Communion of Saints,

Christ Interceding with God the Father for the Humble and the Mighty, Illumination by Maitre.
Intercession prays on behalf of another or asks others to pray on one's behalf.

Holy Trinity (detail) by Balen.
A prayer of thanksgiving shows gratitude to God for his infinite love and filling life with every good thing, both material and spiritual.

anyone can also ask the angels and saints in Heaven—as well as the members of the Church on earth—to intercede with God for all necessities.

> **The witnesses who have preceded us into the kingdom,[18] especially those whom the Church recognizes as saints, share in the living tradition of prayer by the example of their lives, the transmission of their writings, and their prayer today. They contemplate God, praise him and constantly care for those whom they have left on earth. When they entered into the joy of their Master, they were "put in charge of many things."[19] Their intercession is their most exalted service to God's plan. We can and should ask them to intercede for us and for the whole world. (CCC 2683)**

- *Thanksgiving* shows gratitude to God for his infinite love and filling life with every good thing, both material and spiritual. St. Paul advised, "Be thankful."[20] A person who stops to count his or her blessings soon recognizes how grateful he or she must be for the loving kindness shown, especially through Christ's redemption.
- *Praise* gives God glory simply because he is God. Praise often spontaneously arises from a sense of wonder toward the natural world and human beings. Beauty, power, intricate harmony, and intelligence abound in the world. If created things are this wonderful, how great God must be, who is their Creator.
- *Contrition* shows sorrow for sins and offenses committed against God, who is the source of all truth and goodness. These failings can be one's own or those of others. There are many examples of disrespect toward the love and goodness of God and grave offenses against human dignity. In a prayer of contrition, a heartfelt act of reparation expresses sorrow coupled with the desire to make up for offenses by leading a holy life.

DIFFICULTIES IN PRAYER

Prayer is sometimes easy and full of consolation. However, everyone—even the greatest of saints—has at times found prayer difficult. Prayer is part of the spiritual struggle to act habitually according to the will of God. Thus, perseverance in prayer is an expression of great love for God.

There are three principal difficulties most often encountered in prayer:

- lack of time,
- distraction, and
- spiritual dryness.

It is important to have a set time for prayer. Without an established, specific time for prayer, people tend to put it off until later, which usually means praying less frequently, less fervently, or not at all. The experience of men and women well versed in the spiritual life demonstrates prayer should be done at the same time every day, preferably in the morning before the concerns of the day take hold. If it is not possible to pray in a church, then a suitable location should be found, one that is quiet and free from exterior distractions, noise, and interruptions.

> **The church, the house of God, is the proper place for the liturgical prayer of the parish community. It is also the privileged place for adoration of the real presence of Christ in the Blessed Sacrament. The choice of a favorable place is not a matter of indifference for true prayer.**
>
> **For personal prayer, this can be a "prayer corner" with the Sacred Scriptures and icons, in order to be there, in secret, before our Father.[21] In a Christian family, this kind of little oratory fosters prayer in common. (CCC 2691)**

The antidote to spiritual dryness is a humble petition for divine assistance coupled with a commitment to persevere in the effort to be holy.

A suitable place for prayer eliminates many typical distractions. The next hurdle is often mental wanderings, which divert from focused prayer. When faced with these challenges, people should remind themselves nothing is more important than God. If these distractions take the form of worries, faith in the power of fervent prayer can lessen them.

Another kind of distraction, especially during vocal prayer, is not paying attention to the words. This should not be a discouragement to stop praying but should be an impetus to center the focus of life more firmly on Christ. As with any human relationship, communion with God has to be continually renewed. As the habit of prayer grows, there will be fewer distractions.

A final difficulty in prayer is dryness, which is a sense that prayer is of no value, or worse, a waste of time. Almost everyone faces this difficulty at one time or another. In fact, one of the great mystics of the Church, St. John of the Cross, wrote *The Dark Night of the Soul*, in which he discussed the feeling of being abandoned by God. Bl. Teresa of Calcutta (Mother Teresa), the founder of the Missionaries of Charity, also experienced a sense of abandonment by God for many years, though she palpably radiated God's love to everyone in her presence. The antidote to spiritual dryness is a humble petition for divine assistance coupled with a commitment to persevere in the effort to be holy.

Pope Benedict XVI Baptizes a Baby on the Feast of the Baptism of the Lord in the Vatican Sistine Chapel.
Water is the sacramental sign of Baptism; as water cleanses the body, Baptism cleanses the soul of sin—Original and personal—and initiates a new life in Christ.

Last Supper (detail) by Rubens.
Christ remains present even after Mass is dismissed in the consecrated hosts that are reserved in the tabernacle.

THE SACRAMENT OF THE EUCHARIST
by which Christ associates his Church and all her members with the sacrifice of the Cross

In the Gospel of St. John, Christ identified himself with the "bread come down from heaven."[27] These words were brought to fulfillment at the Last Supper when Christ took the bread and the cup filled with wine, and said, "This is my body...this is my blood of the covenant."[28] Each time a priest repeats these words of Christ in the Holy Mass, the substance of the bread and wine is changed into the Body and Blood of Christ by the power of the Holy Spirit. Christ himself, living and glorious, becomes truly and really present on the altar.

After the words of Consecration, there is no longer bread or wine present. Every particle of bread and every drop of wine have been completely changed in substance. Though the appearance of bread and wine remain (taste, weight, color, size, and the like), Christ is truly present in his Body and Blood. This change in the substance of the bread and wine into the substance of the Body and Blood of Christ is called *transubstantiation*. In the Eucharist,

- the whole Christ is present in each and every part;
- the whole Christ is present if the parts are divided;
- the whole Christ is present in his Body, Blood, Soul, and Divinity;
- the presence of Christ is sacramental; and
- the presence of Christ endures as long as the appearance of bread and wine remains.

Christ remains present among his people in the Eucharist because of his great love. His *Real Presence* in the Eucharist is proof he wishes to share himself with us as much as possible. He remains present even after Mass is dismissed in the consecrated hosts that are reserved in the tabernacle. The Eucharist is reserved to take to those who are sick or infirm and so the faithful may adore him outside of Mass.

Because it is Christ himself, the Eucharist is the Church's greatest treasure.

Because it is Christ himself, the Eucharist is the Church's greatest treasure. Therefore, every care must be taken to treat the Eucharist with the utmost respect, especially when receiving Holy Communion. Catholics also show their respect for the Real Presence of Christ in the Eucharist by genuflecting when entering or leaving a church, or when passing in front of a tabernacle.

In order to receive the Eucharist properly, the recipient must:

- be a baptized Catholic;
- believe in Christ's Real Presence;
- fast from all food and drink (except water and medicine) at least one hour prior to reception;
- be in a state of grace; and
- not be under any ecclesiastical censure such as excommunication.

The grave sin of sacrilege occurs by treating holy things as if they were profane. This can occur if someone were to receive the Eucharist in a state of mortal sin. St. Paul warns, "Whoever, therefore, eats the bread or drinks the cup of the Lord in an unworthy manner will be guilty of profaning the body and blood of the Lord....For any one who eats and drinks without discerning the body eats and drinks judgment upon himself."[29]

Communion with Christ in the Eucharist foreshadows the perfect communion Christians hope to enjoy with God in Heaven. Since Jesus Christ is being received, each person should approach the Sacrament with the greatest reverence and devotion. Though every Catholic is required to receive the Eucharist at least once yearly, he or she should desire to receive it as often as possible.

The person who receives the Eucharist is blessed with many graces. The Eucharist:

- not only maintains but also increases intimate union with Christ;
- reinforces the unity of the Church as the Mystical Body of Christ;
- removes venial sins;
- strengthens a person to avoid grave sins;
- increases charity toward God and neighbor;
- strengthens against temptation;
- decreases temporal punishment due to sin; and
- helps control concupiscence.

The entire life of the Church converges on the Eucharist; it is the source and summit of the life in Christ. When a person receives Holy Communion with the proper dispositions, the Eucharist transforms him or her into another Christ: Christ's presence intensifies in the soul, and the person approaches the goal of the New Commandment to love as Christ loved.

The Eucharist is the third of the Sacraments of Initiation; it incorporates the believer fully into the Church. In fact, in the Eastern Rites of the Catholic Church—as in the early Church—Baptism, Confirmation, and Communion are given to infants in one continuous rite.

THE SACRAMENT OF RECONCILIATION
by which sins after Baptism are forgiven

Through the Sacrament of Baptism, a person is cleansed from all sin, both Original and personal. However, the inclination to sin, or concupiscence, remains. Since Christians sin, harming their relationships with God and neighbor, Christ established the Sacrament of Reconciliation as a means to receive God's forgiveness and healing for sins committed after Baptism.

The Sacrament of Reconciliation does not simply remove sin and restore lost grace but actually increases grace in the soul.

Christ entrusted the ministry of Reconciliation to the Apostles. After the Resurrection, he declared to them, "If you forgive the sins of any, they are forgiven."[30] This power is handed on through the Sacrament of Holy Orders. The Sacrament of Reconciliation, or Penance, is a Sacrament of Healing in which Jesus Christ, through the actions of a bishop or priest, forgives sins committed after Baptism. In this way, God restores his friendship with the penitent after he or she had broken it by committing mortal sin or damaged it by committing venial sin. Through this sacrament, a sinner is reconciled with God and the Church.

In order to receive God's forgiveness, the penitent must have contrition for his or her sins. When a person is sorry for sins out of love for God above all else, it is called "perfect contrition." When sorrow arises from fear of Hell or other punishment, it is called "imperfect contrition."

While the Church requires Catholics confess all mortal sins at least once yearly, love of God should lead to the confession of any mortal sin as soon as possible. The Church also recommends frequent Confession even when no mortal sin has been committed. This practice makes it easier to recognize and eradicate venial sins. Frequent Confession helps increase genuine self-knowledge, correct bad habits, purify the conscience, develop Christian humility, strengthen the will, decrease lukewarmness, and augment self-control. The Sacrament of Reconciliation does not simply remove sin and restore lost grace but actually increases grace in the soul. Confessing venial sins and even moral imperfections can gain additional graces.

Regular Confession provides an opportunity to receive spiritual direction, which may be defined as spiritual advice so as to increase in holiness. Spiritual direction should be sought regularly if it is to be effective in the long term. Time should be set aside to discuss recent progress, problems that have arisen, and what goals should be set for the month ahead. Following this advice, especially when given in the Sacrament of Reconciliation, and reviewing the results before the next Confession can lead to great progress in the Christian life.

Reconciliation with God is the whole purpose of the Sacrament of Reconciliation, which

- forgives confessed sins, thereby restoring sanctifying grace lost by mortal sin;
- remits eternal punishment caused by mortal sin;
- imparts actual graces to avoid sin in the future;
- reconciles the penitent with the Church;
- remits part of the temporal punishment due to sin; and
- gives peace of conscience and spiritual consolation.

THE SACRAMENT OF THE ANOINTING OF THE SICK
by which one is strengthened in the face of death

Is any among you sick? Let him call for the elders of the church, and let them pray over him, anointing him with oil in the name of the Lord; and the prayer of faith will save the sick man, and the Lord will raise him up; and if he has committed sins, he will be forgiven. Therefore confess your sins to one another, and pray for one another, that you may be healed. The prayer of a righteous man has great power in its effects. (Jas 5: 14-16)

The purpose of the Anointing of the Sick, the second Sacrament of Healing, is to confer a special grace on Christians who are in danger of death due to grave illness or old age. This sacrament is not only for those who are moments from death; it is fitting to receive it before a serious operation or as soon as there is danger of death from sickness or old age. The Anointing of the Sick may be repeated if a person's condition becomes more serious.

Ideally, the Anointing of the Sick is to be celebrated along with the Sacrament of Reconciliation and reception of the Eucharist. The first sacrament to be received should be Confession, followed by the anointing. Finally, the Eucharist is received as *viaticum* (from the Latin for "traveling provisions"). The faithful should receive the Eucharist as preparation for the moment of passing over from this life to the next; it is the seed of eternal life through the power of the Resurrection.

Christ Healing the Blind (detail) by El Greco.
In the Gospel, Jesus healed people both to demonstrate he is the Messiah and to show compassion for those who were suffering.

Like all of the sacraments, the Anointing of the Sick imparts special graces on those who receive it. The graces of this Sacrament are:

- union of the sick person to the Passion of Christ for his or her own good and the good of the Church;
- strength, peace, and courage to endure, in a Christian manner, the sufferings of illness or old age;
- forgiveness of sins if the person is at least implicitly sorry for his or her sins and unable to receive the Sacrament of Penance;
- restoration of health if it is good for the salvation of the person's soul;
- strength to resist the temptations of the Devil;
- preparation for passage into eternal life; and
- reduction or removal of all temporal punishment due to sin when the ill person is properly disposed.

In the Gospel, Jesus healed people both to demonstrate he is the Messiah and to show compassion for those who were suffering. These healing acts demonstrated the Kingdom of God had arrived. Through the Sacrament of the Anointing of the Sick, Christ brings about a radical healing of the soul amid the pain and suffering due to severe illness and assists the individual to draw strength by uniting his or her suffering to the Cross.

Deacons Are Ordained to the Priesthood in St. Peter's Basilica.
The recipients of this Sacrament are servants of the Word of God and God's sacraments.

THE SACRAMENT OF HOLY ORDERS
by which people serve the faithful in the name of Christ

Those men who receive the Sacrament of Holy Orders are called by God to the ministry of preaching and administering the sacraments in Christ's name in the service of the faithful. Through this sacrament, the mission entrusted by Christ to the Apostles has been handed on to the present day, and it will continue to be handed on until the end of time.

The Sacrament is given in three levels, each with different powers and authority.

- ✠ A *bishop* receives the highest level of Holy Orders and participates fully in the priesthood of Christ. Bishops are the successors of the Apostles and members of the college of bishops, of which the pope is head. A bishop is head of a diocese, or local church. A bishop has the power to ordain deacons, priests, and other bishops.
- ✠ A *priest*, whose role is to assist his bishop, often cares for a community of the faithful called a parish. Priests celebrate Mass and administer the Sacraments of Reconciliation; Baptism; Matrimony; Anointing of the Sick; and, under certain circumstances, Confirmation.
- ✠ A *deacon* is a minister of the Gospel and Holy Communion and is ordained to perform acts of service and charity. Deacons celebrate the Sacraments of Baptism and Matrimony and serve the bishop and parish in many ways.

Service of the faithful by teaching the Faith and administering the sacraments is the main purpose of Holy Orders. Holy Orders is called a Sacrament at the Service of Communion because it primarily exists for the sanctification of others.[31]

The reception of Holy Orders presupposes a divine vocation. "One does not take the honor [of ordination] upon himself, but he is called by God."[32] The recipients of this Sacrament are servants of the Word of God and God's sacraments. They dedicate themselves to a life of self-denial and sacrifice for the good of others. St. Paul goes so far as to call himself as a slave, showing how serious the obligation to serve Christ becomes within the Sacrament of Holy Orders.

In every marriage there are three parties: the husband, the wife, and God.

THE SACRAMENT OF MATRIMONY
by which a man and a woman form an intimate communion of life and love

Matrimony is the second Sacrament at the Service of Communion. Matrimony joins a baptized man and a baptized woman in a covenant for life; it is ordered toward the good of the spouses and the procreation and education of children. By divine design, Matrimony signifies the union of Christ and his Church. Since it is instituted by God, Matrimony is endowed with special graces to enable the couple to love each other with the same self-sacrificing love of Christ for his bride, the Church. This grace enables the spouses to maintain and sanctify their love.

Marriage has been considered sacred from the beginning of creation. The Book of Genesis states man and woman were created for marriage; God observed, "It is not good that the man should be alone."[33] Christ revealed, from the beginning, God intended the marriage covenant to be permanent; no authority on earth can dissolve it.

The effect of the Sacrament of Matrimony is a permanent bond between the spouses, established and guaranteed by God. In every marriage there are three parties: the husband, the wife, and God. A valid, sacramental marriage cannot be dissolved.

Through the Sacrament of Matrimony, Jesus Christ bestows special graces on married couples. The husband and wife each receive graces to fulfill their marital vows. This sacrament helps the spouses give themselves completely in sacrificial love, provided the right dispositions are present. Specifically, the grace of Matrimony gives the couple strength to shoulder the burdens of marital life, especially regarding the education and formation of children. Moreover, Matrimony confers graces to grow in holiness and charity, which is manifested in a spirit of forgiveness, patience, and service.

The family is the first school of the Faith. By the example of the parents, children receive their first instruction in Catholic teaching and, by their conversations, hear the first explanations of Catholic beliefs. The Christian home is called the *domestic church*—a community of love and prayer, a school of virtue and Christian charity.

A family centered on Christ through his Church is an effective training ground for saints, and both parents and children will radiate the light of Christ to their friends and peers. The mutual, generous love of parents can educate the children in the true, self-sacrificing love exemplified by Christ.

Pope Benedict XVI Seated Beneath Bernini's Throne of St. Peter in St. Peter's Basilica, Vatican.
It is important to remember Christ's kingship is not of this world; he rules by serving others and moving human hearts to repentance and conversion.

Pope John Paul II Blesses 83,000 People of God in Giants Stadium, Newark, NJ, on October 5, 1995.
As St. Paul taught, everyone has been called by God to play a special role in the Mystical Body of Christ, the Church.

CONCLUSION

Regardless of personal circumstances, by virtue of the power of the redemption given in the Sacrament of Baptism, everyone is called to be a saint. This is true in the case of deacons, priests, bishops, religious brothers and sisters, cloistered contemplatives, and lay persons. In fact, all the events of life, even the most mundane, can be occasions for serving Christ and neighbor and growing in holiness. As St. Paul taught, everyone has been called by God to play a special role in the Mystical Body of Christ, the Church.

Christ has not only called all the baptized to live a life of sanctity but also supplied them with all the means necessary to accomplish it. In addition, when people cooperate with God's grace, they help others achieve sanctity because the Gospel is spread from person to person. The joy of those who arrive in Heaven is magnified by those for whom one was an instrument of salvation.

There are as many ways to become a saint as there are people, and God gives great freedom to choose any path. Because human beings are fallible, they inevitably experience failures and disappointments along the way. However, as long as anyone begins again, aided by grace, and keeps trying to do his or her best to serve God as he wills, final success is guaranteed. He or she keeps in touch with God along the way by prayer, listening to his Word, and speaking to him. He or she is strengthened during the different stages of life—from infancy through old age—by the sacraments, especially the "everyday" gifts of the Eucharist and Reconciliation. Throughout this lifelong conversion process, he or she will introduce others to the friendship of Christ.

The call to love neighbor through service, reflected in the social teachings of the Church, is not aimed at creating a perfect society according to a false, utopian vision. Rather, it is directed to specific persons with concrete needs, alleviating his or her suffering and enabling him or her to live in the dignity of a person who is a child made in the image of God. Living in accordance with Christ's New Commandment of Love immerses a person more deeply into the heart of Christ.

In this way, both man's exalted stature and his need to serve others can be understood. The Fathers of the Second Vatican Council wrote, "Man, who is the only creature on earth which God willed for itself, cannot fully find himself except through a sincere gift of himself."[46]

SUPPLEMENTARY READING

1. *Purification of Spirit Through Fasting and Almsgiving*

The special note of the paschal feast is this: the whole Church rejoices in the forgiveness of sins. It rejoices in the forgiveness not only of those who are then reborn in holy baptism but also of those who are already numbered among God's adopted children.

Initially, men are made new by the rebirth of baptism. Yet there still is required a daily renewal to repair the shortcomings of our mortal nature, and whatever degree of progress has been made there is no one who should not be more advanced. All must therefore strive to ensure that on the day of redemption no one may be found in the sins of his former life.

Dear friends, what the Christian should be doing at all times should be done now with greater care and devotion, so that the Lenten fast enjoined by the apostles may be fulfilled, not simply by abstinence from food but above all by the renunciation of sin.

There is no more profitable practice as a companion to holy and spiritual fasting than that of almsgiving. This embraces under the single name of mercy many excellent works of devotion, so that the good intentions of all the faithful may be of equal value, even where their means are not. The love that we owe both God and man is always free from any obstacle that would prevent us from having a good intention. The angels sang: *Glory to God in the highest, and peace to his people on earth.* The person who shows love and compassion to those in any kind of affliction is blessed, not only with the virtue of good will but also with the gift of peace.

The works of mercy are innumerable. Their very variety brings this advantage to those who are true Christians, that in the matter of almsgiving not only the rich and affluent but also those of average means and the poor are able to play their part. Those who are unequal in their capacity to give can be equal in the love within their hearts.

— Pope St. Leo the Great

2. *Prayer Is the Light of the Soul*

The highest good is prayer and conversation with God, because it means that we are in God's company and in union with him. When light enters our bodily eyes our eyesight is sharpened; when a soul is intent on God, God's inextinguishable light shines into it and makes it bright and clear. I am talking, of course, of prayer that comes from the heart and not from routine: not the prayer that is assigned to particular days or particular moments in time, but the prayer that happens continuously by day and by night.

Indeed the soul should not only turn to God at times of explicit prayer. Whatever we are engaged in, whether it is care for the poor, or some other duty, or some act of generosity, we should remember God and long for God. The love of God will be as salt is to food, making our actions into a perfect dish to set before the Lord of all things. Then it is right that we should receive the fruits of our labors, overflowing onto us through all eternity, if we have been offering them to him throughout our lives.

Prayer is the light of the soul, true knowledge of God, a mediator between God and men. Prayer lifts the soul into the heavens where it hugs God in an indescribable embrace. The soul seeks the milk of God like a baby crying for the breast. It fulfils its own vows and receives in exchange gifts better than anything that can be seen or imagined.

Prayer is a go-between linking us to God. It gives joy to the soul and calms its emotions. I warn you, though: do not imagine that prayer is simply words. Prayer is the desire for God, an indescribable devotion, not given by man but brought about by God's grace. As St. Paul says: "For when we cannot choose words in order to pray properly, the Spirit himself intercedes on our behalf in a way that could never be put into words."

If God gives to someone the gift of such prayer, it is a gift of imperishable riches, a heavenly food that satisfies the spirit. Whoever tastes that food catches fire and his soul burns for ever with desire for the Lord.

— Pseudo-Chrysostom

SUPPLEMENTARY READING Continued

3. *Our Prayer Is Public and Communal*

Above all, the Teacher of peace and Master of unity did not want prayer to be made singly and privately, so that whoever prayed would pray for himself alone. We do not say My *Father, who art in heaven* or *Give* me *this day* my *daily bread*; nor does each one ask that only his own debt should be forgiven him; nor does he request for himself alone that he may not be led into temptation but delivered from evil. Our prayer is public and common, and when we pray, we pray not for one person but for the whole people, since we, the whole people, are one.

The God of peace and the Master of concord, who taught unity, willed that one should pray for all, just as he himself, being one, carried us all. The three children observed this law when they were shut into the fiery furnace, praying with one voice and with one heart: thus our faith in divine Scripture teaches us, and, as it teaches us how such people prayed, gives us an example that we should follow in our own prayers, so that we may become like them: "Then these three sang a hymn as if with one mouth, and blessed the Lord." They spoke as if with one mouth, even though Christ had not yet taught them how to pray.

And therefore, as they prayed, their prayers were heard and were fruitful, because a peaceful, sincere, and spiritual prayer deserved well from the Lord. Thus, too, we find the Apostles and the disciples praying after the ascension of the Lord: "They all continued with one accord in prayer, with the women and with Mary who was the mother of Jesus, and his brothers." They continued with one accord in prayer, showing, by the urgency and the unanimity of their praying, that "God, who makes the inhabitants" of a house "to be of one mind," only admits to his divine and eternal home those among whom prayer is unanimous.

But, dear brethren—what deep blessings are contained in the Lord's Prayer! How many they are, and how great, collected in so few words but so rich in spiritual power! There is nothing at all that is not to be found in these our prayers and petitions, as it were a compendium of heavenly doctrine. "Thus," he said, "you must pray: Our Father, who art in Heaven."

The new man, re-born and brought back to God by his grace, says *Father* at the very beginning, for he has just begun to be God's son. "He came to his own, and his own did not accept him. But to those who did accept him he gave power to become children of God, to those who believe in his name." Whoever believes in God's name and has become his son, should start here so that he can give thanks and profess himself to be God's son, by calling God his Father in heaven.

— St. Cyprian, *Treatise on the Lord's Prayer*

"Our prayer is public and common, and when we pray, we pray not for one person but for the whole people, since we, the whole people, are one."
(St. Cyprian, *Treatise on the Lord's Prayer*)

SUPPLEMENTARY READING Continued

4. *On the Lord's Prayer*

We need to use words so that we may remind ourselves to consider carefully what we are asking, not so that we may think we can instruct the Lord or prevail on him.

Thus, when we say: "Hallowed be your name," we are reminding ourselves to desire that his name, which in fact is always holy, should also be considered holy among men. I mean that it should not be held in contempt. But this is a help for men, not for God.

And as for our saying: "Your kingdom come," it will surely come whether we will it or not. But we are stirring up our desires for the kingdom so that it can come to us and we can deserve to reign there.

When we say: "Your will be done on earth as it is in Heaven," we are asking him to make us obedient so that his will may be done in us as it is done in heaven by his angels.

When we say: "Give us this day our daily bread," in saying "this day" we mean "in this world." Here we ask for a sufficiency by specifying the most important part of it; that is, we use the word "bread" to stand for everything. Or else we are asking for the sacrament of the faithful, which is necessary in this world, not to gain temporal happiness but to gain the happiness that is everlasting.

When we say: "Forgive us our trespasses as we forgive those who trespass against us," we are reminding ourselves of what we must ask and what we must do in order to be worthy in turn to receive.

When we say: "Lead us not into temptation," we are reminding ourselves to ask that his help may not depart from us; otherwise we could be seduced and consent to some temptation, or despair and yield to it.

When we say: "Deliver us from evil," we are reminding ourselves to reflect on the fact that we do not yet enjoy the state of blessedness in which we shall suffer no evil. This is the final petition contained in the Lord's Prayer, and it has a wide application. In this petition the Christian can utter his cries of sorrow, in it he can shed his tears, and through it he can begin, continue and conclude his prayer, whatever the distress in which he finds himself. Yes, it was very appropriate that all these truths should be entrusted to us to remember in these very words.

— St. Augustine, *Letter to Proba*

Supper at Emmaus by L'hermitte.
"When we say: 'Give us this day our daily bread' in saying 'this day' we mean 'in this world.'"
(St. Augustine, *Letter to Proba*)

VOCABULARY

ANOINTING OF THE SICK
One of the Seven Sacraments. It is administered by a bishop or priest to someone suffering from illness or old age and near death. It includes prayers and anointing with the Oil of the Sick. It is usually administered together with Reconciliation and the Eucharist.

BAPTISM
The first of the Seven Sacraments; it gives access to the other sacraments. It is the first and chief Sacrament of the Forgiveness of Sins because the baptized Christian receives the remission of both personal and Original Sin. It incorporates him or her into the Church, the Mystical Body of Christ (cf. CCC 977, 1213).

CONFIRMATION
One of the Sacraments of Initiation. It completes and confirms the sanctifying grace first received in the Sacrament of Baptism by a special outpouring of the gifts and seal of the Holy Spirit. This Sacrament equips the confirmed for worship and apostolic life in the Church.

CONTEMPLATIVE PRAYER
A form of prayer in which mind and heart focus on God's greatness and goodness in affective, loving adoration; to look on Christ and the mysteries of his life with faith and love.

CORPORAL WORKS OF MERCY
Charitable actions that assist a neighbor in bodily, or corporal, necessities.

EX OPERE OPERATO
Latin for "by the very fact of the action's being performed" (CCC 1128). If the faithful are properly disposed, they will receive grace through the sacraments regardless of the personal sanctity of the person conferring the sacrament since it is really Christ who is acting through the minister.

GOOD SAMARITAN
The "good neighbor" described in Christ's parable (Lk 10: 25-37), who exemplified Christ's teaching, "You shall love...your neighbor as yourself" (Lk 10: 27).

EUCHARIST
From the Greek for *thanksgiving*; called the Mass or Lord's Supper. It is the principal sacramental celebration of the Church, established by Christ at the Last Supper, in which the mystery of salvation through participation in the sacrificial Death and glorious Resurrection of Christ is renewed and accomplished. This term is also applied to the species consecrated during the Mass.

HOLY ORDERS
The Sacrament of Apostolic Ministry by which the mission entrusted by Christ to his Apostles continues to be exercised in the Church through the laying on of hands, which leaves a sacramental character on the soul.

LAW OF CHRIST
An interior law that stems from grace—in connection with life in Christ—and becomes a norm or impulse for imitating him.

LECTIO DIVINA
Reading and meditation on Scripture.

MATRIMONY
The Sacrament by which a baptized man and a baptized woman, in accordance with God's design from the beginning, are joined in an intimate union of life and love, "so they are no longer two but one" (Mt 19: 6). This union is ordered to the mutual benefit of the spouses and the procreation and education of children.

MEDITATIVE PRAYER
A form of prayer in which one tries to understand God's Revelation of the truths of the Faith, the purpose of the Christian life, and the means to adhere and respond to what the Lord is asking.

RECONCILIATION
Also called Penance or Confession; the Sacrament by which Christ forgives sins. Christ gave his Apostles—who passed it on to their successors down to this day—the power to forgive and retain sins. This Sacrament is administered by bishops and priests.

VOCABULARY Continued

SACRAMENTS AT THE SERVICE OF COMMUNION
The Sacraments of Matrimony and Holy Orders, which are directed toward the salvation of others, conferring a particular mission in the Church, and serving to build up the People of God.

SACRAMENTS OF HEALING
The Sacraments of Penance and Anointing of the Sick, which restore body and soul through Christ's work of healing and salvation.

SACRAMENTS OF INITIATION
The Sacraments of Baptism, Confirmation, and the Eucharist, which lay the foundation of the Christian life and bring a person into full communion with the Church. One is born again in Baptism, strengthened in Confirmation, and given the Bread of Life in the Eucharist.

SOCIAL TEACHINGS OF THE CHURCH
Moral teachings of the Church with regard to the dignity of the person and his or her basic rights and the requirements of the common good.

SPIRITUAL WORKS OF MERCY
Charitable actions that assist our neighbors in their spiritual necessities.

TRANSUBSTANTIATION
The scholastic term that designates the unique change—in a true, real, and substantial manner—of the entire substance of the Eucharistic bread and wine into the Body and Blood of Christ, with his Soul and Divinity, leaving intact the accidental appearance of bread and wine.

VOCAL PRAYER
A form of prayer in which the mind, heart, and mouth combine to give thanks, adoration, petition, or contrition to God.

The High Altar Displaying the Eucharistic Miracle of Lanciano.
After thirteen hundred years, the Body and Blood of Christ are in the same perfect condition as at the first moment of Consecration. The Host changed to flesh and the wine changed to blood is a gift to the entire Church to strengthen the faith of all believers.

STUDY QUESTIONS

1. Why is the Lord's Prayer a perfect prayer?
2. What was startling about the way Jesus Christ referred to God the Father?
3. What does *hallowed* mean?
4. To what extent has God's kingdom actually come?
5. How can God's will in a person's life be concretely known?
6. What is included in the petition for *our daily bread*?
7. What is the condition for being forgiven of sins?
8. Can a person be tempted to sin beyond his or her power to resist?
9. What is the literal meaning of *Amen*?
10. Do human beings have an intrinsic desire for God?
11. According to the *Catechism*, no. 27, what is the essence of man's desire for God?
12. What are some benefits of a life of constant prayer?
13. What is the primary way to listen to God?
14. What is *lectio divina*?
15. What are the three traditional expressions of prayer in the spiritual life?
16. What are some examples of vocal prayer?
17. What is the aim of meditation?
18. Is meditation entirely intellectual?
19. What is contemplation?
20. What are the major forms of prayer?
21. What are the major difficulties in prayer?
22. What is a sacrament?
23. Why are the sacraments of the highest importance to the Christian life?
24. How do the sacraments give importance to the Catholic Church?
25. What does it mean to say the sacraments convey grace *ex opere operato*?
26. What two types of grace do the sacraments impart?
27. Why are there *seven* sacraments?
28. Why is Baptism a Sacrament of Initiation?
29. What does Baptism take away?
30. How does Baptism change a person's relationship with God?
31. What are the signs by which Confirmation is accomplished?
32. Why is Confirmation a Sacrament of Initiation?
33. When did Christ institute the Sacrament of the Eucharist?
34. What are the words of the institution of the Eucharist?
35. What is the doctrine of transubstantiation?
36. Why is the Eucharist reserved in consecrated hosts in the tabernacle outside of Mass?
37. What does St. Paul say about a person who receives the Eucharist in a state of mortal sin?
38. Why should everyone receive the Eucharist as often as possible?
39. Why did Christ establish the Sacrament of Reconciliation?
40. What is the difference between perfect and imperfect contrition?
41. How often should a person go to Confession?
42. When should a person receive the Anointing of the Sick?
43. Can the Anointing of the Sick be repeated?

STUDY QUESTIONS Continued

44. How are Penance, the Anointing of the Sick, and the Eucharist related?
45. What is the Sacrament of Holy Orders?
46. What are the three levels of Holy Orders?
47. What is the relationship between a modern-day bishop and the Apostles?
48. What is the main purpose of Holy Orders?
49. What is the purpose of Matrimony?
50. Can a sacramental marriage be dissolved?
51. Who are the three partners in a sacramental marriage?
52. Why is the Sacrament of Matrimony good for the spouses?
53. Why is the Sacrament of Matrimony good for the children?
54. What is the New Commandment?
55. What are the two Great Commandments?
56. According to the Parable of the Good Samaritan, who is one's neighbor?
57. To what extent has the Church been faithful to the command to love a neighbor in need?
58. With what kinds of poverty and suffering is the Church concerned?
59. How can it be known that witnessing to Christianity is necessary for salvation?
60. Who is called to witness to Christ?
61. What is the basis of Christian witness?
62. What is the only real failure in life?

PRACTICAL EXERCISES

1. Many Christians have written commentaries on the Lord's Prayer. One example is St. Augustine's *On the Lord's Prayer—A letter to Proba* (cf. Supplementary Reading 4 in this chapter). Write your own commentary on the Lord's Prayer, providing one or two sentences on each of its petitions, explaining it in your own words and relating it to modern life.

2. Use the concepts of thanksgiving, reparation, adoration, and petition for ten minutes of silent vocal prayer. Find a place that is quiet and conducive to prayer. First, thank God for the good things for which you are grateful. Second, make acts of reparation for all the evil in the world, especially your own and others' offenses of which you are aware. Third, adore God simply for being God, for his goodness and greatness. Finally, ask God for the things you and those you love need.

3. God always gives what is best but not always exactly what people think they want. Think of three petitions God might not answer in the manner the petitioner hopes. What might be God's answer to each?

4. List one concrete way you could practice each of the corporal and spiritual works of mercy in your life.

5. Read about the seven themes of Catholic social teaching provided by the United States Conference of Catholic Bishops. It is located at the following Web site:

    www.usccb.org/sdwp/projects/socialteaching/excerpt.shtml

For each theme, list one example of how Catholic social teaching is violated in the world today and one example of how it is upheld. If you cannot think of a way it is upheld, list a practical way it could be.

FROM THE CATECHISM

1253 Baptism is the sacrament of faith.[47] But faith needs the community of believers. It is only within the faith of the Church that each of the faithful can believe. The faith required for Baptism is not a perfect and mature faith, but a beginning that is called to develop. The catechumen or the godparent is asked: "What do you ask of God's Church?" The response is: "Faith!"

1254 For all the baptized, children or adults, faith must grow *after* Baptism. For this reason the Church celebrates each year at the Easter Vigil the renewal of baptismal promises. Preparation for Baptism leads only to the threshold of new life. Baptism is the source of that new life in Christ from which the entire Christian life springs forth.

1257 The Lord himself affirms that Baptism is necessary for salvation.[48] He also commands his disciples to proclaim the Gospel to all nations and to baptize them.[49] Baptism is necessary for salvation for those to whom the Gospel has been proclaimed and who have had the possibility of asking for this sacrament.[50] The Church does not know of any means other than Baptism that assures entry into eternal beatitude; this is why she takes care not to neglect the mission she has received from the Lord to see that all who can be baptized are "reborn of water and the Spirit." *God has bound salvation to the sacrament of Baptism, but he himself is not bound by his sacraments.*

1285 Baptism, the Eucharist, and the sacrament of Confirmation together constitute the "sacraments of Christian initiation," whose unity must be safeguarded. It must be explained to the faithful that the reception of the sacrament of Confirmation is necessary for the completion of baptismal grace.[51] For "by the sacrament of Confirmation, [the baptized] are more perfectly bound to the Church and are enriched with a special strength of the Holy Spirit. Hence they are, as true witnesses of Christ, more strictly obliged to spread and defend the faith by word and deed."[52]

1324 The Eucharist is "the source and summit of the Christian life."[53] "The other sacraments, and indeed all ecclesiastical ministries and works of the apostolate, are bound up with the Eucharist and are oriented toward it. For in the blessed Eucharist is contained the whole spiritual good of the Church, namely Christ himself, our Pasch."[54]

1325 "The Eucharist is the efficacious sign and sublime cause of that communion in the divine life and that unity of the People of God by which the Church is kept in being. It is the culmination both of God's action sanctifying the world in Christ and of the worship men offer to Christ and through him to the Father in the Holy Spirit."[55]

1326 Finally, by the Eucharistic celebration we already unite ourselves with the heavenly liturgy and anticipate eternal life, when God will be all in all.[56]

1422 "Those who approach the sacrament of Penance obtain pardon from God's mercy for the offense committed against him, and are, at the same time, reconciled with the Church which they have wounded by their sins and which by charity, by example, and by prayer labors for their conversion."[57]

1524 In addition to the Anointing of the Sick, the Church offers those who are about to leave this life the Eucharist as viaticum. Communion in the body and blood of Christ, received at this moment of "passing over" to the Father, has a particular significance and importance. It is the seed of eternal life and the power of resurrection, according to the words of the Lord: "He who eats my flesh and drinks my blood has eternal life, and I will raise him up at the last day."[58] The sacrament of Christ once dead and now risen, the Eucharist is here the sacrament of passing over from death to life, from this world to the Father.[59]

FROM THE CATECHISM Continued

1527 The sacrament of Anointing of the Sick has as its purpose the conferral of a special grace on the Christian experiencing the difficulties inherent in the condition of grave illness or old age.

1536 Holy Orders is the sacrament through which the mission entrusted by Christ to his apostles continues to be exercised in the Church until the end of time: thus it is the sacrament of apostolic ministry. It includes three degrees: episcopate, presbyterate, and diaconate.

1601 "The matrimonial covenant, by which a man and a woman establish between themselves a partnership of the whole of life, is by its nature ordered toward the good of the spouses and the procreation and education of offspring; this covenant between baptized persons has been raised by Christ the Lord to the dignity of a sacrament."[60]

1931 Respect for the human person proceeds by way of respect for the principle that "everyone should look upon his neighbor (without any exception) as 'another self,' above all bearing in mind his life and the means necessary for living it with dignity."[61] No legislation could by itself do away with the fears, prejudices, and attitudes of pride and selfishness which obstruct the establishment of truly fraternal societies. Such behavior will cease only through the charity that finds in every man a "neighbor," a brother.

2599 The Son of God who became Son of the Virgin also learned to pray according to his human heart. He learns the formulas of prayer from his mother, who kept in her heart and meditated upon all the "great things" done by the Almighty.[62] He learns to pray in the words and rhythms of the prayer of his people, in the synagogue at Nazareth and the Temple at Jerusalem. But his prayer springs from an otherwise secret source, as he intimates at the age of twelve: "I must be in my Father's house."[63] Here the newness of prayer in the fullness of time begins to be revealed: his *filial prayer*, which the Father awaits from his children, is finally going to be lived out by the only Son in his humanity, with and for men.

2600 The Gospel according to St. Luke emphasizes the action of the Holy Spirit and the meaning of prayer in Christ's ministry. Jesus prays *before* the decisive moments of his mission: before his Father's witness to him during his baptism and Transfiguration, and before his own fulfillment of the Father's plan of love by his Passion.[64] He also prays before the decisive moments involving the mission of his apostles: at his election and call of the Twelve, before Peter's confession of him as "the Christ of God," and again that the faith of the chief of the Apostles may not fail when tempted.[65] Jesus' prayer before the events of salvation that the Father has asked him to fulfill is a humble and trusting commitment of his human will to the loving will of the Father.

2607 When Jesus prays he is already teaching us how to pray. His prayer to his Father is the theological path (the path of faith, hope, and charity) of our prayer to God. But the Gospel also gives us Jesus' explicit teaching on prayer. Like a wise teacher he takes hold of us where we are and leads us progressively toward the Father. Addressing the crowds following him, Jesus builds on what they already know of prayer from the Old Covenant and opens to them the newness of the coming Kingdom. Then he reveals this newness to them in parables. Finally, he will speak openly of the Father and the Holy Spirit to his disciples who will be the teachers of prayer in his Church.

2610 Just as Jesus prays to the Father and gives thanks before receiving his gifts, so he teaches us *filial boldness*: "Whatever you ask in prayer, believe that you receive it, and you will."[66] Such is the power of prayer and of faith that does not doubt: "all things are possible to him who believes."[67] Jesus is as saddened by the "lack of faith" of his own neighbors and the "little faith" of his own disciples[68] as he is struck with admiration at the great faith of the Roman centurion and the Canaanite woman.[69]

2611 The prayer of faith consists not only in saying "Lord, Lord," but in disposing the heart to do the will of the Father.[70] Jesus calls his disciples to bring into their prayer this concern for cooperating with the divine plan.[71]

Sacred Conversation by Bellini.
Meditative Prayer is a form of prayer in which one tries to understand God's Revelation of the truths of the Faith, the purpose of the Christian life, and the means to adhere and respond to what the Lord is asking.

ENDNOTES - CHAPTER SEVEN

1. Tertullian, *De orat.* 1: PL 1, 1155.
2. Tertullian, *De orat.* 10: PL 1, 1165; cf. Lk 11: 9.
3. Schneider, Reinhold, *Das Vaterunser*, 10.
4. Mt 6: 25.
5. Jn 6: 35.
6. Cf. Rev 2: 17.
7. Cf. Gn 1: 26.
8. Vatican Council II, *GS* 19 § 1.
9. St. Gregory of Nazianzus, *Orat. theo.*, 27, 1, 4: PG 36, 16.
10. St. John Chrysostom, *Ecloga de oratione* 2: PG 63, 585.
11. Lk 1: 28.
12. Lk 1: 42.
13. Cf. Heb 5: 7; 7: 25; 9: 24.
14. Cf. Mt 11: 25-26; Mk 14: 36.
15. St. Teresa of Jesus, *The Book of Her Life*, 8, 5 in *The Collected Works of St. Teresa of Avila*, tr. K. Kavanaugh, OCD, and O. Rodriguez, OCD (Washington, DC: Institute of Carmelite Studies, 1976), I, 67.
16. Sg 1: 7; cf. 3: 1-4.
17. Cf. CCC 2626.
18. Cf. Heb 12: 1.
19. Cf. Mt 25: 21.
20. Col 3: 16.
21. Cf. Mt 6: 6.
22. St. Leo the Great, *Sermo.* 74, 2: PL 54, 398.
23. Cf. St. Thomas Aquinas, *STh* III, 65, 1.
24. Cf. Council of Florence: DS 1314: *vitæ spiritualis ianua*.
25. *Roman Catechism* II, 2, 5; cf. Council of Florence: DS 1314; CIC, cann. 204 § 1; 849; CCEO, can. 675 § 1.
26. 2 Cor 2: 15.
27. Jn 6: 41.
28. Mt 26: 27-28.
29. 1 Cor 11: 27, 29.
30. Jn 20: 23.
31. Cf. CCC 1534.
32. Heb 5: 4.
33. Gn 2: 18.
34. Mt 22: 36.
35. Mt 22: 37-39.
36. Cf. Lk 10.
37. Mt 5: 42; 10: 8.
38. Cf. Mt 25: 31-36.
39. Mt 11: 5; cf. Lk 4: 18.
40. *LG* 42; cf. *DH* 14.
41. Mt 10: 32-33.
42. Cf. Eph 1: 22.
43. Eph 4: 13; cf. *LG* 39.
44. Jn 13: 35.
45. Cf. 1 Cor 13: 4-7.
46. *GS* 24.
47. Cf. Mk 16: 16.
48. Cf. Jn 3: 5.
49. Cf. Mt 28: 19-20; cf. Council of Trent (1547) DS 1618; *LG* 14; *AG* 5.
50. Cf. Mk 16: 16.
51. Cf. *Roman Ritual*, Rite of Confirmation (*OC*), Introduction 1.
52. *LG* 11; cf. *OC*, Introduction 2.
53. *LG* 11.
54. *PO* 5.
55. Congregation of Rites, instruction, *Eucharisticum mysterium*, 6.
56. Cf. 1 Cor 15: 28.
57. *LG* 11 § 2.
58. Jn 6: 54.
59. Cf. Jn 13: 1.
60. CIC, can. 1055 § 1; cf. *GS* 48 § 1.
61. *GS* 27 § 1.
62. Cf. Lk 1: 49; 2: 19; 2: 51.
63. Lk 2: 49.
64. Cf. Lk 3: 21; 9: 28; 22: 41-44.
65. Cf. Lk 6: 12; 9: 18-20; 22: 32.
66. Mk 11: 24.
67. Mk 9: 23; cf. Mt 21: 22.
68. Cf. Mk 6: 6; Mt 8: 26.
69. Cf. Mt 8:10; 15: 28.
70. Cf. Mt 7: 21.
71. Cf. Mt 9: 38; Lk 10: 2; Jn 4: 34.

The Mystery of Redemption

EPILOGUE

The Paschal Mystery in the Holy Mass

Everyone should prepare well for the Mass since it is the most important "meeting" one can ever have, a participation in the Body, Blood, Soul, and Divinity of Christ.

The Mystery of Redemption

EPILOGUE

The Paschal Mystery in the Holy Mass

INTRODUCTION

The Sacrifice of the Mass is the very same sacrifice that was offered by Christ on Calvary nearly 2000 years ago. Christ's perfect and unrepeatable sacrifice is perpetuated sacramentally in an unbloody manner in the liturgy of the Mass. Through this incredible gift, Christ has given his Church the means to offer God a pure and acceptable sacrifice of adoration, thanksgiving, atonement, and petition. This possibility of sharing in Christ's redemptive sacrifice through the liturgy of the Mass is one of the many marvelous effects of the redemption.

The redemption Christ merited by his Passion, Death, and Resurrection is a free and undeserved gift. Out of his great love, he offers forgiveness of sins, reconciliation with God, and eternal salvation. The Mass is a means to participate in the propitiatory sacrifice of the Cross, which is offered in atonement for sins.

Eleventh Station of the Cross.
Jesus is nailed to the cross.

By offering God adoration through the Eucharistic sacrifice, the faithful acknowledge his sovereignty in their lives. God does not *need* our worship—no one or nothing can add or detract from his happiness, glory, and greatness—rather, worship is an expression of the need and desire to render to God the glory he deserves.

It is not possible to thank God adequately for his many magnificent gifts. However, in the Mass, Christ has given a means to thank the Father for all his benefits. As the word *eucharist* comes from the Greek for *thanksgiving*, in the Mass, the faithful offer God a perfect gift—the pure and unspotted Lamb of God—in thanksgiving for all his blessings, spiritual and material. They join their imperfect thanksgiving with Christ's perfect act of thanksgiving to the Father.

The Holy Eucharist as a sacrifice is inseparable from the Holy Eucharist as a sacrament. In the Mass, Christ's redemptive sacrifice on Calvary is made present through the words of consecration: "This is my Body. ...This is my Blood." Through the sacrifice on the altar, Jesus Christ becomes truly and substantially present under the appearances of bread and wine. The Real Presence constitutes the Eucharist as a sacrament and means, following the words of consecration, Christ is present in his Body, Blood, Soul, and Divinity. Those who are properly disposed are encouraged to receive the Body and Blood of Christ in the Eucharistic banquet.

The Mass is the perfect occasion to pray for oneself, family, and friends. United to the sacrifice of Christ and the prayers of the whole Church, prayer takes on an eternal value. The prayers of the faithful, joined with those of the angels and saints in Heaven, are effective. When united to Christ's redemptive sacrifice, prayer becomes the prayer of Christ.

The Last Supper by Tissot.
As the word *eucharist* comes from the Greek for *thanksgiving*, in the Mass, the faithful offer God a perfect gift—the pure and unspotted Lamb of God—in thanksgiving for all his blessings, spiritual and material.

THIS CHAPTER WILL ADDRESS SEVERAL QUESTIONS:

- Why did Christ give his Apostles the Eucharist?
- How does Christ's sacrifice relate to Old Testament sacrifices?
- What happened at the Last Supper?
- What is the relationship between the Mass and the sacrifice of Christ?
- What are the ends, or purposes, of the Mass?
- How does one best prepare for Holy Mass?
- What are some titles of the Blessed Virgin Mary, and why does she have them?

Christ in the Garden of Olives by Champaigne. Christ offered himself as a sacrifice, pouring out his own Blood to inaugurate the New Covenant between God and man.

SACRIFICE IN THE OLD COVENANT

The practice of offering ritual sacrifice was established by God and played a major role in the worship of the Israelites. In fact, the Books of Exodus and Leviticus describe in great detail the altar of sacrifice, the furnishings of the tabernacle, the responsibilities of the priests, and the types of sacrifices that were required for the forgiveness of different types of sins.

These sacrifices could be defined as the offering of a *victim* or *host* to God in a manner that destroyed it in some way. For example, the Old Testament prescribed animal sacrifice in which the victim was to be slaughtered and its body burnt on the altar. Other sacrifices included the offering of grains, wine, or oil. Sacrifices were offered in recognition of the divine sovereignty of God and were intended to render him homage and worship as well as to obtain forgiveness of sin.

Sacrifices were also offered to seal the covenants between God and his people. After receiving the Law, Moses offered a sacrifice of oxen, pouring half the blood on the altar and sprinkling the other half on the people to seal the Old Covenant.

> **Moses came and told the people all the words of the Lord and all the ordinances; and all the people answered with one voice, and said, "All the words which the Lord has spoken we will do." And Moses wrote all the words of the Lord. And he rose early in the morning, and built an altar at the foot of the mountain, and twelve pillars, according to the twelve tribes of Israel. And he sent young men of the people of Israel, who offered burnt offerings and sacrificed peace offerings of oxen to the Lord. And Moses took half of the blood and put it in basins, and half of the blood he threw against the altar. Then he took the book of the covenant, and read it in the hearing of the people; and they said, "All that the Lord has spoken we will do, and we will be obedient." And Moses took the blood and threw it upon the people, and said, "Behold the blood of the covenant which the Lord has made with you in accordance with all these words." (Ex 24: 3-8)**

In like manner, Christ offered himself as a sacrifice, pouring out his own Blood to inaugurate the New Covenant between God and man.

> **"This is my blood of the covenant, which is poured out for many for the forgiveness of sins." (Mt 26: 28)**

THE SACRIFICE OF CHRIST FORESHADOWED

In the Old Covenant, sacrifices of primarily animal or cereal offerings were presided over by priests selected from the tribe of Levi. These ritual sacrifices expressed the worship and repentance of the Chosen People and, therefore, had religious value. They were imperfect by nature, however, and had to be continually repeated; they were powerless to effect a true reconciliation between God and man or to make reparation for the sins of the world.

God accepted these sacrifices as a foreshadowing, or prefiguration, of the sacrifice of the New Covenant—a perfect sacrifice of infinite value. Through these Old Covenant types, or foreshadowings, God prepared his people for the one sacrifice of Jesus Christ, who is the "high priest, holy, blameless, unstained, separated from sinners, exalted above the heavens."[1]

When the New Testament calls Christ the Lamb of God,[2] it references the Passover lamb, which was sacrificed on the night the Israelites were delivered from slavery in Egypt and each year thereafter as a memorial of this event. This lamb was a type of Jesus Christ, the Lamb of God, who would be sacrificed to take away the sins of the world.

SACRIFICE IN THE OLD AND NEW TESTAMENTS	
Old Testament Sacrifices	**The Sacrifice of the Mass**
God accepted the sacrifice of Abel offered in faith.	**Christ offers himself as a pure oblation, acceptable to God the Almighty Father.**
The priest-king Melchizedek offered a sacrifice of bread and wine.	**Christ offers his own Body and Blood under the appearances of bread and wine. He is a priest "after the order of Melchizedek."[3]**
Obedient to God, Abraham offered his son Isaac.	**God the Father sent his Only-Begotten Son, Jesus Christ, to be offered as a sacrifice on the Cross. Christ was perfectly obedient to this mission.**
The Passover lamb was sacrificed as a memorial of deliverance from slavery in Egypt.	**Christ is the Lamb of God who delivers people from slavery to sin.**
The Prophet Malachi foretold, "From the rising of the sun to its setting my name is great among the nations, and in every place incense is offered to my name, and a pure offering."[4]	**The pure oblation of the Mass is offered throughout the world. There is always a Mass being said somewhere.**

REDEMPTION REQUIRES A PERFECT SACRIFICE

In order to redeem mankind, God willed to offer an adequate satisfaction for sin. Satisfaction refers to reparation for offenses committed. Since human beings offended God (our first parents with Original Sin and each individual person with actual sin, save the Blessed Virgin Mary and Christ), a human being had to offer satisfaction.

Because sin constitutes an offense against God, who enjoys infinite dignity and transcendence, the satisfaction for sin must also have an infinite value. Man cannot offer such a sacrifice on his own, which is why the sacrifices of the Old Testament were imperfect by their nature. They could not make satisfaction for sins against the infinite dignity of God.

Only a divine Person, who also shared fully in human nature, could offer a sacrifice of infinite value. For this reason, God sent his Son, Jesus Christ—true God and true man—to be offered as a sacrifice for the sins of the world. Christ became man in order to offer himself in satisfaction for sins, and, in this way, his whole life was directed toward the sacrifice of the Cross.

The Mocking of Christ by Doré.
While Christ freely offers his redemption and gives the grace and the means to respond, he allows everyone the freedom to accept or reject it.

As the Psalms attest, everyone could spend his or her entire life doing penance and never offer adequate satisfaction for the infinite offenses against God.

> **Truly no man can ransom himself, or give to God the price of his life, for the ransom of his life is costly, and can never suffice.** (Ps 49:7-8)

This does not mean people should not do acts of penance. On the contrary, acts of penance have merit when united to the sacrifice of Christ. His sacrifice alone offers adequate satisfaction for the sins of the world.

> **There is one God, and there is one mediator between God and men, the man Christ Jesus, who gave himself as a ransom for all.** (1 Tm 2:5-6)

While the redemption merited by the sacrifice of the Cross is adequate for the reparation of sin, it must be applied to those properly disposed. The redemption must be applied to the person for whom it was offered. Christ suffered and offered himself as a sacrifice for *all* people—past, present, and future—but each person must freely desire and accept the benefits of his sacrifice. While Christ freely offers his redemption and gives the grace and the means to respond, he allows everyone the freedom to accept or reject it.

ST. BENEDICT OF NURSIA

St. Benedict was born in the year 480 at Nursia, Italy. As a young man, he went to Rome to be educated, but the moral decay of the city impelled him to withdraw to a cave in Subiaco to live as a hermit. As time passed, others joined him in his reclusive life, and his reputation for sanctity spread.

Before he died, St. Benedict founded twelve monasteries, the most famous of which is his first at Monte Cassino. Though he probably did not intend to found a religious order, he did compose a *Rule* for monks, which became the standard for monastic life in the Western Church. In fact, the *Rule of St. Benedict* was adopted by almost every monastic community in the medieval period and continues in wide use today.

The *Rule of St. Benedict* has been lauded for its spirit of peace and love as well as its moderation in the ascetical life. For example, it instructs monks to sleep six to eight hours each night and have a bed, pillow, and sufficient food. The *Rule* divides the schedule of a monk into four parts: chanting the Psalms and reciting prayers in community (four hours), private prayer and reading Scripture (four hours), physical labor (six hours), and meals and sleep (ten hours). According to the Benedictine model, the monastic life is lived in common. No one is allowed to own property, though the monastery itself can. The *Rule* makes provision for an abbot, who governs the monastery. All monks make vows of poverty, chastity, and obedience after undergoing a novitiate.

St. Benedict intended a monastery to be a family and self-sustaining community. Different monks have different tasks and functions, which are organized and distributed in such a way as to ensure self-sufficiency. Working together for the good of the whole and the glory of God, the monastery is a place where the nobleman and commoner labored, each in his own and separate way but always for the common good.

The rise of Benedictine monasticism during the decline of the western half of the Roman Empire proved vital for the spread of Christianity and the formation of a new

Christian culture in Europe. As communities of monks spread throughout the continent, they became centers of spirituality, education, and learning. They even began to convert barbarian tribes to the Christian Faith.

Monasteries were the chief centers of learning in Europe until the rise of universities beginning in the thirteenth century. Monks meticulously copied manuscripts in *scriptoria*, large rooms set aside for that purpose. It can be said monasteries singlehandedly saved Western culture during the Middle Ages.

Through their educational work, monks taught the surrounding population how to read and write. The monks elevated them intellectually, which facilitated the development of a new culture expressed in a fusion of the old Greco-Roman tradition with a newer Germanic culture.

As a consequence of their work of evangelization, the monasteries also had a great civilizing effect on these Germanic peoples. Attracted by the holiness of the monks and nuns, the Germanic tribes proved willing pupils in many practical disciplines. Monks taught trades such as agriculture, carpentry, stone masonry, and ironwork. They also infused a spiritual meaning into the act of work itself and thus taught the dignity of work as a form of adoration and emulation of Jesus Christ, who was himself a worker.

St. Benedict's feast day is celebrated on July 11 (March 21 in the extraordinary form of the Latin Rite; March 14 in the Eastern Rites of the Catholic Church).

Illustration: *St. Benedict at Supper with His Monks* (detail) by Il Sodoma.

The Last Supper (detail) by Tiepolo. The Paschal lamb was replaced by the Lamb of God.

THE LAST SUPPER AND THE PASSOVER

While they were at supper, he took bread, blessed and broke it, and gave it to his disciples.[5]

The Passover meal was an annual celebration commemorating the deliverance of the Israelites from slavery in Egypt. This ritual meal was celebrated at home and included a lamb, unleavened bread, wine, and bitter herbs, each symbolizing different elements of the original Passover. While it looked back at a past deliverance, it also celebrated the hope of a more magnificent deliverance yet to come.

The Last Supper, which Christ shared with his Apostles, took place during a Passover meal. By instituting the Sacrament of the Holy Eucharist during the Passover, Christ, the true Lamb of God, gave this ancient feast its full meaning. The Paschal lamb was replaced by the Lamb of God.

Lamb of God, you take away the sins of the world. (*The Roman Missal*, 1975)

That which was foreshadowed in the Old Covenant became a reality. The imperfect sacrifices of the Old Law came to an end and were replaced by a new sacrifice. The New Covenant, established by Christ's Blood, is everlasting and effectively reconciles God and man.

Jesus took bread, and blessed, and broke it, and gave it to the disciples and said, "Take, eat; this is my body." And he took a cup, and when he had given thanks he gave it to them, saying, "Drink of it, all of you; for this is my blood of the covenant, which is poured out for many for the forgiveness of sins." (Mt 26: 26-28)

Christ commanded his Apostles, "Do this in remembrance of me."[6] With these words, Christ instituted both the Sacrament of the Holy Eucharist and the Sacrament of Holy Orders. This made it possible for Christ's sacrifice on the Cross, offered once and for all on Calvary, to be perpetuated sacramentally until he comes again.

When the Church celebrates the Eucharist, the memorial of her Lord's death and resurrection, this central event of salvation becomes really present and "the work of our redemption is carried out."[7] This sacrifice is so decisive for the salvation of the human race that Jesus Christ offered it and returned to the Father only *after he had left us a means of sharing in it* as if we had been present there. Each member of the faithful can thus take part in it and inexhaustibly gain its fruits. (*Ecclesia de Eucharistia*, 11)

Christ's instructions at the Last Supper—to repeat his words and actions—have been observed faithfully in the Church and will be until the end of time. The earliest Christians "devoted themselves to the Apostles' teaching and fellowship, to the breaking of bread and the prayers."[8] The *breaking of bread* was the term they used for the Eucharistic liturgy.

Golgotha by Van Dyck.
The Mass is neither a repetition of nor a substitute for Christ's redemptive sacrifice of the Cross; it is the same sacrifice.

THE HOLY MASS IS THE SACRIFICE OF THE CROSS

Look, O Lord, upon the Sacrifice which you yourself have provided for your Church.[9]

In the Mass, the Church continues to fulfill Christ's mandate to offer the Eucharist sacrifice. The Mass is neither a repetition of nor a substitute for Christ's redemptive sacrifice of the Cross; it is the same sacrifice. At Mass, the faithful are present at the foot of the Cross in a real way, and the graces from the Eucharist are obtained from the redeeming sacrifice of Jesus Christ.

> **The Mass is a sacrifice because it *re-presents* (makes present) the sacrifice of the cross, because it is its *memorial* and because it *applies* its fruit:**
>
> > **[Christ], our Lord and God, was once and for all to offer himself to God the Father by his death on the altar of the cross, to accomplish there an everlasting redemption. But because his priesthood was not to end with his death, at the Last Supper "on the night when he was betrayed," [he wanted] to leave to his beloved spouse the Church a visible sacrifice (as the nature of man demands) by which the bloody sacrifice which he was to accomplish once for all on the cross would be re-presented, its memory perpetuated until the end of the world, and its salutary power be applied to the forgiveness of the sins we daily commit.[10] (CCC 1366)**

The sacrifice of the Mass and the sacrifice on Calvary are the same sacrifice because the Priest and the Victim are the same. On the Cross, Christ offered himself to redeem man. In the Mass, Christ, through the ministerial priest acting in the Person of Christ (*in persona Christi*), brings the Paschal Sacrifice to the present moment in an unbloody manner to redeem the faithful. Christ's sacrifice on Calvary is re-presented at Mass as it was at the Last Supper.

Crucifix by Donatello.
At Mass, the faithful are present at the foot of the Cross in a real way.

> **"The sacrifice of Christ and the sacrifice of the Eucharist are *one single sacrifice*."[11] Saint John Chrysostom put it well: "We always offer the same Lamb, not one today and another tomorrow, but always the same one. For this reason the sacrifice is always only one... Even now we offer that victim who was once offered and who will never be consumed."[12]**

Jesus Christ's redemptive sacrifice on Calvary and its re-presentation in the Mass are one and the same sacrifice. The manner in which this sacrifice is offered, however, has some accidental differences. (*Accidental* means the only differences are those of appearances rather than substance or reality.) While Christ's sacrifice on the Cross was a historical event that cannot be repeated, it is made present on the altar in a sacramental, or mystical, way, transcending time and space. For this reason, the Mass is called an unbloody sacrifice. Another accidental difference is the Holy Sacrifice of the Mass includes the whole Church. In other words, the Mass allows all of the baptized to unite themselves to Christ, their head, in his redemptive sacrifice.

In speaking of the Sacrifice of the Mass, words such as "renewal" and "re-presentation" are used with respect to the sacrifice of Calvary. When using these terms, people must be careful not to interpret them as a mere symbolic representation. Rather, the Mass incorporates the faithful into the present redeeming action of Christ, which is the same in substance as the sacrifice of the Cross. In the Mass, the sacrifice of Christ becomes a present reality, and its redeeming grace is applied to individual souls for their sanctification.

Pope Benedict XVI Celebrates Holy Mass in the Valley of Josaphat, opposite the Garden of Olives, Jerusalem.
The ministerial priest acts in the Person of Christ (*in persona Christi*), and he alone has the power to "confect" the Eucharist, changing the bread and wine into the Body and Blood of Christ.

THE PRIEST AND THE FAITHFUL

Christ on the Cross (detail) by Velázquez.
On the Cross, Christ was both the Priest who made the offering and the Victim who was offered.

Jesus Christ, the Eternal High Priest, is the primary minister of the Eucharistic sacrifice. On the Cross, Christ was both the Priest who made the offering and the Victim who was offered. In the Mass, Christ continues to offer himself through the ministerial priesthood. For this reason, the priest does not say, "This is the body and blood of Christ"; rather, he declares, "This is my body," and, "This is my blood."

While both the ordained priest and the faithful who assist at Mass exercise the priesthood of Christ, they do so in different ways. The ministerial priest acts in the Person of Christ (*in persona Christi*), and he alone has the power to "confect" the Eucharist, changing the bread and wine into the Body and Blood of Christ. Nevertheless, all who attend the Mass are called to be active participants. First and foremost, their hearts and minds should be united to the liturgy unfolding before them on the altar. The faithful should not be present as spectators but should offer themselves in union with Christ, both Priest and Victim.

The faithful also offer a sacrifice: the sacrifice of good works; sufferings; faith, hope, and love; and the like. They unite their living sacrifice to Christ's. St. Paul witnessed this truth: "I appeal to you...to present your bodies as a living sacrifice, holy and acceptable to God, which is your spiritual worship."[13] By doing so, the faithful become not only co-offerers with the priest and with Christ but also co-victims with him.

The faithful participate more fully in the sacrifice of the Mass and exercise their common priesthood by entering into the mystery of the Mass, following the words of the liturgy, responding in those parts proper to the faithful, and receiving Holy Communion.

> **Although all those who participate in the Eucharist do not confect the sacrifice as He does, they offer with Him, by virtue of the common priesthood, their own spiritual sacrifices represented by the bread and wine from the moment of their presentation at the altar. For this liturgical action, which take a solemn form in almost all liturgies, has a "spiritual value and meaning."[14] The bread and wine become in a sense a symbol of all that the eucharistic assembly brings, on its own part, as an offering to God and offers spiritually. (*Dominicæ Cenæ*, 9)**

THE ENDS OF THE MASS

The Eucharistic sacrifice includes four ends, or purposes, that correspond to the four principal objectives of prayer. The first is to give *adoration* to God the Father. The second is *thanksgiving* in recognition of God's many gifts, above all his redemption and communion with him in the Eucharist. Thirdly, since the sacrifice of the Mass is Christ's redemptive sacrifice performed sacramentally, the Eucharist is offered in reparation, or *atonement*, for sin. Lastly, the celebration of the Eucharist is the prayer above all others to *petition* for favors, especially those that involve growth in Christian discipleship. Through the incredible gift of the Mass, Christ has given his Church the means to offer to God a pure and acceptable sacrifice of adoration, thanksgiving, atonement, and petition.

a. The Mass offers perfect adoration to God

The Mass is a perfect act of adoration and praise of God. Jesus Christ is the High Priest at every Mass, who offers his Body and Blood to God the Father in an act of adoration. Through the Liturgy of the Eucharist, the faithful can offer God fitting adoration because they adore him through Christ's redemptive sacrifice.

At the Holy Sacrifice of the Mass, the angels and saints in Heaven join their prayer of adoration to Christ's. It follows that each person can become part of this prayer of adoration in the company of all the angels and saints, who offer continual worship to God before his throne in the heavenly liturgy.

> **Holy, Holy, Holy Lord God of hosts. Heaven and earth are full of your glory. Hosanna in the highest.**[15]

Through the Mass, honor is given to the angels and saints in Heaven:

> **Receive, O holy Trinity, this oblation which we make to Thee, in memory of the Passion, Resurrection, and Ascension of our Lord Jesus Christ, in honor of Blessed Mary, ever Virgin, blessed John the Baptist, the holy Apostles Peter and Paul, and of all the Saints, that it may avail unto their honor and our salvation, and may they vouchsafe to intercede for us in heaven, whose memory we celebrate on earth.** (*The Roman Missal*, 1962)

b. The Mass offers perfect thanksgiving to God

The *Gloria*, which forms part of the Introductory Rites, is a prayer of adoration and thanksgiving.

> **Glory to God in the highest, and on earth peace to people of good will. We praise you, we bless you, we adore you, we give you thanks for your great glory.**[16]

The second purpose of the Mass is to offer thanksgiving. The faithful give thanks to God for the many gifts received, both spiritual and material, including those hidden from their eyes. There can be no greater act of thanksgiving than Christ's sacrificial offering in the celebration of the Eucharist.

Recall the word *eucharist* means *thanksgiving*. Only Christ our Lord, the Son of God made flesh, can offer God the Father perfect thanksgiving. At the Last Supper, he gave thanks to the Father in anticipation of his sacrifice of the Cross. At Mass, the faithful unite their thanksgiving to that of Christ and thus, with Christ, offer fitting thanksgiving to the Father.

> **Father, all-powerful and ever-living God, we do well always and everywhere to give you thanks through Jesus Christ our Lord.**[17]

Through the Liturgy of the Eucharist, the faithful can offer God fitting adoration because they adore him through Christ's redemptive sacrifice.

c. The Mass offers perfect atonement to God

> **May this Sacrifice of our reconciliation, we pray, O Lord, advance the peace and salvation of all the world.**[18]

The Mass is a propitiatory sacrifice of atonement or reparation. Though God is lavish in his mercy and forgiveness, the damage and disorder inflicted on the human soul by sin needs to be repaired. Moreover, sin wreaks havoc on human society, causing strife, division, hatred, and violence. The graces that flow from the Holy Sacrifice of the Mass have the power to heal these wounds. This reparation or atonement begins with those directly participating in the Mass and are applied according to each one's desire and eagerness to be united to the Lord's Eucharistic sacrifice.

d. The Mass offers perfect petition to God

Listen graciously to the prayers of this family.[19]

The Mass is the ideal occasion to petition God for material and spiritual needs, including the needs of others.

The fourth purpose of the Mass is petition. While on earth, Christ "offered up prayers and supplications...and being made perfect he became the source of eternal salvation to all who obey him, being designated by God a high priest after the order of Melchizedek."[20] In Heaven, Christ "lives always to make intercession for us."[21]

The Mass is the ideal occasion to petition God for material and spiritual needs, including the needs of others. These pleas for God's help and assistance should include prayers for the sick, the poor, and those suffering from natural disasters or catastrophes. We can also ask for material necessities such as rain in time of drought, an end to an epidemic, or an increase in employment. Through the renewal of the sacrifice on the Cross, the faithful should also pray for peace and for those who suffer from war. A very urgent request would include the respect for human life, especially an end to abortion.

In addition to material needs, prayers should be offered for spiritual necessities. The Mass is an ideal time to pray for the conversion of a family member or friend. One of the best ways to show charity to another is to pray for him or her. Extending the Kingdom of God in the world depends on the prayers of the faithful. The challenges of evangelization are certainly overcome by the graces requested through the Eucharistic sacrifice.

The following excerpt from Eucharistic Prayer II indicates some of the formal petitions in the Mass:

> Lord, remember your Church throughout the world; make us grow in love, together with...our Pope,...our bishop, and all the clergy.
>
> Remember our brothers and sisters who have gone to their rest in the hope of rising again; bring them and all the departed into the light of your presence. Have mercy on us all; make us worthy to share eternal life with Mary, the virgin Mother of God, with the apostles, and with all the saints who have done your will throughout the ages. May we praise you in union with them, and give you glory through your Son, Jesus Christ. (*The Roman Missal*, 1975)

PROPER DISPOSITIONS TO PARTICIPATE IN THE MASS

The Eucharist is the "source and summit of the Christian life."[22] It is the center around which the Christian life revolves. The reception of the sacraments, prayer and liturgical life, devotions, visits to the Blessed Sacrament, mortifications, penitential practices, and the apostolate all have the Eucharist as their focus. If the Mass were to be abandoned, the Christian life would collapse.

With spiritual benefits in mind, the Third Commandment and the first Precept of the Church require the faithful to attend Mass on Sunday. The Church also warmly recommends the faithful receive Holy Communion each time they participate in the celebration of the Eucharist and obliges them to do so at least once a year.[23]

While the Sacrifice of the Mass adds nothing to the redemption gained by Christ on the Cross (objective redemption), it is a means for each person to accept and apply this redemption in his or her own life (subjective redemption). In the Sacrament of the Eucharist, as in all the sacraments, the ends are accomplished *ex opere operato*, i.e., by the very fact that it is celebrated. However, the benefits are received *ex opere operantis*, i.e., according to the dispositions of those participating. The more a person surrenders him- or herself to the will of God and the more he or she is united to Christ in the Mass, the more he or she will be disposed to receive the fruits he offers through the Mass. For this reason, sin and the attachment to sin are obstacles to receiving the enumerable benefits of the Mass and to achieving sanctity of life.

In the Mass, the faithful are called to unite their personal sacrifices to that of Christ and, in this manner, transform them into an acceptable, atoning offering to God the Father. As St. Paul reminded, "Present your bodies as a living sacrifice, holy and acceptable to God."[24] Through the Mass, every action, even the most insignificant, takes on an eternal value when united to Christ's redemptive sacrifice. Therefore, works, sufferings, illnesses, failures, humiliations, fatigue, and the like should be offered as part of the Eucharistic sacrifice, where they become absorbed into the perfect sacrifice of Our Lord. Precisely in the Mass, the sacrifice of the whole Church is joined to that of Christ, the head of his Mystical Body.

When the faithful's offerings are united to Christ's, they take on a redemptive value; thus, they cooperate in his work of redemption, becoming co-redeemers with him. In the words of St. Paul, "I rejoice in my sufferings for your sake, and in my flesh I complete what is lacking in Christ's afflictions for the sake of his body, that is, the church."[25] Christians gain another glimpse into their great dignity as children of God—children permitted take part in the redemption won by Our Lord, Jesus Christ.

At Mass, people should try to have the same disposition Christ had when he offered himself on Calvary. This means cultivating a life of charity and self-sacrifice and having a spirit of penance in reparation for sin. Through this effort to identify with Christ on the Cross, his divine life intensifies within their hearts.

Precisely in the Mass, the sacrifice of the whole Church is joined to that of Christ, the head of his Mystical Body.

Remember also our brothers and sisters who have fallen asleep in the hope of the resurrection.[26]

The atoning fruits of the Mass are available for all those for whom it is offered. This includes the faithful who are present, those not present, and the Holy Souls in Purgatory. As St. Cyril of Jerusalem (d. 386) attested in Mystogogical Catechesis, the faithful have always offered the Mass for the needs of others and for the Holy Souls in Purgatory.

> **After the spiritual sacrifice, the un-bloody act of worship, has been completed, we bend over this propitiatory offering and beg God to grant peace to all the Churches, to give harmony to the whole world, to bless our rulers, our soldiers and our companions, to aid the sick and afflicted, and in general to assist all those who stand in need; we all pray for all these intentions and we offer this victim for them...and last of all for our deceased holy forefathers and bishops and for all those who have lived among us. For we have a deep conviction that great help will be afforded those souls for whom prayers are offered while this holy and awesome victim is present. (St. Cyril of Jerusalem, *Mystogogical Catechesis*, "On the Mysteries," V, Lecture XXIII, 8-9)**

Necessary Conditions to Receive Holy Communion

Anyone who desires to receive Christ in Eucharistic communion must be in the state of grace. Anyone aware of having sinned mortally must not receive communion without having received absolution in the sacrament of penance. (CCC 1415)

Silent mediation can serve as an excellent immediate preparation for the Holy Mass.

Receiving the Eucharist in a state of mortal sin is the grave sin of sacrilege. Therefore, if a person is aware of having committed a mortal sin, he or she should make a sacramental Confession as soon as possible. As long as a person is not aware of having committed a mortal sin since the last Confession, he or she may receive Holy Communion.

In order to receive Holy Communion, it is necessary to have the right intention and to keep the Eucharistic fast. The right intention would include, at a minimum, the intention to receive the Body, Blood, Soul, and Divinity of Jesus Christ present in the Blessed Sacrament. The faithful are also required to abstain from all food and drink, except water and medicine, for a period of one hour before receiving Holy Communion.[27] In addition to being a small act of penance, the Eucharistic fast reminds the recipient the Eucharist is not ordinary food and drink but supernatural nourishment for our souls.

"Truly, truly, I say to you, unless you eat the flesh of the Son of man and drink his blood, you have no life in you." (Jn 6:53)

The Church wants her members to receive the Holy Eucharist frequently, even daily, if possible. To this end, over the past century and a half, the Church has lowered the age at which the Eucharist can first be received and reduced the Eucharistic fast to one hour.

Preparation for Mass

In order to offer the Holy Mass with greater fruitfulness, everyone should prepare him- or herself spiritually. Therefore, it is good to keep in mind the following:

- Of all the wonderful devotions Christians have at their disposal, *participating in the sacrifice of the Mass* is the most pleasing to God. He calls his people to participate in the Mass not as strangers or passive spectators but as active disciples who want to understand it better each time and in a conscious, pious, and active manner. Participating in the Mass with a lively faith and ardent love provides the right dispositions to receive God's grace.
- *The faithful should prepare for Mass by prayer.* Silent meditation can serve as an excellent immediate preparation for the Holy Mass. If it is not possible to spend a prolonged time in prayer, plan to arrive at the church a few minutes early to pray and recollect thoughts in order to better focus on the liturgy that is about to begin.
- *The faithful should offer the Mass in union with the whole Church.* Therefore, every person's intentions should be united with those of the bishop and the pope, the Vicar of Christ.
- As hearts and minds are joined to Christ in the Sacrifice of Mass, the faithful offer to God the Father, through the assistance of the Holy Spirit, all their works, charity, sacrifices, sufferings, self-denials, and tribulations of each day.

Proper Participation at Mass

At Mass, everyone should also participate properly in the following ways:

- Attend the Mass in a spirit of piety by reciting the prayers appropriate to the faithful and reflecting on what is being said. Closely following the prayers and gestures of the priest fosters full participation of both mind and heart.
- To avoid distractions, it is often helpful to use a missal or missalette. This helps a person be one with the words, actions, and gestures of the priest, who acts in the Person of Christ.
- Listen, respond, acclaim, sing, and keep appropriate silence as a way of penetrating and reflecting on the Word of God and the meaning of the Mass.
- Stand, sit, and kneel as directed by the rubrics of the Mass. For example, slouching (half sitting and half kneeling) can be a mark of irreverence to Our Lord.
- Being punctual—arriving a few minutes before Mass begins and leaving only after Mass has ended—helps assure the entire liturgy is being prayed with reverence and respect. Every part of the Mass has meaning and purpose.
- Dress properly as befits the occasion. Dress ought to convey the respect, solemnity, and joy of the Mass; moreover, it is a sign of love and respect for God.

Communion and Thanksgiving

Because Jesus Christ is present within the recipient in Holy Communion, it is most fitting to spend time in silent thanksgiving after Mass. Along with the presence of Christ, he or she is also a beneficiary of the graces received from the Sacrament of the Eucharist.

Receiving Holy Communion increases union with Christ and with all the faithful, forgives venial sins, and helps preserve the recipient from grave sins. Since receiving this sacrament strengthens the bonds of charity between the communicant and Christ, it also reinforces the unity of the Church as the Mystical Body of Christ.

Though the emotions may not always react sufficiently to such a privileged time, these minutes spent in prayer are the high point of the day. What would someone say to Our Lord if he or she actually were to see him in the flesh? Undoubtedly, he or she open his or her heart in adoration and thanksgiving. He or she would ask for physical and spiritual healing. He or she would ask for favors and make acts of contrition for infidelities. Though the Lord is not seen in this way, he is just as accessible in the Eucharist as when he walked through the towns and villages of Palestine. These few minutes spent in prayerful thanksgiving will have a strong impact on being aware of the presence of God during the day through love and kindness toward everyone.

The Institution of the Eucharist (detail) by Poussin.
What would someone say to Our Lord if he or she actually were to see him in the flesh?

The Coronation of the Virgin by Velázquez.
The Blessed Virgin Mary's Assumption into Heaven is a natural consequence of her Immaculate Conception; since she never sinned, there was no reason her body should suffer corruption. Now in Heaven, the Blessed Virgin Mary is honored as Queen of Heaven and earth.

THE BLESSED VIRGIN MARY

Our Lord allows his people to participate in the redemption of the world, completing "what is lacking in Christ's afflictions," as St. Paul wrote. In the case of the Blessed Virgin Mary, this is true to the highest degree possible for a human being.

Sin's entry into the world was made possible through the prideful disobedience of Eve; redemption was made possible through the humble obedience of the Blessed Virgin Mary. Her indispensable *yes* to the Archangel Gabriel made it possible for our Savior to enter into the world. This act of obedience occasioned the conception of Jesus Christ by the power of the Holy Spirit. The Blessed Virgin Mary provided the human Body and Blood of her Son. His Body and Blood paid the exorbitant price of redemption. Because of her intimate role in the immediate preparation for the redemption, Sacred Tradition has given her the title of Co-redemptrix.

The Adoration of the Christ Child (detail) by Bartolomeo.
The Blessed Virgin Mary was a virgin when Christ was conceived, and she remained a virgin throughout her life.

As Mother of God, the relationship between the Blessed Virgin Mary and the sacrifice of Jesus Christ is unique. As she participated fully in the Incarnation, Our Lady—the *woman* of the *Protoevangelium*—cooperated fully in the redemptive sacrifice of Christ. At the foot of the Cross, she embraced the Father's will fully and stood suffering with her Son, consenting to his sacrifice. At this moment, St. Simeon's prophecy, "A sword will pierce through your own soul also,"[28] was fulfilled.

The *woman* of the *Protoevangelium* united herself to her Son, and she continues to do so. In this way, the Blessed Virgin Mary is present in a mystical way at every Mass. As she stood by Christ at Calvary, each person is able to unite him- or herself to Christ in the renewal of the same, albeit unbloody, sacrifice of the Mass.

The Privileges of Mary

The Blessed Virgin Mary's greatest privilege is her divine maternity and, thus, her greatest title is **Mother of God** (*Theotokos*, literally, Bearer of God). Because she is the Mother of Christ, she is also the **Mother of the Church**, the Mystical Body of Christ, and of all Christians. From this divine maternity flow all of her other privileges.

- **Ever-Virgin:** The Blessed Virgin Mary was a virgin when Christ was conceived, and she remained a virgin throughout her life. Christ's *brothers* are actually his cousins or close relatives; the Aramaic language did not distinguish between the two. The Blessed Virgin Mary's Perpetual Virginity has been the constant belief of Christians and is attested to by numerous early Christian writings. It was solemnly defined at the Second Ecumenical Council of Constantinople (553-554) and re-emphasized by Pope St. Martin I at the Lateran Synod in 649.
- **Immaculate Conception:** In his Apostolic Constitution *Ineffabilis Deus*, Pope Bl. Pius IX declared this universal belief of Catholics: the Blessed Virgin Mary was conceived without any stain of Original Sin, and this is a dogma of the Faith. He wrote: "The most Blessed Virgin

Mater Dolorosa: The Sorrowful Mother by Tissot.
The Blessed Virgin Mary is present in a mystical way at every Mass. As she stood by Christ at Calvary, each person is able to unite him- or herself to Christ in the renewal of the same, albeit unbloody, sacrifice of the Mass.

Mary, in the first instance of her conception, by a singular grace and privilege granted by Almighty God, in view of the merits of Jesus Christ, the Savior of the human race, was preserved free from all stain of original sin, is a doctrine revealed by God and therefore to be believed firmly and constantly by all the faithful." At no time was the Mother of God under the power of Satan or the slavery of sin: rather, from the moment of her conception, she was *full of grace*. This privilege enabled her to cooperate fully in God's plan of redemption.

- **Assumed into Heaven** and **Queen of Heaven and Earth:** In 1950, Pope Pius XII solemnly defined the dogma of the Assumption of the Blessed Virgin Mary in his encyclical *Munificentissimus Deus*: "The Immaculate Mother of God, the ever Virgin Mary, having completed the course of her earthly life, was assumed body and soul into heavenly glory." Her Assumption into Heaven is a natural consequence of her Immaculate Conception; since she never sinned, there was no reason her body should suffer corruption. Now in Heaven, the Blessed Virgin Mary is honored as Queen of Heaven and earth.
- **Co-redemptrix, Mediatrix,** and **Advocate:** Because of the Blessed Virgin Mary's unique role in God's plan of salvation and her cooperation in the redemptive sacrifice of her Son, she is Co-redemptrix. She is Mediatrix because, by her consent, God became man; she continues to intercede, participating in the dispensation of graces merited by her Son. In Heaven, the Blessed Virgin Mary continues to pray for the People of God; therefore, she is called Advocate. In these roles, she serves as the Mother of Christians and the model of the Christian life.

PRAYER TO THE VIRGIN MARY BEFORE MASS

O mother of devoted love and mercy,
Most blessed Virgin Mary,
With all my heart and all my affection
I take refuge in you,
Though I am a poor and undeserving sinner.
You stood by your most dear Son
As he was hanging on the cross.
Stand mercifully by me,
Poor sinner though I am,
And by all the priests
who today offer this sacrifice,
Here and in all our holy Church.
With the help of your gracious presence,
May we offer a sacrifice that is right and acceptable
in the presence
of the most high and undivided Trinity.
Amen.

From the *Roman Missal*

Thirteenth Station of the Cross.
Jesus' body is removed from the cross.

Entombment of Christ (detail) by Weyden.
Through proper and conscious participation in the Mass and the Eucharist, the faithful unite themselves with Our Lord and the saints and angels in Heaven.

CONCLUSION

Christ's sacrifice on the Cross to redeem the world is the fulfillment of the sacrifices of the Old Covenant, which foreshadowed Christ's atoning sacrifice. The Sacrifice of the Mass makes the sacrifice of Calvary present but in an unbloody manner.

The Mass and the Eucharist are the "source and summit" of the Christian Faith. Through proper and conscious participation, the faithful unite themselves with Our Lord and the saints and angels in Heaven, offering perfect adoration, thanksgiving, atonement, and petition. Everyone should prepare well for the Mass since it is the most important "meeting" one can ever have, a participation in the Body, Blood, Soul, and Divinity of Christ.

The Blessed Virgin Mary was Christ's closest collaborator in his redemption; Christians, too, can co-redeem with Christ if they say yes to his plans.

> The holy Mass brings us face-to-face with one of the central mysteries of our faith, because it is the gift of the Blessed Trinity to the Church. It is because of this that we can consider the Mass as the center and the source of a Christian's spiritual life.
>
> It is the aim of all the sacraments. The life of grace, into which we are brought by baptism, and which is increased and strengthened by confirmation, grows to its fullness in the Mass. "When we participate in the Eucharist," writes St Cyril of Jerusalem, "we are made spiritual by the divinizing action of the Holy Spirit, who not only makes us share in Christ's life, as in baptism, but makes us entirely Christ-like, incorporating us into the fullness of Christ Jesus."[29]

INDEX

INDEX